THEOLOGICAL INVESTIGATIONS

Volume XIII

THEOLOGICAL INVESTIGATIONS

THEOLOGICAL INVESTIGATIONS

VOLUME XIII
THEOLOGY, ANTHROPOLOGY, CHRISTOLOGY

by
KARL RAHNER

Translated by
DAVID BOURKE

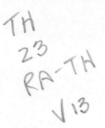

CROSSROAD • NEW YORK

1983
The Crossroad Publishing Company
575 Lexington Avenue, New York, NY 10022

A translation of the first part of
SCHRIFTEN ZUR THEOLOGIE, X
published by Verlagsanstalt Benziger & Co. A.G., Einsiedeln

This translation © Darton, Longman & Todd Ltd. 1975
First published 1975
Reprinted 1983

Library of Congress Catalog Card Number: 61-8189
ISBN: 0-8245-0389-9
Printed in the United States of America

CONTENTS

PART THREE *Christology*

FOREWORD

The thirteenth (the first half of the tenth in German) volume of my *Theological Investigations* is here presented. I have hardly anything to say in this foreword which has not already been said in the forewords to the previous volumes. The purpose and aim of these volumes has in fact remained unaltered. The great majority of the articles included in the present volume stem from the few years which have elapsed since the publication of the eleventh and twelfth (ninth in German) volumes. Only a few earlier articles have been included as and when I have felt it appropriate to incorporate them here. As before, details concerning the origins of the various studies are supplied in the list of sources at the end. It is ultimately intended to publish a detailed index to all fourteen volumes, and preparations for this have already commenced. This general index is too large to admit of its being included as a supplement to this present volume. My heartfelt thanks are extended to my collaborators, Roman Bleistein S.J. and Karl Neufeld S.J., for all the labours which they have devoted to the preparation of the present volume. In conclusion it remains only for me to say this: Even in fourteen such widely ranging volumes I have not in any sense attempted a systematic presentation of theology. Given the necessary conditions in terms both of my own physical powers and of external circumstances, I do indeed hope to be able to produce such a systematic presentation in the not too distant future, but it will be extremely modest in scope and size, and at a relatively popular level. At the same time, however, it may legitimately be asked whether it is nowadays possible to undertake any such systematic presentation at all, if one is to write theology in a way that corresponds to the needs of the times.

Munich, 20 March 1972 Karl Rahner

PART ONE

Theology as Science

I

ON RECOGNIZING THE IMPORTANCE OF THOMAS AQUINAS

T HE purpose of the present study must be defined here right at the
outset so that everyone can know what he has to deal with in it. It
is intended as a call to contemporary Catholic theologians not to
forget Thomas Aquinas. From the time of Leo XIII onwards he has been
the teacher in Catholic theology, the *Doctor Angelicus et Communis.*[1]
Formerly his position as such was laid down in ecclesiastical law: the study
of theology should be practised *ad mentem* Thomas Aquinas.[2] And although the tone adopted by the Second Vatican Council was already far
less forceful, nevertheless it singled Thomas out for special mention in the
course of its pronouncement on ecclesiastical studies.[3] Even the past few
years have seen the appearance of serious studies on his theology, which
rank higher than that type of doctorate thesis which consists in the presentation of various historical details but is incapable of making any dynamic
impact on the theology of the future. In Rome too one more Congress of
Thomists[4] was recently added to the many which have already been held
in the past. Yet even so, in contemporary theology regarded as a whole,
there is a strange silence on the subject of Thomas. We need only to
glance at the catalogue of recent major publications in theology to recognize the extent to which Thomas has receded into the background among
all those many theologians from whom it is found necessary to quote at

[1] Leo XIII, *Aeterni Patris,* dated 4 August 1879; cp. DS 34, 3135–3140.
[2] CIC c 1366 § 2.
[3] Vatican II, 'Gravissimum educationis' (*Declaration on Christian Education*), no.
10, and the references there adduced to the address of Pope Paul VI to the Sixth
International Congress of Thomists on 10 September 1965; cf. also 'Optatam totius'
(*Decree on Priestly Formation*) no. 16, and also the references to addresses of Pope
Pius XII (24 June 1939), and Pope Paul VI (12 March 1964).
[4] The Seventh International Congress of Thomists held at Rome from 7 to 12
September 1970; on this cf. the report by H. Beck in *Philos. Jahrbuch* 78 (1971),
pp. 181–184.

various points in any scholarly presentation of theology. Is this state of affairs so satisfactory? Should it be allowed to remain unchanged? That is the question.

We shall not be in a position to give a negative answer to this question until we have made one proviso. Right down to the most recent times it has been possible to regard Thomas as in a peculiarly direct sense *the* teacher in the schools of theology and for his *Summa* to be used as *the* textbook. All that the lecturer had to do in order to discharge his duties as a lecturer in theology was merely to supply a commentary on what he had written. Whether this approach was *de facto* universally adopted is another question. It was possible to adopt it, and to a large extent it actually was adopted, and, moreover, with the recommendation and approval of the official Church. And once this approach was adopted it was possible for great benefits to be reaped from it. Whether changes should have been introduced at an even earlier stage is again a question which does not concern us here. Today we neither can nor should adopt precisely *this* approach any longer, and do not in fact do so. From being, in this peculiarly direct sense, *the* teacher of theology in the theological schools themselves, Thomas has acquired the status of a Father of the Church. He has receded into the background and become more remote. And this is something which we cannot alter. From this point of view any restoration of the former seminary Thomism, or of a direct and almost naïve commitment to Thomas as to a contemporary figure, would be a betrayal of the Church and of the men of today. From having formerly been a teacher in this direct sense he has become a Father of the Church, an authority belonging to the same dimension as the great philosophers such as Plato or Aristotle, or the great theologians such as Augustine or Origen, more remote, less readily accessible, more isolated than he was before. And this remains true even though this authority which he carries is of a quite specific, peculiar, and unique kind of which we shall have to treat further. This state of affairs is quite inevitable. For after all between him and us lie seven hundred years of further and forceful developments in the history of ideas and the history of the world. Hence we cannot simply ignore all that lies between him and us. And of course this applies to theology too. The methods of teaching and the scientific approach envisaged by the Second Vatican Council for theology no longer ascribe to Thomas a status such that his works can be regarded simply as *the* textbook of theology for today.

But while recognizing all this we are still very far from being justified on this account in more or less forgetting Thomas, or only allowing him still to have a place in our discussions as the subject of theological dissertations. He must remain alive in contemporary theology even though his function in it is more or less that of a Father of the Church. For in saying this we can still recognize that his function is of a unique kind by comparison with the other Fathers of the Church. The reason why it is necessary to recognize this is not merely that Thomas is one of the initiators of that anthropocentric approach which already has been for centuries, and still continues to be even today, a decisive influence on the cultural and intellectual life of Europe; not merely, in other words, that for anyone who seeks to reach back to the roots of his own situation, Thomas is one of the factors which he must not ignore. There are other reasons too, simpler than that which we have mentioned, to which Metz and others have already drawn our attention.[5]

Even in the speculative disciplines or arts there is a spirit of the age which raises problems. Even here, and not least in theology itself, it is inevitable that there should be historical development and change. The gospel has to be preached in ever fresh forms, adapted to the changing historical situations of its hearers. And hence theology is confronted again and again with fresh tasks. And, with the best will in the world – seeing that man and his capacity for attention are finite – such fresh tasks cannot simply be added on to those we already have, and so be fulfilled in such a way as to leave what has gone before totally unaffected. Whether we like it or not, fresh tasks tend to squeeze out former tasks and aims, which inevitably recede into the background. A theology which was not one-sided in any sense would be a bad theology. If we were so balanced as to accord an equal measure of our attention and capacities for work to every possible approach, this would merely be a secret excuse on our part for being reluctant, or even totally unwilling, to come to grips with the new tasks and duties that press in upon us. What we are saying here, then, does not imply any rejection of a legitimate one-sidedness, or of laying very strong emphases on particular aspects of a question, even in the study of theology. But there are also wrong kinds of one-sidedness, and to forget Thomas would be one such. To forget Thomas might be fashionable, but it could only lead to a blurring and circumscribing of that awareness of the past which is so fragile, the maintaining of which is

---

[5] A survey on the question of 'anthropomorphism' is provided by J. Splett in *Sacramentum Mundi* I (New York and London, 1968), pp. 40–41; on the same subject cf. J. B. Metz, *Christliche Anthropozentrik* (Munich, 1962), and the discussion arising from this, H. Meyer, 'Zur chrislichen Anthropozentrik', *Th. Rv.* 61 (1965), 9–12, and J. B. Metz, 'Nochmals: Christliche Anthropozentrik', *ibid.*, pp. 13–16.

precisely the function of theology, and which, according to Metz, is the indispensable precondition for any genuinely enlightened attitude towards the present, and so too towards present-day theology.[6] Often that which we leave unspoken is precisely that which, in a strange way, we are suppressing, that which we do not want to consider because it calls for a critical questioning of our own position. In view of the silence of contemporary theologians on the subject of Thomas, this is a point to be borne in mind.

To put it more precisely: in the speculative disciplines it is necessary, if they are to remain alive, for us to maintain contact not merely with the ideas, but with the thinkers too, of earlier ages. In the physical sciences the learned figures of the past still continue to figure only through the busts set up to them at the entrances to laboratories or as names that are given to laws or units of measure. But with the speculative disciplines the situation cannot be the same. For in these the essential meaning of an idea is not present wholly and solely in the terms in which it is expressed. The actual process of thought leading up to the idea must be taken into account as well. For we always acquire deeper insights into the idea itself in and through this than in the proposition resulting from this thought process taken by itself. And we can always make the idea our own in a more satisfying way by taking the thought process behind it into account. Again and again we must think with a thinker if we are to achieve a genuine and radical insight into his ideas. In this field of the speculative disciplines the process of thinking with the thinker at the personal level is an intrinsic factor in the process of thinking objectively. It entails a dialogue that is constantly renewed with the great thinkers of the past who can never, properly speaking, be wholly out of date since the questions they raise can never be answered in such a way that the question in itself can be set aside as a problem that has definitively been solved. On these grounds alone, then, and abstracting from all other considerations, the history of philosophy, and *a fortiori* of theology, constitute intrinsic elements in philosophy and theology themselves such that without them these disciplines would always be subject to the contingent character of their own present, and, in the end, to destruction, and, moreover, precisely at that point at which their practitioners considered them so modern and relevant to the present that they imagined that they could dispense with that dialogue with their own past which is so necessary.

Thomas Aquinas is to be numbered among the great figures of theology

---

[6] Well treated of by J. B. Metz, 'Political Theology', *Sacramentum Mundi*, V (New York and London, 1970), pp. 34–38, together with the bibliography there adduced.

with whom any contemporary theology must engage in a genuine dialogue. This despite the interval of seven hundred years which separates him from us. Certainly he is not the sole partner with whom we so engage. There are others too. Nevertheless I believe that even today Thomas still remains, in a quite special and *unique* sense, a theologian of such magnitude that he must not cease to have a place in our discussions. In support of this opinion I will adduce only a few quite simple reasons. Thomas is first and foremost a theologian who, if the paradox may be permitted, is interested in that which is for the moment uninteresting. He is not the kind of theologian who is influenced by a mere fashion or succumbs to a monomania that blinds him to all other aspects except one. His attitude of balance and calm is such that he can give his attention to *a whole number* of theological questions. However true it may be to call him a *systematic* theologian, it is no less true that the importance he attaches to system never leads him to omit questions and valid findings which at first sight do not seem to be prompted either by his basic approach or by any special relevance they may have for him. It is consistent with this attitude that Thomas' reading and range of studies and general knowledge should also have been extraordinarily wide for his time. Points of common knowledge, points already made by others, and seemingly quite unexciting, are just as interesting to him as those which *he himself* recognizes for the first time or manages to embody in his system. So much is this the case that even when he brings out a point that is absolutely original to himself, he either never mentions the fact at all, or at most gives some indirect indication of it. Among the ancient Fathers of the Church, and among the theologians of his own age as well as of later ages, there may be not a few whom we find more immediately striking than him in virtue of their originality and creativity, their capacity for sudden fresh discoveries, the element of challenge and passionate commitment to their theories. But the theologian of today could learn certain simple lessons from him: to think *in breadth*, to have enough boldness to be modest and self-critical, to give devoted consideration to points which seem uninteresting or not relevant to the moment, to listen to, and take seriously, the views of others, even when they may at first be on a different wave-length from oneself in the arguments they put forward, to recognize genuinely and sincerely that one can only exercise self-criticism, and so be truly modern and avoid merely following the fashions of yesterday with the rest, by bearing in mind the ideas of earlier ages. This is why Thomas' tone is gentle and restrained. He is not concerned to dress his ideas up in impressive terms. In speaking of great matters he does not find it necessary to make them still greater by the greatness of his words. His ideas are consistently developed in the perspective of, and orientated towards, the whole. He does not seek to make an impression, but is rather himself impressed by the matters he is treating of. Even as he seeks to express and impart his ideas to others he is still meditating upon them and making their reality his own. And because of all this he is almost speaking to himself, patient with himself and the question he is treating of, and courteous towards his opponents insofar as he either has, or ever could have, any such at all in view of the intrinsic breadth and magnitude of his spirit. He is the systematic theologian who consistently considers each individual point in the light of clearly conceived ultimate principles; the theologian who, in his questioning, is preoccupied with fundamentals and not much concerned with the complexities and variegations of the concrete world. But because he is a realist, the specific point of detail represents something more for him than merely an occasion for discoursing on abstract principles. He still continues to accord it all due respect even when, at first sight, it seems that it cannot, without further modification, be brought into line with the great *leitmotivs* of his thought.

In this sober realism of his we find concealed, or rather betrayed, a sense of reverence and yearning for the eternal light which does not yet illumine our minds directly here below; an awareness that even in theology all the theologian's insights are theological only to the extent that he remains consistently conscious of their provisional character. For the theologian must remain conscious of this even when *that* dimension of inconceivability which, properly speaking, it is his sole province to consider, is not being acclaimed in lyrical outpourings.

Thomas is the mystic, whose message is one of adoration of that mystery which transcends all powers of expression. He does not hold that because theology is concerned with this incomprehensible mystery of God it should speak of it in terms that are vague or imprecise. But neither does he hold that precision of language in theology should give the impression that one has penetrated the divine mystery and caught it within the subtle convolutions of theological concepts. Thomas knows (even though he may not repeat it every other moment) that the utmost precision and the soberest realism which is achieved in true theology are ultimately designed simply to serve a single end: to force man out of the brightness of the dimension which he can comprehend, and into the mystery of God where he no longer grasps but rather is grasped, where he no longer rationalizes but rather adores, where he no longer controls but rather is himself subject to a higher control.

When we say the words '*Adoro te devote*, latens *Deitas, quae sub his figuris vere latitas*' we must not always speak them in a lyrical sense, but recognize that they also express the innermost essence of all theological thought and perception. This will continue to be the case for all eternity. Even when we behold face to face, that which we behold, love, and praise will be the eternal mystery which continues to be such. Indeed, so far from diminishing, once it is present in itself, and no longer merely in signs and parables, it will be still more incomprehensible and more consuming. And because of all this the theology of pilgrim man must not be at variance with this recognition of God as mystery. It must point us on to the experience of the mystery in the absolute, albeit the mystery that has been brought near to us. It is not for the idle, the soulless, or the heartless to say that what is said in theology is all straw, though St Thomas himself did in fact say this. Yet, measured by the ineffable reality which it seeks to make its concern, all that theology has to say is, after all, mere '*paleae*', straw. And to recognize this is a pain that slays us and raises us from the dead. And unless a man has himself, in heart and spirit, with zeal and energy, endured this pain with Thomas, then he has never given himself to theological study as a disciple of Thomas either. His theology may perhaps be ingenious, but it will never be really spiritual theology, the theology of the Pneuma, theology in the true sense. From an historical point of view it may be Thomism, but it will never be the kind of theology that is Thomas-inspired.

Obviously a Thomism that has become petrified has manifested itself in various forms and at various points in the course of history. Its practitioners have set themselves to keep Thomas alive, but in the very act of so doing have in fact brought him into discredit with their own contemporaries. But this is, after all, a fate that befalls other thinkers and other schools as well. The Jansenism of the 17th century is a petrified Augustinianism. The philosophy of such figures as Wolff is a 'boiled-down' version of the philosophy of Leibniz, truncated and adapted for pedagogic purposes, and so on. We must precisely avoid judging a great philosopher or a great theologian by the minor school which invokes his name, and the members of which are prone to deny that anyone unwilling to be associated with their pettifogging systems can be a disciple of their master at all. We must avoid viewing Thomas simply in the light of a Cajetan (though in itself his contribution is far from insignificant) – still less in the light of the Thomism of a Billuart or any other theologian of a similar kind. We must reject the attempt to reduce the truly great philosophy of a Thomas to that potted version of it produced under Pius X in the so-called Twenty Theses published by the Congregation of Studies at Rome in 1914, and purporting to be the genuine philosophical teaching of Thomas.[7] In response to all such forms of circumscribed, over-systematized, and so petrified Thomism, we must insist on the point that in his own period, and measured by the philosophy and theology then accepted as traditional, Thomas himself must have been felt to be uncompromisingly progressive, if not actually revolutionary. This must have been so even though he himself never proclaimed his own theology and philosophy *as* progressive or revolutionary with drums and trumpets. Instead, calmly confining his attention solely to the question under investigation, and without any strident partizanship, he said what he had to say. Yet precisely in virtue of this he stood at the centre of a theological current, and was never the upholder of any final and definitive system, an edifice within which men of all subsequent ages could live. In this respect too Thomas can be an example and a consolation to those of today who seek to practise, at their own cost and at their own risk, a type of theology that has come to be discarded, and in doing so refuse to be 'modern' in the sense of falling in with mere fleeting fashions of the hour, thereby giving their work a spurious acceptability.

Certainly we should not adopt the approach of Leo XIII in regarding Thomas as the one great ocean into which all conceivable streams of wisdom and knowledge flow and converge, so that it is from *this* ocean alone that we must draw our knowledge and inspiration, all other sources now being superfluous. Again, he is obviously conditioned by his own age, and has not pronounced upon all those questions which we of today have to raise and to find answers to. Yet we do need to be aware that even in those factors which, from a Christian and theological standpoint, we have to recognize, act upon, or endure as characteristic of our own age, we are not far removed from Thomas. The philosophical apparatus (emanating from Greek sources) which he uses in his theology may to a large extent be derived from an approach that is orientated towards objects and an objective world, an approach, therefore, belonging to a stage *prior to* Copernicanism, when philosophy became reorientated towards the subject and existence. In his approach Thomas may still have few explicit reflections to offer on the historicity of man and of his thought, so ingenuously – almost naïvely – near is he to history itself. Yet for all this he does stand at the threshold of that world which still remains ours of today as well, the world which is essentially secular, and not immediately

[7] cf. DS 34, 3601–3624 (Decree of the Congregation of Studies of 27 July 1914).

apprehensible as sacral in character. It is true that Thomas may be regarded as the great philosopher and theologian of a comprehensive system of ideas in which all that is genuinely real is duly recognized as such, but at the same time assigned its appropriate place within the system in all its breadth. But while Thomas is all this, he is also first and last the theologian who, in the teeth of the conservatism and pietism of his contemporaries, recognized philosophy as an autonomous discipline, one which sees God not as one particular element (albeit the highest) within the world, but rather as him who produces effects in the world only through those 'second causes', those realities and forces which themselves belong intrinsically to the world as having power over its own course. This means that Thomas himself stands at the origins of that reflexive process in theology in which Christian faith explicitly recognizes the status of the world as autonomous and responsible for its own destiny. It is true that, by a process of synthesis, this world, while still remaining autonomous and secular, is nevertheless subsumed, in Thomas' system, within the order of God as revealing himself and creating salvation. And while this synthesis may still be over-static and, as it stands, not something that we can simply accept without modification, the fact still remains that Thomas stands at the beginning of a period in the history of ideas in which his system, taken in conjunction with Scotism and Nominalism, and as developed between the earlier period and the High Middle Ages, can be set down as the beginning of that age which, in a true sense, remains ours also. Today, for instance, we are living in the age of rationalism, and of a methodological atheism, the outcome of the empiricism of the natural sciences. In our theology of creation and grace we think of God not so much as him who inserts himself into the world, as it were perforating an otherwise closed system from without, but rather as the infinite incomprehensible mystery and absolute future, present intrinsically in the world all along as that which provides its ultimate consummation and so sustains its movement towards this from within. And if all this is true, then we must feel that we are not far removed from Thomas. At the same time we must recognize in him a consoling confirmation of the fact that in the last analysis that which is special and proper to our age derives from the spirit of Christianity. Whatever disagreements there may be on points of detail – and all too often both sides are guilty of misrepresentations here – these special characteristics of our own age do not involve any rebellion against Christianity. On the contrary, they have already been accepted and recognized, at least incipiently and in principle, by him whom the Church recognizes as her 'doctor communis'. And this even though much of what is said so simply and quietly would surely still seem revolutionary even today to the more timid and conservative elements in the Church if they only realized to the full the true import of his message.

As we said right at the outset, what we need in theology, if we are to practise it aright, is not only great theologies but great theologians also, so that in fellowship with them we may reflect upon the ineffable in a spirit of reverence.

I do not believe that some spectacular Thomist renaissance is on the point of breaking out in the Church. But at the same time I do hope that there will always be enough independent thinkers constantly emerging afresh in theology. And by 'independent thinkers' I mean such as will also have the courage to be unmodern, to enter the arduous school of a great master and, when they are confronted with goals which can be achieved only slowly and at the cost of toil, will not regard them merely as a bore. So long as the Church can number such men and such theologians in her ranks and in her theological schools, so long will Thomas Aquinas always have disciples and constantly be acquiring fresh ones. For today too he still has something to say. One element in that awareness of what Christ means in the Church which renders us free and immune to the cult of mere modernism is safeguarded in the works of Thomas.

2

THOMAS AQUINAS ON TRUTH

OUR purpose here is to present, in brief outline, the essence of truth as seen by Thomas.[1] For this it should be unnecessary either to point out *in extenso* where the relevant statements are to be found, or to draw attention to the limits imposed upon us by the very nature of an article of this kind. It should be equally unnecessary to spend much time in justifying the point that all that is possible here is to provide a few summary indications – necessarily, therefore, in simplified form. What is more important is to draw attention right from the outset to two difficulties which any such attempt necessarily entails. First, Thomas Aquinas is by profession a theologian rather than a philosopher. It is true that he consciously draws upon certain explicit philosophical tenets in that he continually incorporates them into his theology, but he had never developed this philosophy in itself into a positive system in its own right. He has not written any major work such as could, in any true sense, be said to be exclusively philosophical in character. Even the *Summa Contra Gentiles*[2] is, measured by the essential message which inspires it, not a philosophical work but a work of Christian apologetics.

This conclusion does not for one moment imply any pre-judgement as to the intrinsic value of Thomas' philosophy. But it does give us some intimation of the difficulties entailed in attaching a philosophy which is so much subordinated and assimilated to theology, and in presenting it in its own intrinsic significance and, corresponding to this, the principles it lays down. This state of affairs in fact leads to the position that even

[1] The text of this essay – a lecture first delivered in 1938 and here lightly revised in certain unimportant details – belongs to the period of the author's basic works: *Geist in Welt* (Innsbruck, 1939) and *Hörer des Wortes* (Munich, 1941). The reason for publishing it here for the first time is that apart from its documentary importance it has a special value as indicating the basic preoccupations of the author in the development of his thought.

[2] In German, *Thomas von Aquin, Die Summa wider die Heiden*, Vols I–IV (Leipzig, 1935–1937).

though a point may be crucial from a philosophical point of view in Thomas' works, it does not always follow that it is also the main point at issue. This also applies to the subject of our present investigation. It is true that we have the *Quaestiones Disputatae de Veritate*[3] and for some years a good translation of these has been available, that namely by Edith Stein, the pupil of Husserl. This does provide us with certain important pointers (especially in the case of the first *Quaestio*, articles 1–12, where truth is explicitly treated of). But many of the arguments here would be quite out of place in a philosophical discussion. Of course further and more comprehensive passages are to be found which throw an important light on the epistemology of Thomas Aquinas.[4] A further factor in his teaching which the historian of philosophy cannot, properly speaking, neglect, is his teaching on angelic knowledge. For it is here, despite the fact that the context seems to be of its nature exclusively theological, that Thomas Aquinas presses his theory of knowledge to its ultimate limits in developing the concept of a finite knowledge that is not based on sense experience. This teaching on angelic knowledge in Thomas represents, so to say, a counterpart to the monadology of Leibniz.

In view of this situation and the difficulties it entails, we are justified in approaching the question in such a way that our presentation seems unconnected (at least to all outward appearances) with any specific individual passages in Thomas' writings. Instead our exposition of his basic position will be through a freer approach, and one which, in fact, in view of the difficulties described, we are obliged to adopt.

To this initial difficulty in achieving any adequate presentation of the thought of Aquinas a second must now be added: the question of its interpretation. A point which applies to Plato, Aristotle, Kant, and others

---

[3] German, *Des hl. Thomas von Aquino Untersuchungen über die Wahrheit*, Edith Steins Werke, III (Louvain/Freiburg i. Br. 1952; first published in 1931).

[4] The relevant passages have been assembled and set forth by Jos. de Vries, *De Cognitione Veritatis Textus Selecti Sancti Thomae Aquinatis*, Op. et Textus, Ser. Schol. XIV (Munster, 2nd ed. 1953). Cf. *Summa Contra Gentiles* I, cc. 44–71 (metaphysics of the divine knowledge); II, cc. 46–90 (anthropology and the metaphysics of human knowledge); *Summa Theologiae* I qq. 14–17 (the knowledge of God; ideas; truth; falsehood), *Summa Theologiae*, Eng. transl. Vol. 4, *Knowledge in God* (London, 1964); qq. 79 (the powers of reason), *Summa Theologiae*, Eng. transl. Vol. II (London); qq. 84–88 (how the soul, in conjunction with the body, comes to know the physical world which is subordinate to it by reason; the modes and consequences of rational knowledge; what does our reason know of material things?; how does the soul endowed with intelligence come to understand itself and its powers?; how does the human soul come to know what is above it?), *Summa Theologiae*, Eng. transl., Vol. 12 (London, 1968).

is just as true of Thomas here. In all cases we can discuss how far the philosopher's teaching is correct only to the extent that we find it easy to answer, and to achieve general agreement upon, the question of what he actually taught. We can never arrive at the true philosophical content of what is being taught merely by assembling and summarizing the relevant statements. The only way of doing this is creatively to reconstruct the original line of reasoning of the philosopher himself. And this principle applies to Thomas too, for unfortunately his justly acclaimed clarity also entails a constant temptation to assume that his philosophy is easier than it in fact is. Our only reason for pointing this out in the present context is that we wish right from the outset to emphasize that in the present interpretation of Thomas nothing that we have to say either can or should be regarded as spoken in the name of scholasticism. All that we seek to convey is that particular interpretation of Aquinas which, as we personally believe, must be correct. That is our sole aim. The question of whether our understanding of the master is right or wrong cannot be decided by invoking some illusory consensus of 'the' scholastics, but only by a fresh examination of Thomas' own writings and of the matter itself.[5]

[5] In addition to textual studies and translations we find a whole series of attempts to provide a comprehensive presentation and interpretation of Aquinas' teaching on truth, belonging chiefly to the period of the thirties, but also, in part, both to earlier and later periods. Mention may be made of certain important works which are not without significance for the thought of the present author as well: P. Rousselot, *L'intellectualisme de Saint Thomas* (Paris, 2nd ed., 1924); J. Maréchal, *Le point de départ de la metaphysique* (Bruges/Louvain – Paris, 1923–1926); G. Söhngen, *Sein und Gegenstand. Das scholastische Axiom: ens et verum convertuntur als Fundament metaphysische und theologische Spekulation* (Munster, 1930); P. Wilpert, *Das Problem der Wahrheitssicherung bei Thomas von Aquin* (Munster, 1931); P. Wilpert, 'Das Urteil als Träger der Wahrheit nach Thomas von Aquin', *Philos. Jahrbuch* 46 (1953), pp. 56–75; A. Hufnagel, *Intuition und Erkenntnis bei Thomas von Aquin* (Munster, 1932); G. Siewerth, *Die Metaphysik der Erkenntnis nach Thomas von Aquin I: der sinnliche Erkenntnisakt* (Munich/Berlin, 1933); idem, 'Die transzendentale Selbigkeit und Verschiedenheit des ens und des verum bei Thomas von Aquin', *Philos. Jahrbuch* 66 (1957), pp. 22–23; idem, *Der Thomismus als Identitätssystem* (Frankfurt, 3rd ed. 1961); J. B. Lotz, *Das Urteil und das Sein*, Pullacher *philos. Forsch.* II (a second edition, revised and expanded, of *Sein und Wert* I, 1938) (Pullach, 1957); M. Müller, *Sein und Geist. Systematische Untersuchungen über Grundproblem und Aufbau mittelalterlicher Ontologie*, Beiträge zur Philosophie und ihrer Geschichte, 7 (Tübingen, 1940); J. Pieper, *Wahrheit der Dinge. Eine Untersuchung zur Anthropologie des Hochmittelalters* (Munich, 1947); W. Kern, 'Das Verhältnis von Erkenntnis und Liebe als philosophisches Grundproblem bei Hegel und Thomas von Aquin', *Scholastik* 34 (1959), pp. 394–427; E. Coreth, 'Das Sein als Wahrheit', *Metaphysik* (Innsbruck, 1961), pp. 399–422; J. Fellermeier, 'Wahrheit und Existenz bei Thomas von Aquin', *Münch. theol. Zeitschrift* 20 (1969), pp. 136–145.

Our ideas will be developed in three stages. If we were to name each stage in accordance with the basic ideas of Thomism itself they might be classified as follows: 1. Judgement, 2. The Light of the Active Intellect (*Intellectus Agens*), and 3. God: Pure Being and Pure Thought. In terms of Hegelian terminology we might bring our threefold classification into line with the three divisions of his phenomenology of the mind as follows: 1. Awareness, 2. Awareness of Self, and 3. Absolute Mind. The first section is discarded because Thomas regards truth as present only in the judgement. The second section is justified on the grounds that according to Aquinas judgement consists not in any mere passive acceptance of an impression, but in a creative synthesis between the transcendental *a priori* of the mind (the light of the active intellect) and sense experience. Finally the inclusion of the third section is justified by the fact that Thomas recognizes, side by side with the truth of judgement, the further ontological truth of being in itself, an intrinsic illumination of that which is inasmuch as, and to the extent that it is being, an illumination which finds its absolute fulness and ultimate original norm in that absolute being which is the absolute intelligence.

1. *The Judgement*

'If truth consists in the agreement of an act of cognition with its object....' Thus even Kant opens his argument.[6] We should not, therefore, be surprised that in the Thomistic metaphysic of the nature of truth the same sentence should provide the starting-point and, so to say, the definition of truth: '*adaequatio rei et intellectus*'.[7] Ultimately speaking, however, what we have here is a mere provisional approximation, a mere description, of something which we are aware of from the first when we begin to ask what truth is. The situation here is the same as with all metaphysical enquiries. It is an enquiry into something which is already familiar to us from the first, and which we fail to comprehend precisely for this reason. For what do we mean when we say that truth is present where intellect and object agree? In real terms, what is intellect? What is being? What is agreement? And how can these particular entities agree with one another? It is self-evident, therefore, that even though this initial definition is familiar to us from the first, we can only grasp its true meaning once we have comprehended the particular concepts of which it is composed in themselves, and

[6] I. Kant, *Kritik der reinen Vernunft*, BS. 83.
[7] cf. e.g. Thomas Aquinas, *Summa Theologiae* I, q. 21, art. 2 c, and *Quaestiones Disputatae de Veritate*, q. 1, art. 10.

also precisely as components of this statement considered as an unity.

We find an initial indication of what Thomas means by intellect (*intellectus*) when we find him saying that truth at the human level is located in the judgement. It is self-evident that in the normal act of human cognition it is the content of the judgement, and not the act of judging as such, that is made to correspond to the object: '*Illud quod intellectus intelligendo dicit et cognoscit oportet esse rei adaequatum . . . non operatio qua id dicit*'.[8] For Thomas a meaningful content of this kind, such as – under certain circumstances at least – can claim to constitute truth, is possible of attainment only in judgement and not in the forming of a concept, i.e. what he calls *simplex apprehensio* or *incomplexum*. We must emphasize, therefore, that point in Thomas' doctrine on judgement which is most important for our enquiry. For Aquinas a judgement does not consist merely in a synthesis between two concepts so as to form a single concrete idea. In Thomas' eyes a concretizing synthesis of this kind – Heidegger would call it a predicative synthesis – would still be an *incomplexum* of the type, for instance, to which definition belongs. In order for judgement and truth in the true sense to be present, the concretizing synthesis must further be related to the reality itself; there must be a *comparatio vel applicatio ad rem per affirmationem vel negationem*. An affirmative or objectifying synthesis of this kind (and it is only through this kind of synthesis that a *complexio* or judgement is arrived at) is therefore a constitutive element of judgement and so too of truth (with Heidegger we might also call it a veritative synthesis), though admittedly only provided that this affirmative synthesis is also in fact a valid one. Of course the subject and predicate do not have the same place or function in the statement involved, a point which can be demonstrated by an analysis of the Thomist doctrine of the concretizing synthesis. The known content of the concept forming the predicate is applied to the object itself in its ontological reality as pointed to by the affirmative synthesis and as designated by the concept forming the subject, so that the affirmative synthesis is just as much the enabling condition of the concretizing synthesis as the other way round.

Now for Thomas Aquinas it is only in such judgements that truth exists, for it is only in them that this affirmative and objectifying application can be made of the consciously entertained content of our ideas to a reality existing in its own right, and independently of the concept as such that we form of it at the psychic level. As applied to such an ontological reality, therefore, the reason that our judgement is valid is that the

[8] *Summa Contra Gentiles* I, c. 39.

concretizing synthesis is merely the reproduction in the conceptual dimension of that synthesis achieved in the objective one between a subject (a *hypokeimenon*) and a quiddity (*quidditas, forma* etc.) by which that subject is specified.

But how does the subject making the judgement know that his reproduction and application of the objective synthesis is actually valid, does in fact correspond to it? Clearly there can be no question – at least in all ordinary cases – of proceeding straightway to compare the reality as known in the act of judgement with the reality in itself.

In order to understand Thomas' answer to this question we must begin by laying down, in accordance with his teaching, that every one of our judgements and every one of our concepts contain two elements: a sensible element and an intellectual one (representation and conception, to the extent that this is based on the spontaneity of the understanding, as we might say with Kant). Aquinas would wholeheartedly subscribe to the following statement by Kant: 'Thoughts without content are empty; perceptions without conceptions are blind.'[9] The point Kant is seeking to make here is treated of by Thomas under the heading of the necessity of a *conversio* to the *phanatasma* in spontaneous thinking.[10] As for Kant, so too for Thomas, there are no perceptions other than sensible ones. This proposition calls for some explanation at this point, at least in passing, since time does not admit of any fuller discussion of it. According to Thomas sensibility as such, to the extent that it apprehends the existing thing at all, apprehends it as it truly is in itself. The 'impression upon the receptivity of our mind' is, as a single and undivided reality, present at one and the same time both in the sensible object itself and in sensibility as such. This seemingly 'naïve' realism is in truth profoundly metaphysical, for the conception of sensibility on which it rests is metaphysical and ontological in character, and is not merely derived from an empiricist-sensualist approach in which the senses are regarded as instruments. This metaphysical and ontological conception in its turn stems from the conception of a finite act of perception that 'takes in' an individual object as such as it presents itself in its own identity; only so does it arrive at the metaphysical conception of what it is to be material: the materiality of the object that exhibits itself, and the necessary materiality, and thereby sensibility, of a knowledge that 'takes in' and perceives. Unfortunately it is impossible here fully to carry through this transcendental deduction of the sensibility inherent in a finite act of perception. Hence, even though

---

[9] I. Kant, *Kritik der reinen Vernunft*, B S. 75.
[10] *Summa Theologiae* I, q. 84, art. 7.

our approach at this point is, properly speaking, quite unphilosophical, all that we can do is to give the following assurance: when we speak of the apprehending, by a subject endowed with sensibility, of certain determinations in a material object in itself, this involves no contradiction for philosophy because, as contrasted with popular notions, it regards the essential metaphysic of the process by which one material being is affected by another material being as consisting precisely in the fact that absolutely one and the same reality is present in both agent and patient. Now if a determination of the patient of this kind is recognized to be such, then, since the 'patient' in this case is sensibility, this means that we are recognizing and experiencing a determination of the agent as such, and, in the case we are considering, as a determination of the sensible object.

If it were pointed out that after all, as the most universal experience attests, that which is immediately observed by the senses (the sensible qualities) is to be regarded as present only in the sensible experience itself, Thomas would surely have disposed of this by replying that the determination of a being does not cease to belong to it because it belongs to that being only inasmuch as it is posited as a specification of itself *and* of the patient at the same time. Two points follow from this position: first, scope is given, on a totally different scale, for a physics in the metaphysical sense, i.e. regarded as critical enquiry into the determinations of a material being, which belong to it independently of its reality, and as being the kind of thing it is and shows itself to be in the medium of the sensory cognition of the knowing subject. The second point, however, is that even prior to any physics an answer is given to the metaphysical question of how the knowledge of another being can apprehend by taking something into itself, a question which must, in principle, be resolved prior to any physics, since any physics, whatever critique it has to offer of outward appearances, basically presupposes an outside world that is already realized as such, and so a knowledge that is already present from the outset emanating from that which is other to itself. This remains true even when it supposes that what it experiences is, in itself, merely a subjective affection, for even this is still external to the knowledge we have of it. The metaphysic of sensibility that is presupposed in Thomas' theory of cognition is, then, of this kind. According to it sensibility is a finite experience in which a finite being reveals itself and is 'taken in', a kind of knowledge in which a sensible object is possessed in its manifestation of itself as it is in itself. Once we assume such a metaphysic of sensibility it is immediately evident why, according to Aquinas, sense knowledge as such can never be false and, for this very reason, never true either in any proper sense.[11]

The purely passive process of consciously 'taking in' – it would be called receptivity without spontaneity by Kant, or awareness without self-awareness by Hegel – in virtue of its passivity, makes it possible for the real thing to imprint its image upon the receptivity of the knower, and so to reveal itself of itself. But precisely in making this possible, this passive process makes it impossible for sensibility to stand back, so to say, from the impression it has received and from its object, and so to judge of it as it is in itself. What sensibility experiences is always a genuine reality, yet it cannot express any judgement upon it, which means that strictly as such it never rises to a level at which it is capable of being true or false. Sensibility possesses things in a single uninterrupted projection from the things themselves, but for this very reason it is also at the mercy of their obtuse particularity, their lack of reference to anything beyond themselves. Of course when such sensibility is linked with an intellectual and spontaneous power of knowledge within the unity of conscious awareness, as with man, this sub-logical certainty, inherent in the material reality itself and manifesting itself of its own power at the level of sensibility, can have a certain significance for the establishing of truth. But taken in itself and in isolation from this, it merely supplies the basis for the truth of the material content of a particular judgement. The formal structure even of such a judgement, and *a fortiori* the structure and content of universal, and especially metaphysical judgements, are too advanced to find any basis in this sureness of perception at the sensible level.

2. *The Light of the Active Understanding*

We are faced, then, with a further question: what is the truth of a judgement based upon, to the extent that the judgement constitutes something more than the mere passive receiving of the impression of a particular sensible object as such? As in every major metaphysic of knowledge from Plato to Hegel, so too with Thomas Aquinas, we here arrive at a principle of truth which is prior to the sensible impression. But Thomas departs from the tradition of Plato, Plotinus, Augustine, Bonaventure, and Malebranche in refusing to regard this as consisting in any objectified *a priori* postulated as a second objective sphere immediately accessible to man, over and above the individual thing as perceptible by the senses. Thomas

---

[11] *Quaestiones Disputatae de Veritate,* q. 1, art. 11, and *Summa Theologiae* I, q. 16, art. 2.

stands, rather, in the line of the tradition of Aristotle, Thomas, Kant, and Hegel in regarding this principle of truth as consisting in a formal *a priori* of the spontaneous intellect itself. In other words it consists not in a *fundamentum* of truth viewed as an object, as for instance an idea, a light of God, God himself, etc., but rather – to express it in Thomist terms – in a light of the understanding itself which permeates and informs the material of the sense knowledge, and raises it in acts of judgement to the level of objective apprehension and conceptuality.

It would be possible to work out a transcendental deduction of this formal *a priori* of the understanding in the Thomist sense in various ways. With Aquinas himself we might enquire into the *a priori* conditions which make it possible to raise the individual object as apprehended by the senses to the conceptual level. This is the normal way in which Thomas arrives at the concept of the spontaneity of the understanding, the *intellectus agens* as he calls it (following an Aristotelian conception in this), as well as the essential structure which this has. Again we might – likewise in the Thomist sense – enquire into the conditions enabling that process to take place which Thomas recognizes as the *reditio subjecti in seipsum*, that which sets the intellect apart from all that is non-intellectual, and which, in modern terms, and in the Hegelian sense, might be called self-awareness: the capacity which the knowing subject has to stand apart from that which he experiences with his senses so as to maintain a position of free transcendence over the sense impression, even though inevitably 'lost' at this level, to evaluate it and estimate its truth, to be conscious of himself being 'over against' the world – in brief the knowing subject's capacity to enjoy that which in Heidegger's terminology is called '*Dasein*' (personal existence). We may say that the act of judgement consists in the applying of a cognitive faculty to a being as it is in itself so as to find meaning in it. In itself the being involved is set 'over against' cognition as the content of subjective awareness. Now if we accept this, then it is in fact self-evident that this act of judgement always involves a simultaneous awareness of the self as 'over against' the known object, and that for this reason any enquiry into the transcendental conditions which make a true judgement possible also involves an enquiry into the enabling conditions of self-awareness too.

We have reached a point at which we have to recognize the entire problem in the context of which the question of achieving an assured truth has to be viewed. But at this point another line of approach must at least be indicated, which is still more immediately connected with this question of an assurance of truth. The assurance of the truth of any given judgement, to the extent that this is not to be derived from the evidence of sense perception, is achieved, according to Thomas, by a reduction to the first principles. These come first in the *via intentionis*, and in critically evaluating his own judgement, the person making the judgement returns to them '*resolvendo*'.[12] It is impossible here to enter in any greater detail into the content of these first principles. We may confine ourselves to noticing that in the view of Thomas Aquinas we have in them something more than the mere principles of formal logic such as, for instance, the principle of non-contradiction. We are dealing, rather, with first principles of an ontological kind, with the ultimate and apodictic axioms of metaphysics, which claim to apply necessarily and absolutely to every existing thing. But where do we find the basis for the assurance of truth of these first principles themselves? At this stage there can no longer be any question of syllogistic justification. They must, therefore, be 'seen' as evident in themselves: *dicendum quod omnis scientia habetur per aliqua principia per se nota et per consequens visa*.[13] They are '*per se nota*', as Thomas also says frequently in other contexts.

Now for any right interpretation of the Thomist argument in support of this assurance of truth in judgement it is crucially important to know what the real import of this word 'evident' is as applied to first principles. Above all a clear grasp of first principles does not consist in the mind recognizing an obvious state of affairs in the sense of being confronted with a complex entity having being (albeit not 'existence') in its own right, or a proposition having meaning in its own right. It is not as though such a complex or such a proposition were being seen by the mind in some objective or ideal mode of being of their own. Propositions, 'values', or 'ideas' existing in their own right have no place in Aquinas' system. The reason he rejects them is that, as he sees it, there is, in principle, no objective dimension of subsistent ideas such as, in terms of being and knowledge alike, would ultimately be independent of the dimension of being already in existence. To accept any kind of vision of ideas objectively subsisting in themselves (a theory with which Thomas is familiar from Plato and Augustine, but contests) must, therefore, as he sees it, logically lead to ontologism, to the doctrine of a direct vision of absolute being in itself, in other words to a conception which he rejects from the outset on theological grounds, as well as on grounds of the Aristotelian metaphysic of epistemology.

A further point is that Thomas does not recognize that the first prin-

---

[12] *Summa Theologiae* I, q. 79, art. 8 c.
[13] *Summa Theologiae* II-II, q. 1, art. 5 c.

ciples are evident in virtue of their objective conceptual content as such in the sense that once we have realized the intrinsic meaning of the individual concepts or of the propositions as a whole in which these first principles are expressed as such, we have immediate grounds for recognizing them as having an objective existence and validity in their own right. This thesis of the classic pre-Kantian rationalism of the 17th and 18th centuries would not have gone unopposed by Aquinas any more than it did by Kant. Thomas, no less than Kant in a later age, and for the same reasons, rejected the ontological argument for the existence of God, an argument which, according to the principles of the classical rationalism, would have been regarded as sound. Indeed it is accepted as valid even by Leibniz and Wolff, and in just the same way in the rationalism of the Middle Ages, with its tendency to an objectifying mysticism, easily turning to ontologism. This is exemplified in Anselm of Canterbury, Albert the Great, Aegidius of Rome, Thomas of Strasbourg, and Bonaventure. As with the ontological proof of the existence of God, the realization – in itself certainly reasonable – of the connection which necessarily has to be established between various conceptions and the first principles, only has an ontological significance provided that this connection is valid for the individual conceptions. And for Thomas this connection is not simply and *ipso facto* established in cases in which these conceptions transcend the level of concrete individual sense experience, being something more than mere pointers to such experience. These universal conceptions, which lie at the roots of the first principles, impinge upon man in his apprehension of individual sensible reality and in connection with this. To that extent (but only to that extent) the universal concepts of metaphysics are ultimately abstractions from the individual object as apprehended by the senses. In holding this Thomas Aquinas is no Platonist but an Aristotelian. But it would be totally to misunderstand his Aristotelianism if we sought to go on from this and to jump to the over-hasty conclusion that Thomas regards the particular meaning at the level of sense perception as providing an adequate basis for the ontological validity of individual metaphysical conceptions. Thomas leaves no room whatever for doubt that the only meaning which the individual, taken simply as such, can convey is that of its own self. And because of this, while the experience of a multiplicity of individual things simply as such may perhaps be capable of providing a basis for an empirical, inductive, and so assertive, generalization of experience as expressed in propositions, it is still quite incapable of providing a basis for the validity of conceptions which are universal in a metaphysical sense, and so could be in turn the

basis for an apodictic universality and validity of metaphysical propositions, namely the first principles. For such metaphysical conceptions to
have universal validity it would be necessary to find a basis for them in a
principle that was prior to the individual case, in other words an *a priori*
principle. But, as we have already pointed out, Thomas' system is such as
to exclude any *a priori* principle of this kind, having an objective existence
of its own and independently of other being. It follows that it can only be
a formal *a priori* principle of the spontaneous intellect itself. Aquinas calls
this the *lumen intellectus agentis*. The light he refers to here is the *a priori*
form in which an intellect, of its own spontaneity, apprehends the sensory
material – Thomas actually calls the sense impression itself the *materia* of
the *intelligibile* – that which can be understood. The intellect gives conceptual form to this material, and so makes it that which is *intelligibile
actu*, that which is known at the conceptual level and emerges as a synthesis of the sensory material and the *a priori* of the intellect. And in
Thomist metaphysical epistemology this *a priori* form in which the
sensory material is apprehended is, ontologically speaking, nothing else
than the dynamic movement of the intellect as such outwards towards the
absolute totality of all possible objects of the human intellect, the *tendentia
in objectum formale adaequatum intellectus*, to express the matter in the
Latin terms of Thomism. To this extent, in this dynamic outward movement of the intellect as a 'hunger' (for so it might be called with Hegel),
the individual object as sensibly experienced is apprehended, recognized
as that which is finite, and as failing, by reason of its limitations, to measure
up to the capacity of the dynamic force in all its fulness and depth. Once
the absolute epistemological ideal is applied to it as a standard, it is shown
to be *a* being as compared with being itself, and so as a 'this', a finite
individuum, the limitations of which are such as to admit of other possible
objects being experienced together with itself. Now in the very act of
recognizing it as particular in this sense, the universal is, by implication,
recognized too and *vice versa*. The process of transcending the particular
and attaining to the totality of all possible knowable objects appears, then,
as the transcendental condition enabling abstraction to take place, and so
the condition of expressing a judgement, i.e. of understanding something
as a 'something', and finally of thereby arriving also at the *reditio completa*
of knowledge of the self.

At this point an initial question arises as to the extent and range of this
transcendence, and of what limits can be set to this totality of all possible
objects of human knowledge as opened up by the light of the *intellectus
agens*. And here Thomas departs from Kant. For, as the latter sees it, the

transcendence of the understanding and of its formal *a priori* does not in principle extend beyond the basis provided by the power of the imagination, of sensory perception. Kant's view, expressed in Thomist terms, is that the *objectum formale* of the human spirit is *ens principium numeri, ens materiale*, that which is and which has, as an intrinsic principle of its being, that *materia* which Thomas too regards as the metaphysical basis for conceiving of space and time. Now for Thomas the intellect's transcending power avowedly bears upon being in the absolute. It extends beyond the sphere of the senses, thereby opening up a knowledge of being as such, and providing the basis on which metaphysics, with its specifically human characteristics, becomes possible.

Regrettably we cannot spend any further time at this point in carrying through the transcendental deduction of this extent and range of the intellect's transcending power. For this we must refer to that work by Maréchal[14] which probably constitutes the best example of a philosopher in the spirit of Aquinas coming to terms with the central problem of Kant. Here we must confine ourselves to remarking that even according to Thomas the opening up of the sphere of human thought so as to make room for a metaphysic extending beyond the sphere of sense experience, and embracing all being in the absolute, is not achieved by any direct view of metaphysical being in the sense of classical rationalism or ontologism. According to Aquinas it is of such a nature, rather (and this is precisely something that would have to be shown by any transcendental deduction of the range of transcendence in this sense) that to accept this range of transcendence and, concomitantly with it, a knowledge of being in the absolute and in its most ultimate and formal structures, is numbered among the transcendental conditions enabling an intellect endowed with self-knowledge to make objective judgements upon, and so know, the objects of sense perception. In other words it would have to be shown that that transcendence which is the enabling condition of judgements upon, and *a priori* knowledge of, objects of the world of perception, must necessarily be a transcendence extending beyond this world, and hence is accepted to be such in every kind of knowledge belonging to this world. Once this transcendental deduction is carried through, then that condition is fulfilled under which even Kant is prepared to recognize a metaphysic as valid. While it is true that knowledge of the world based on judgement – Kant calls it physics – does not afford any direct view of the metaphysical dimension, still it does implicitly involve what is the enabling condition of this, namely the acceptance of transcendental being and of its

[14] See n. 5.

ultimate structures. Thomas' primary and most fundamental way of expressing these is not through the categories (for him, in fact, these apply primarily to material being), but through what he calls the transcendental determinations of being. For him they are the ultimate 'categories' of metaphysical being. It is from these metaphysical concepts that the first principles are formed. These are, then, valid in their application to being in the absolute, and also, by the same token, to the being touched upon in direct sense experience.

In the light of this we are now in a better position to state the precise sense in which the first principles are said to be 'evident', for according to Thomas the assurance of truth in all our true judgements is based upon this character which they have of being evident once we abstract from the evident character of sense experience as such. For this latter, of itself and taken in isolation, is incapable of any judgements at all, much less any true judgements.

The character of any judgement as evident is ultimately based on the character of the first principles as evident. As principles these are, of their nature, metaphysical, i.e. they purport to apply to being as such. Their claim to have this kind of application cannot be regarded as justified by any 'evidentness' inherent in the reality of which they treat in itself, for this would presuppose that we were able to compare the concept with the metaphysical object, and so were capable of metaphysical intuition. Or again, it would necessarily mean being able to interchange the concept and the object for which it stands. The 'evidentness' of the first principles, rather, is the objective recognition that in every judgement which man makes as an act of cognition within the material world, the metaphysical validity of these principles is asserted, and this assertion constitutes the *a priori* condition, implicitly posited, which makes knowledge possible within the material world. Thus in the very act of recognizing his judgements as necessary, man is also asserting, as something posited and asserted as a necessary corollary of this, the metaphysical validity of the *a priori* structures of being as such. And since it is totally impossible for man to achieve an existential 'epoch' in his attitudes of judgement upon the world, he is necessarily, albeit implicitly, committing himself to an assertion of these metaphysical principles such that, if in his thinking he were explicitly to deny, or cast doubts upon, the ontological laws of being which he implicitly asserted, he would be breaking that law of formal logic which is the principle of non-contradiction. The 'evidentness', at the human level, therefore, of these metaphysical principles, is ultimately based not upon any recognition of an evident identity between the concepts (even for Thomist epistemology, rightly understood, these principles are a synthetic *a priori*), but on the 'evidentness' of a manifest contradiction, in terms of formal logic, between the positing as such of their validity and their content and the denying of this. If anyone were in a position to arrive at a metaphysical and existential 'epoch' from which to judge (and to doubt is also a form of judging), the metaphysical principles would cease, so far as he was concerned, to have any claim to validity. But at the selfsame moment such a one would cease to be that which he proclaimed himself to be in every act he performed: a finite being endowed with intellect, '*Dasein*' (in the sense of modern existentialist philosophy).

In the light of this conception of 'evidentness' in finite human knowledge, it is easy to understand that Thomist epistemology cannot be accused of basing its theory of the adequateness of truth upon the naïve assumption that it is possible to compare the reality in itself with the reality as known, and so to establish an agreement between the two. This objection has no basis in the Thomist interpretation of sense knowledge strictly as such, because here the reality as experienced and the reality in itself are strictly one and the same. With regard to the objects of metaphysical enquiry and their 'evidentness', the objection has no force since, on a Thomist interpretation, the 'evidentness' of these for finite knowledge is based not upon the reality in itself, but on the *a priori* of the intellect; in other words at no stage is there any attempt whatever to institute a comparison. In fact such a comparison can only be based on a misinterpretation of the nature of intellect, for it is first and foremost in this that anything in the order of truth can reside. Thomas states that in the act of understanding truth is achieved by the judgement as it bears upon the reality in itself,[15] and this statement alone serves to show how far he is from attempting at any stage to institute a comparison between the reality in itself and the reality as apprehended. Ultimately speaking, however, this truth, this *proportio ad rem* of the act of judgement, is realized not, as we would expect, by a reflecting upon, or looking at, the reality itself, but by the understanding reflecting upon itself. We do not seek, at this point, to give a precise interpretation of the actual text of Thomas, on which so incalculably much has already been written. To conclude the point we are making, we may confine ourselves merely to observing that what has here been presented as the process of transcendental reflection upon the conditions which make knowledge possible (on the *natura intellectus*, as Thomas expresses it) is, in our view, the same as that process

[15] *Quaestiones Disputatae de Veritate*, q. 1, art. 9 c.

which, in the passages just referred to, Thomas calls the '*supra seipsum reflecti*' of the understanding.

If, therefore, truth at the individual level consists in a judgement upon the 'thing in itself', where judgement is a veritative affirmative synthesis, then it is based upon the metaphysical first principles of being which constitute the sustaining basis for individual judgements. These principles, however, are rooted in the formal *a priori* of the intellect, the *lumen intellectus*, and their validity is recognized by the fact that our implicit assent to them is apprehended as being the transcendental condition making it possible for there to be objects of knowledge as such. Hence we can say that in all cases truth is possible only in self-awareness. The discovering of truth is always the discovering of the self as well on the part of the intellect.

But it also appears from this what truth signifies for Thomas at this level of the self-awareness which is always and necessarily involved in any true judgement. So far as human cognition is concerned, truth is found in the judgement alone. Judgement presupposes abstraction and self-awareness. Both are possible only in virtue of the transcendental *a priori* of the intellect, which opens up the perspective of being in the absolute. Thus a true particular judgement on a being is possible only in and through an implicit estimation of being in the absolute, at however formal a level, only in a comprehensive awareness of being itself, and so, on any definitive understanding, in an implicit acceptance of pure being, God himself. *Omnia cognoscentia implicite cognoscunt Deum in quolibet cognito.* Truth is possible only in being as such.

3. *Pure Being and Pure Thought*

These remarks are still not enough to bring our argument to its completion. That which, for the Thomist system, constitutes the heart and centre of the metaphysical concept of truth still remains to be discussed. As Thomas sees it, truth in human judgement essentially presupposes an *a priori* formal principle as its enabling condition, in any understanding arrived at through judgement, and one which must be accepted as such. Yet at the same time truth consists in judging of a being as it is in itself. This means that the intelligence adduces the ultimate formal and metaphysical structure of its possible objects of its own power and concomitantly with its judgement upon them, yet must accept this structure as that of its objects, i.e. as that of being in the absolute and in itself. Now at basis this implies nothing else than accepting an ultimate unity of being and knowledge, for it is only on this assumption that the validity of the formal *a priori* of the intellect is wholly reasonable and intelligible. Our chief point in saying this is that man, by the very fact of accepting the validity of his own transcendental *a priori*, and thereby the first principles of being as such, in every act of judgement he makes, accepts also that it is in principle possible to know a being as such. *Quidquid est intelligi potest.*[16] Furthermore, as a corollary of this, he is also assenting to the proposition that every being, as a possible object of knowledge at some level, has, as a determination of all beings necessarily present in the very nature of being itself, an intrinsic orientation to possible knowledge and a possible knower. Now if this is the case, then being and knowing (ultimately in the form of pure being, and also as realized in the existing thing to the extent that it is being and not non-being) must constitute an ultimate unity, must be *unius generis*, as Thomas puts it. For wherever a correlativity is found between two realities, such that it arises from their very natures, it can, in the last analysis, only have its basis in an original unity between the two. Now what this means as applied to our present question is that the reason that being and knowing are correlative is that they are originally and radically identical.

Pure being and pure knowing are the same reality, and we call it God. A finite being is endowed with knowledge, and in fact with knowledge of itself, in that it is, in a certain measure and according to a certain 'analogy', being. Now it is here that, taken at their ultimate metaphysical level, the concepts of knowledge, and so too of truth, are realized in their radical significance; it is here that the ultimate truth of truths is finally discerned. If being and knowledge (pure being in the absolute and *a* being in the measure that it is being) constitute an original unity, then knowledge cannot at its ultimate basis consist in a state of having something intentionally 'over against' one as an object; the only way still open to us to conceive of it is as a state in which the being concerned is 'with' or 'beside' itself, in which being is inwardly illumined to itself, in which knowing and the state of what it truly is to be known are identical, in which the knower in the true sense and the known in the true sense are one and identical in being. At its metaphysical roots, then, true knowledge consists in the unquestioning 'being with itself' of being. But knowledge and truth consist in thinking out and forming at the intentional level concepts different from the knower himself only to this extent: that that knower, in virtue of being finite, and so of the element of non-being intrinsic to him, does not *ipso facto* and from the outset know everything by the inner light of

[16] *Summa Contra Gentiles* II, c. 98.

his own intrinsic possession of himself. For he himself is not everything.

At the same time, however, to the extent that it is constantly extending itself, and to the extent that it actually 'loses itself' in the object, the act of cognition never ceases to remain a conscious 'taking possession of himself' on the part of the knower, for it is in this that knowledge first and last consists. For Thomas Aquinas the extent to which such a conscious return to the self in knowledge is possible is the essential factor showing the degree of existential power to be ascribed to a given being.[17] Thus for Aquinas an item of knowledge is true, i.e. comprehensive of being as such, to the extent that it simultaneously constitutes an opening up of the personal being of the knower, of the knowing subject. And because of this every true item of knowledge is – to put it in modern terms – always, and *ipso facto* an existential factor in the life of man as well. For the more it confronts him with being itself, the more it confronts him also with his own self, and brings him to self-realization.

Once this is recognized, namely that knowledge constitutes, in an ultimate unity, the 'being to itself' of being, we might go on to achieve an understanding of what ontological truth signifies on Thomas' theory. We might explain how ontological and logical truth are essentially interconnected. A being is, in the measure of its being, inwardly illumined to itself and possesses itself as an object of logical truth. It is in virtue of this fact that a being is ultimately knowable, a possible object of knowledge, and so ontologically true. This is why logical and ontological truth absolutely coincide in the pure being of God.

We must break off our considerations at this point. If we may make one further attempt briefly to recapitulate what we have been trying to say here, then it must be stated in conclusion that for Thomas Aquinas truth is primarily a state of having reality before one in judgement, the process of applying the concretizing synthesis between two concepts to the reality as it is in itself.

From this the following conclusion may be drawn: since truth, with the insights it offers, exists at the human level only in the judgement, it is always rooted in a transcendental *a priori* which is formal in character. The first effect of this is that being as such is always assented to in its most formal structures. Assent precisely to this is a necessary condition of realizing truth, and necessarily present, by implication, in every judgement. And this assent itself represents the ultimate assurance of truth at the human level. From this the second effect follows, namely that this trans-

---

[17] cf. *Summa Contra Gentiles* II, c. 101, and III c. 51.

cendental *a priori* is *ipso facto* the transcendental condition enabling man to have knowledge of himself.

Finally, therefore, truth is, in its ultimate depths, that state of inner illumination, that intelligibility, which belongs to any being in itself and in the degree of its being. It is the self-confrontation of being as present to itself, such that pure being and pure thinking are one and the same, the absolute intelligence before which we stand in virtue of the transcendence of our intellect. And because truth exists only where being as such is attained to in transcendence, therefore that root which is most hidden, yet which is present and active in all truth, is this one single reality: God.

Therefore the most personal of existential factors, and the most metaphysical at the same time, is that which Thomas has expressed in these words: *Adoro te devote latens Deitas, quae sub his figuris vere latitas.* Everything is a parable – *figura* – of God, who is constantly being unveiled yet at the same time constantly concealed in the parable.

3

POSSIBLE COURSES FOR THE
THEOLOGY OF THE FUTURE

FOR anyone seeking to achieve a balanced view of Christian theology in the 20th century[1] it becomes relevant to look to the future too, for any such attempt gives rise to the pressing question of what future can be foreseen for this theology in the next few decades. Certain forces in contemporary Christianity, as described, for instance, by the Second Vatican Council,[2] and which, moreover, are among the decisive factors for Christian theology, will certainly persist. There are many tasks which theologians of all Churches have always regarded as their special concern. Either they have been discharging them all along or they have now begun to take them in hand. From this point of view and many others besides it is, of course, possible to attempt some estimate of what form the theology of the future will take, at least to the extent of expressing certain fragmentary prognostications, desires, and conjectures. But surely the first point (this at least is my view) which any theologian must lay down for this theology of the future is that ultimately speaking it is unknown to us, not only in practice but in principle as well.[3] If it is in any

---

[1] The original lecture, of which this is a lightly re-edited version, first appeared under the title of 'Ausblick', *Bilanz der Theologie im 20. Jahrhundert*, H. Vorgrimler and R. van der Gucht edd., Vol. III (Freiburg im Breisgau, 1970), pp. 530–551.

In what follows the impression may at times be given that it is the future of Catholic theology only that we are discussing here. No one speaking of the future from the basis of his own convictions and concrete desires would ever dare to speak on behalf of all theologies. Nevertheless the considerations which follow may, from a material point of view, evince many connections with non-Catholic theologies and – *mutatis mutandis* – include their special subject-matter within its purview. Y. Congar is concerned with the same theme, though he concentrates more upon the aspect of tradition, in his book, *Situation et taches présentes de la théologie* (Paris, 1967).

[2] cf. e.g. Conc. Vat. II, *Gaudium et Spes (Pastoral Constitution on the Church in the Modern World)*, Nos. 4–10: 'The Situation of Men in the Modern World'.

[3] On this cf. the author's essay, 'The Question of the Future', *Theological Investigations* 12 (London and New York, 1974), pp. 182–201.

sense true that Christianity as a whole acts as the guardian of the '*docta ignorantia futuri*' for the history of mankind in general, if it represents the most radical critique of the theory that we are either able, or have the right, to work out an absolute plan for the course of history (seeing that any such plan would represent the end of history itself), then it follows that the Church must also go on to state in ever clearer terms that she herself is vitally involved in history, and yet that whatever possibilities or duties there may be to make plans for it to a certain limited extent, the future of history still remains unknown.

This precise point, then, applies to the future history of Christian theology as well. So far the Church has never, properly speaking, worked out any effective plans for it. But surely it both can and should engage in a little more planning and do a little more to provide institutions for such planning to be worked out for the future. In other words some kind of futurology for theology should be engaged in at both the theoretical and the practical level. But the future of theology as a whole, and on the longer view, will still remain unknown for the Church too. And this as a matter of principle. However obvious this point may be, it nevertheless has a practical importance as well. Just as other sciences work out scientific plans for their own spheres, so too (to the extent that all this is applicable to theology) theology itself (and the Church which upholds it) can lay down programmes of research or set up teams of researchers and, where necessary, find the resources to finance these (with greater generosity and understanding, as we may hope, than has formerly been the case). And if this course is adopted, then it can only be praiseworthy and, properly speaking, obvious as well. This is, of course, equally true of international theological periodicals if they decide to cease from publishing articles in a haphazard way simply as they are contributed and without any planned programme. It would also apply to the setting up of an international theological commission at Rome which could set itself quite specific tasks. Or again to projects, either envisaged or already in hand, to publish whole series of earlier theological literature presented according to modern principles. Or again it would apply to any scheme for using the most modern technical aids for theology as well, including even computers for verbal statistics or perhaps even for analyses of style, researches into the history of ideas, etc. (We can say this even while recognizing how large the question looms of the extent to which the financial situation of the Church of the future will really allow us to keep up in this sense with the technical side of modern science.) But all this should not blind us to the fact that the future of theology is properly speaking unknown to us. The abiding character of the Church, and so of her theology as well, does not set either the Church or theology apart from human history in general. The history of the Church and theology develops essentially as the reaction of both to the historical situation of the world which they have to serve. Indeed the Church and theology have to help in shaping this situation in certain limited areas even though they cannot really or totally manipulate or control this situation.[4] Even abstracting from the free movement of the Spirit that disposes in the Church, guiding it but never being guided by it, and remaining always the uncircumscribed Lord of its history, the very fact that, despite all the plans and estimates of futurology, the history of the world ultimately remains unknown, is in itself enough to ensure that the history of the Church and its theology is likewise ultimately unknown. Now this has practical consequences. Neither theology itself nor the Church's teaching office should be over-energetic in attempting to plan or direct theology. Such a course would have very little effect. Nor should we seek too hastily, or without due thought, to organize or institutionalize the whole development of theology by devising mammoth programmes for it. I do not say this idly. For instance at the first session of the International Theological Commission at Rome it was declared, right from the outset, that this commission set itself the task of covering what I felt to be more or less the whole of theology, or at any rate its fundamental themes, embracing all the rest. My personal opinion was against this. *Theology as such* can really be pursued only by *theologians as such*, and it can never be subjected to a standard imposed upon it by planning of a totalitarian or authoritarian kind. Moreover the Church's teaching authority has never laid claim to any such authority, and will be less than ever in a position to do so in the future. It will do no harm if in the future the Church becomes the place where the original and surprising findings of the freely creative spirit can most of all be looked for and welcomed in her theology. So far from any ideological petrifica-

---

[4] There is nothing derogatory in this statement for the Church or theology. First, reaction also implies considered and responsible action upon an already existing situation. So universal is this law that it is quite impossible for there to be any action in human affairs which is not also a reaction. Hence it is, to a large extent, an open question how the Church will 'react' to its situation. Second, the Church is aware that this situation in which it stands in the secular world is ultimately speaking willed by the Lord of history whom the Church itself serves, and whom it must precisely acknowledge as greater than itself, not claiming to be his representative in a totalitarian sense, or pretending to decide everything that takes place. Third, every reaction also implies that the situation to which the Church is reacting is itself having an influence upon it in its turn.

tion of its own understanding or itself, theology must, precisely in the future, continue to be the guardian of the *'docta ignorantia theologiae futurae'*. Precisely because now, in contrast to earlier ages, it is possible and tempting to try to achieve the opposite of this, this manifest fact should be stated here at the beginning of this section.

However true it may be that the future of theology is unknown to us, one factor that belongs to it of its very nature is its attitude of hopeful belief that it will endure and keep its own identity in the future too. We must not dwell too long on this here, for we cannot offer a theology of the nature of theology within the present context. Nevertheless it does seem important in this context to emphasize that even though theology does endure and keep its own identity throughout all temporal changes, this precisely does not shield it from the surprises which its unknown future will bring. The fact that it keeps its own identity, continues in the future too to be what it has been in the past, is, indeed, not simply to be accounted for by an abiding nature which is devoid of any real historical development whatever. On the contrary, it is to be ascribed to the true historical development of this nature itself. Let us take, for instance, the following statements,[5] in themselves justified: that this Christian theology has to be the kind of theology that never ceases to have its roots in the revelation of Jesus Christ; that it never ceases to have its source in Scripture and the Church's own understanding of her faith; that this theology is a theology of the Church, and one which never ceases to be bound up with the teaching office of the Church, even though its relationship with this is constantly subject to critical reappraisal; that it must not lose its living contact with the kerygma of the Church; that it is, with a unity that cannot be dissolved, at once positive, historical, and yet at the same time genuinely theoretical, or 'speculative'; that it must never become too far removed from that theology which has been called a theology of 'genuflection', and so on. All these statements are, and will continue to be, perfectly true. Yet we must not imagine that having made them we know exactly the concrete lines of development which the theology of the future will follow.

A. GENERAL TRAITS IN A THEOLOGY OF THE FUTURE

Having made these provisos and reservations, then, what can now be said about the theology of the future? The term 'future' as used here

[5] cf. e.g. K. Rahner, 'Theology' and 'History of Theology', *Sacramentum Mundi*, VI (New York and London, 1970), pp. 233–246.

stands for a relatively proximate future. Even secular futurologists, provided they are scientists and not writers of science fiction, do not in fact extend their prognostications much beyond the year 2000. What we have to say about the future as thus defined consists, as we have already pointed out, in a certain haphazard and unsystematic amalgam of prognostications, conjectures, and even desires. Even desires, for it is permissible to have these too, and, as compared with 'prophecies', for the most part more reasonable. But where are we to find any kind of basic principle to reduce such conjectures and desires in some sense to a basic common denominator, and put them on a legitimate footing? Surely we cannot dispense ourselves from the quest for a key idea of this kind. For if we sought simply to analyse theology as it *de facto* exists today into its various individual disciplines, and to adduce a futurology of theology on this basis, then surely all that we would achieve would be one of two things: either we would produce programmes of work for the individual theological disciplines which were already familiar to them, and which cannot be developed here, or such an analysis would lead once more to the question of how we should seek in order somehow to be able to define the basic trend of the theology of the future. In the light of this let us begin by pondering the following proposition: the future theology of the Church will become less and less that which it formerly has been, namely the theology of a society which is culturally and regionally homogeneous. In other words the theology of the Church (or the Churches) will be the theology of a world Church, yet one which will never again be in a position to find any obvious basis for itself in any one specific culture, and which will never again simply constitute an obvious social and cultural phenomenon belonging to a particular region, one which is guarded by the society concerned as its own special possession and its own tradition. It will be the theology of a world Church, therefore, which, wherever it exists, will be (albeit in very varying degrees) a diaspora Church, one which will have to maintain itself in a neutralist and secularist world. These social conditions under which the Church, and thereby her theology too, will operate, seem to me to be already present in part, and indeed to a large extent. I suggest that in a world dominated by rationalism and technology they can only increase. For the immediate future all this seems to me to be a manifest truism. In any case I cannot, at this point, enter into dispute with those Christians or theologians who believe that even in the future there will still be, in many great areas of the world, societies which, taken as a whole, will, in their outward character, constitute a Christian or Catholic milieu for the Church and theology in the sense familiar to us up to the present. (There is a quite different question, and one which cannot be treated of here, namely whether there ever can or will be a society such that, though wholly secularist, it is nevertheless subject at a quite radical and hidden level to 'anonymous' Christian influences as one of its determining factors.) The only problem with which we have to concern ourselves here, therefore, is what the implications are of this social situation for the theology of the future. It is, of course, also obvious that such a question could be answered with much greater precision and probability by a specialist in sociology and futurology (assuming that he also understood something of theology) than it can be here, where it is being treated of by one who is a mere theologian and nothing more.[6] We must explicitly emphasize once more that we can treat only, or almost only, of theology in general. Without wishing, therefore, to underestimate other theological disciplines, their necessity or their importance,

[6] Obviously this pluralist, secularized, rational, and technological world which we are regarding as the situation of the theology of the future cannot be described or analyzed in greater detail here. Let us confine ourselves to emphasizing one point: the fact that an individual, e.g. a cleric, speaks about this world does not in itself mean that he is really living in it. It is only when he is actually living in it as well (though this does not mean identifying himself totally with it in every respect) that he can write *that* theology which the future needs. Now this attitude of accepting the intellectual and social situation necessarily involves something precisely more than a mere awareness of the existence of alien 'opinions' which remain just as alien to one as Tibetan medicine might to the average European who has come to know of it through indirect sources. Also, and more than this, this attitude of acceptance involves the ability spontaneously to enter into the basic attitude of mind of a man of tomorrow who is not a Christian, a man who, for instance, is astonished at the sound of church bells on Sunday morning, at the sight of religious habits in the street, which strike him as the costume of folklore; one whose impression of Rome, with its countless clerics clothed in all kinds of habits, and its innumerable churches, is not at all that of a 'holy city'. On the contrary it gives him the sort of feeling that a European might have on arriving as a tourist at Lhasa, and so on. Obviously in such cases a Christian of the kind we are thinking of will still willingly bear the scandal which his faith represents, not regarding it as interchangeable with that other scandal which arises from an obsolete culture which is not his any more than it is the non-Christian's. If he meets a cardinal who still decides to appear in his traditional 'uniform' (if there still are any such) he will not find him any more important, on this account, for his Church or his life (though in saying this we are not falling into a 'fanaticism of desacralization', for an attitude of this kind is not modern but rather inhuman). And so on. These are examples the details of which are not worth disputing over, and are merely intended to illustrate the sort of situation in which the theology of the future too will have to be pursued. But unless we have this truly living feeling for the situation, even those examples will remain incomprehensible which will shortly have to be adduced from the immediate context of theology itself.

the disciplines which are of most concern to us here are those which have the greatest possible relevance to the Church's task of missionary preaching – above all to the extent that she does effectively perform this.

1. Pluralism in Theology

The theology of the future will be a *pluralist* theology,[7] even though obviously it will have to maintain the unity of the Church's creed. This statement should not for one moment be taken to convey that the pluralism we are speaking of (one which, admittedly, should be rightly understood, and should not in practice lead to anarchy) is capable of representing something of the Church's riches, or is in itself to be regarded as something especially welcome. Our intention is simply to recognize this pluralism as a fact. We accept that the Church is, or is destined to be, a world Church, and that too not merely in the sense of having a geographical universality. It also has this character (and this is something which may soon become far more important if the Church intends to be really true to its missionary task) in the sense that it is genuinely and unreservedly committed to recognizing the plurality of life-styles among men within one and the same geographical region, variations of life-style which the Church can no longer be as swift as formerly, and especially as she has been in the last few centuries,[8] to regard as valueless, preferring

[7] cf. K. Rahner, 'Pluralism in Theology and the Unity of the Creed in the Church', *Theological Investigations* XI (London and Baltimore, 1974), pp. 3–23.

[8] This conditional clause does, of course rest upon assumptions which it is the task of the sociologist and futurologist rather than the theologian to investigate. It is becoming ever clearer that we are involved in a culture of the masses of a rational, technical, and cybernetic kind. But however much we may assume that this will lead to uniformity and reduce all to the same level, it will presumably still at the same time offer the individual numerous opportunities for exercising his freedom such as formerly he did not have; opportunities to shape his life-style even though it may be true that the varied forms of life-style which emerge are based upon this universal and technical culture for all. Now these life-styles, which each individual is free to develop for himself within a pluralistic society, will certainly include among others some which are (either wholly or in part) anti-Christian in character, and constitute the 'reproach of the Gentiles'. And in response to these, Christians will have to find courage of a quite new kind in developing a manifest non-conformism. At the same time, however, there will also be precisely the kind of life-styles which on the one hand strike us of today as being still, perhaps, 'impossible' or 'unchristian', while on the other they are capable of fully integrating Christian faith within their framework. The situation will be similar to that of former times, when an actor who was at the same time a Christian was regarded as a contradiction in terms. Unless we can bring a missionary élan to bear, we are inclined too hastily to regard certain social classes

instead to replace them with a single type of society characterized chiefly as that of peasants or petit-bourgeois. Now if all this is true then the theology of the Church is confronted with the most varied points of departure, ranges of perspective, conceptual models, and the most diverse criteria for distinguishing between that which can be taken for granted and that which cannot. These are genuine assumptions, from which theological thought must proceed, and they cannot in the concrete be reduced to any one 'system'. Likewise they give rise to a number of theologies which cannot, in any adequate sense, be reduced to a single theology. In respect of the axioms from which they proceed, and also of those factors in them which can never adequately be expressed at the philosophical, scientific, or sociological level, their intellectual approach, the degree of importance they assign to the various points they deal with, and their terminology, all these theologies differ very vitally among themselves. It obviously follows from this that the question of how theology is related to the Church's teaching office, to the credal formulae, and to the cultic life of the community as a whole, needs in many respects to be set on quite a fresh footing, and this in itself, once more, raises problems of language and communication in these theologies. Likewise it is obvious that these theologies must, for all this, continue to maintain a dialogue with one another not merely because of the unity of the Church and her creed, but also because of the state of interdependence and mutual influence which exists between the various outlooks and schools of thought in the secular world. This pluralism of theologies is in itself enough to justify us in the assumption and the conclusion that no one of these theologies, taken in isolation, any longer has the capacity to work out fully and explicitly in terms of fundamental theology all the ideological and philosophical assumptions to which the situation of pluralism in secular life at the social and individual level gives rise (and in fact a further reason is that no one individual any longer has time or intellectual resources enough to master all these theologies). Every such theology, taken as an autonomous system in its own right, must, in a certain sense, and within certain limits, have the courage to be 'unscientific', and, indeed, is fully justified in being so. At the same time, however, it must make this clear and, in a special (we might say a transcendental) way, show explicitly (as is perfectly possible) why it may legitimately claim to have this right. The very fact that no one

---

or groups as more or less disqualified for Christianity. Yet often all that they are disqualified from in fact is a certain very restricted section of Christendom which we have regarded as the only possible one. All this too will emerge in the theology of the future.

individual man either does live or can live merely by those principles which he has proved right in conscience by a process of scientific reflection after the pattern of the present-day sciences – this fact in itself is enough to justify theology's right to be 'unscientific' in this sense.

2. *Missionary and Mystagogic Theology*

The theology of the future will, in a more direct sense than hitherto, be a missionary and mystagogic theology, and no longer be so willing as has been the case in the past few centuries to consign this department of missionary mystagogy to the realm of personal practice or ascetic and mystical literature.[9] For in the future the Church will no longer be upheld by traditions that are unquestioningly accepted in secular society, or regarded as an integral element of that society. The community Church will be transformed into a Church made up of those who believe as a matter of personal conviction and individual decision. (We are stating all this in a somewhat simplified form.) Again theology has to make a contribution to preaching. And whereas formerly it was possible to depute a large part of this task to the traditional practice and the strength of society in general, in the new situation it will no longer be in a position to do this. And for all these reasons theology (or the theologies) must itself be far more missionary and mystagogic in outlook than it has formerly had to be. I believe that theology, wherever and whenever it still remains alive, no longer has the time, the inclination, or even the right to write such large-scale studies on the Trinity as were written in former ages, for instance, by a D. Ruiz de Montoya. In the unceasing life-and-death struggle within a secularized society it is inevitable that theology should be fully preoccupied with having to raise and answer ever afresh the ultimate questions of a personal decision for God, for Jesus Christ, and (of course in a very derived sense) for the Church. This does not, of course, mean that we will not also have to engage in very intensive 'specialist' studies in the field of dogmatics, a point which we shall discuss more fully at a later stage. But this must be done in such a way that a strong and explicit contact is constantly maintained with the ultimate questions confronting

[9] In this respect theology from the age of the Fathers to the High Middle Ages can perhaps in its turn provide a new model, though of course always recognizing the necessity for having to speak in more 'abstract' and 'formal' terms than in that period. In what has been said a question which has, of course, not really been brought to the surface in any effective sense is the question of the future of the 'religious book'. On this cf. K. Rahner, 'The Future of the Religious Book', *Theological Investigations* VIII (London and New York, 1971), pp. 251–256.

theology today. 'Mystagogy' means that the *fides quae* of today can be expressed only in a very explicitly recognized unity with the *fides qua*. Obviously it is not those preoccupations of 'modern' man which his own inclinations have fixed upon and determined that provide the criterion for deciding what should be studied in theology. But if it is true that everything that is expressed in objective concepts in theology has a reference to the interior self-communication of God in every man, then the *fides qua* both can and must constitute a theme in all departments of dogmatic theology and, moreover, from a different aspect according to each department involved. The point we are seeking to make is that it does not merely signify a subject of some pious interest operating in an area outside theology properly so called. For in all departments of dogmatic theology we have to ask 'What does this mean for me (and society)?' 'How does this really affect me?' 'How precisely can I myself really believe this?' Once such questions as these are raised, once the theologian ceases to identify himself in his studies, in a manner which is at basis out of date, with a quite specific, but ever diminishing social group (which nevertheless still continues to survive in a ghetto-like existence), then theology of itself will become something quite different from what it formerly was. It will of itself become more mystagogic, more missionary, and this is something which in practice is in accordance with the contemporary and future situation. Of course we should supply examples to make our meaning clear. But this is impossible here. Yet we have only to read some teaching about the nature of God or some treatise in fundamental theology or dogmatic christology, or a substantial part of moral theology in the seminary textbooks, to receive the inescapable impression that something is being expounded and proved here about which the author has never seriously entertained any doubts. Now what this means is that the author is, without himself noticing it, sustained by that 'ideology' of his group in Christian society which is still relatively undisturbed. For what other source could there be for his certainty of the compelling force of his all-too 'binding' arguments and ideas? Now a theologian does not necessarily need to be a doubter in the sense in which moral theology treats of culpable doubts on points of faith. But how is a theologian to write a theology capable of being, in any effective sense, missionary and mystagogic if he does not maintain a constant and vital inward sympathy with those for whom, after all, he is really writing, in other words for those who have still to make their way towards belief, and who for the most part still stick fast in their position in the face of those who, from the point of view of their place in society, regard themselves as good Christians and

Catholics. But we have not yet achieved such contact so long as, in our dealings with confirmed non-Christians of this kind, we behave towards them as I might behave, for instance, towards a Hindu or Zen Buddhist acquaintance, or as they might behave towards one of us nowadays on any secular occasion which is not concerned with religious or philosophical questions, and at which no one speaks of religious matters or has the slightest intention of attempting to 'convert' the others.

3. 'Demythologizing' Theology

The theology of the future must be a 'demythologizing' theology. In saying this I am fully aware of the disadvantages which this term has come to have. On the one hand, as a result of the use to which it has been put in the theology of Bultmann, it has nowadays come to acquire a sense which is, to a large extent, unacceptable to Catholics. On the other hand, however, we must recognize that theology as such (and beginning with the New Testament itself) has all along engaged in 'demythologizing'. But if we try to avoid these connotations in choosing the concepts we need to express what we mean, how are we to prevent these other concepts from becoming, so to say, a protective layer of cotton-wool within which a comforting theology can continue simply to reproduce itself in its attachments to those traditional forms of Christianity which do of course still exist, with some variations according to the particular countries in which they are found. When we use the term 'demythologizing' here we are taking it to signify nothing else whatever than the attempt to ensure that the essential and primary statements of faith which must be preached, will be preached in a form which will be credible and acceptable to modern man (though we must recognize to the full the radical responsibility we are taking upon ourselves in this). But this is the chief and primary task for which theology must prepare the ground. It must be stated boldly and explicitly that, at least for the *initial* preaching of the faith which is so necessary, the expressions of that faith which have become traditional are now, and always will be, to a large extent unsuitable. Obviously they will continue to provide – and, moreover, precisely and more particularly for theology – a starting-point and a norm for theological thinking. But if theology is to make a contribution to preaching, the traditional formulae of faith can no longer constitute the outcome and conclusion of theological speculation in the same way as has formerly been the case. In our preaching we cannot continue to present these statements, which come at the beginning and end of theology, more or less as they stand, or provided only with a few additional explanations. In the future too the traditional formulae of faith, the official and definitive doctrinal declarations in force up to the present, will continue to constitute again and again, not merely the starting-point and the norm, but the final goal of theology and preaching as well (the more so since it is quite impossible totally to dispense with them in the liturgy). They will continue to have this function whenever, on the occasion of some fresh theological pronouncement, the following statement is made: 'When such and such a pronouncement was made in the past (or is made in the present in the form of a cultic formula) this was what is meant.' Catholic theology must be upheld by the conviction in faith that a 'demythologizing' of this kind is possible even in an approach that is unambiguously orthodox. The task may be difficult. It is only barely in its incipient stages. Nevertheless it is possible. In order to express our meaning once more in different terms: preaching and cult have drawn their living force more or less from those traditional statements and formulae of faith which emerged in the first five centuries of Christendom in a world of ideas which was more or less homogeneous in character. At the time theology provided, as it were, a musical accompaniment to these formulae (of course in circumstances of mutual interdependence) which was certainly enlightening, but which (as every catechism shows) carried no very great significance so far as understanding and the will actively to believe were concerned for the normal Christian. Today, however, theology must accept as its new and primary task (albeit in the context of a pluralism of theologies within the unity of the Church and her creed) the duty of devising fresh statements of the content of the ancient faith. As we have already said, theology has been engaged in 'demythologizing' activities right from the first. But properly speaking it is only today that such activities have come to have the status of a consciously defined task which can only be discharged in terms of this pluralism. The only question which Thomas Aquinas had to deal with, for instance, was whether God exists. He did not have to answer the question of who and what he is. Anyone undertaking to develop a theology of the nature of God must be willing to proceed very slowly in bringing his hearers to a gradual understanding (capable of being made real in terms of their own concrete lives) of what the very term 'God' is intended to signify. Obviously in any such approach he will still all along be retaining some connection with what was formerly called the proofs of God's existence and the doctrine of the nature of God. Nevertheless his approach will not be the same. For there are very many points with regard to the nature of God and his relationship with the world (for instance that

God takes 'responsibility' even for the wicked in the world in a quite specific way etc.) which were accorded a fairly secondary place in advanced theology and regarded as altogether too much for the average Christian. Today, however, in a mystagogic teaching on the nature of God of the kind we have in mind, such points must be brought into the discussion right from the outset if we are to avoid, once more, either presupposing or implying an idea of God which will appear unacceptable to modern man precisely by presenting God as one particular factor in the world itself. A theology which is 'demythologizing' in the right sense should clearly recognize the effect of such statements as 'there are three Persons in God; God has sent his Son into the world; we are redeemed by the Blood of Jesus Christ', when we continue to make them the beginning and end of the statement of Christian belief in the manner of the old theology and preaching. When he encounters them in this guise, modern man will find them simply incomprehensible, and they will give him the impression of belonging to the crude mythology of a religion of former ages. Of course for many of our contemporary Christians and theologians it would be necessary to provide further explanations and elucidations of this statement. And here this is impossible. All that we can manage in the present context is simply to draw attention to examples of this kind, and so indicate the quite radical difficulties which the task of a future theology will involve. And in such a context it does nothing to make such basic statements of Christian belief acceptable for us to invoke the element of mystery in them. For first the concept of 'mystery' must not be used as a facile excuse for the flabby thinking of a theology that merely repeats traditional arguments, and second, a point that precisely calls for demonstration is how such 'mysteries' have an intrinsic connection with that ultimate mystery which man really feels as an effective part of his life at the depths of his existence, and which he can discover and, in a certain sense, 'verify'. In the results it is designed to achieve the 'demythologizing' envisaged here has little or nothing to do with that residue of Christianity which survives from Bultmann's existential interpretation (even though this may perhaps amount to far more than over-hasty critics have supposed). The crucial point in what we are calling for here – to reiterate it once more – is the conviction that however true it may be that the Christian faith of yesterday and today is materially speaking one and the same, the actual expression of that faith in preaching, the conceptual models employed for it, its connotations and perspectives, will assume a radically different form in the future from that which they have formerly had. This is what theology must work to achieve, though obviously in doing so it must maintain a constant hold on Scripture and the officially binding doctrinal statements of the faith of the Church of former times. To retain this hold is primarily the task of theology, and presumably it is only in a very secondary sense that it is the concern of preaching, to the extent that cultic formulae, which develop according to a tempo of their own, make it necessary. On the whole preachers will proclaim the beliefs of Christianity without constantly falling into the style and parlance of the ancient credal formulae, as preachers and catechists formerly tended to do. Thus what is truly and properly signified by the two natures or the hypostatic union in christology, or by transubstantiation etc., must always be retained. Moreover such ideas must constantly be the subject of fresh studies on the part of theologians in respect both of their history and their content. Yet is it so certain that fifty years from now preachers will still have to operate with these terms? An idea which is constantly being put forward is that while, in our use of such ideas, we do indeed have to recognize that they belong to past history, we also have to recognize at the same time that we can neither replace them nor do without them in the present, seeing that they correspond to a general common sense which has a universal philosophical validity. This thesis, however, though often stated, is still far from having been proved.

4. Transcendental Theology

The theology of the future will be, in a far more explicit sense than hitherto, a transcendental theology:[10] not in the sense that a transcendental theology will be presented as the whole of theology, or that the Christian faith will be reduced to the private and personal dimension by an individualizing philosophy which views the individual as a monad-like 'subject'. The theology of the future will not fail to recognize that the Christian faith has from its origins, side by side with its solicitude for the salvation of the individual, a social relevance, and is, at least in this sense, a 'political theology'. One of the factors belonging intrinsically to transcendental theology is precisely its conscious recognition of its own limitations. And this means that as the outcome of its own principles it arrives at an understanding of the fact that an individual cannot draw his lifeforce solely from some abstract metaphysic, or even from some philosophy of his historical mode of existence. He can only be fully alive in consciously accepting his own history as something which he must

---

[10] cf. *Sacramentum Mundi*, VI (New York and London, 1970), pp. 275-285, with bibliography.

endure and act responsibly in, yet which can never in any adequate sense be consciously comprehended either in its past or its future dimensions by the speculative reason. Nevertheless some form of transcendental theology will have to be worked out for the future in a more consciously reflective and methodical sense than has been the case hitherto. This does not mean the mere taking over of a transcendental philosophy into theology. As a matter of history this transcendental theology may find its point of departure in such a philosophy, and in fact it would have nothing to be ashamed of precisely in this. But the true source of any transcendental theology is itself genuinely theological. For the question theology enquires into is properly speaking this and nothing else: the salvation of man to the extent that this consists in the self-bestowal of God, and therefore the consummate wholeness which man can achieve. If man in this sense is to be taken as a subject in the strict sense of the term, and not merely as one particular individual factor among others, then we can only understand what salvation means to the extent that it (including, by the same token, all the elements in this salvation) is conceived of as applying to the subject as such. Now to understand the reality of salvation in this way means nothing else than to conceive of it as transcendental, applying, that is to say, to the transcendental subject, which is such a subject 'of its very nature', and precisely as so constituted achieves its most radical dimension through that which we call grace. All this has nothing to do with any false 'anthropocentricity' of theology, a fact which will be immediately clear to anyone who (in terms of philosophy and theology) conceives of man precisely as the subject of a radical orientation to the absolute mystery which bestows itself as such upon man in grace, without which man fails to discover his own self, and which is called 'God'. A transcendental theology could be defined as that kind of systematic theology which (a) avails itself of a transcendental philosophy as its instrument, and at the same time (b) is more explicit than formerly and, unlike fundamental theology, not wholly concerned with general principles in defining its themes for investigation on the basis of questions arising at a genuinely theological level. For these themes are the *a priori* conditions in the believing subject which enable him to recognize the fundamental truths of his faith. (A transcendental enquiry of this kind can be extended to all areas except one: that namely in which it is in principle and from the outset impossible to enquire into the *a priori* conditions on which a given piece of theological knowledge depends by reason of the nature of the subject. In such cases man has to recognize that here and now at this particular point, and in fact even in its bearing upon his own salvation, he is confronted by the inescapable factualness of a free historical event, and of his faith accepts this as salvation despite the 'relativity' inherent in it.) It is impossible here to point to individual fundamental dogmas of Christianity in order to exemplify what such a transcendental theology can achieve and must achieve. For this we must refer to other studies.[11] One concluding point remains to be emphasized, however, namely that the need for a transcendental theology is not simply one and the same as the need for a transcendental philosophy in one particular historical form, as though this constituted the indispensable basis of our thinking. To that extent a transcendental theology would not even need to constitute one particular theology within the pluralism of theologies, but could represent an approach and a task which is present in every such theology according to its particular mode.[12]

B. POINTS OF EMPHASIS IN A THEOLOGY OF THE FUTURE

Having pointed to four general and formal characteristics of the theology of the future, we may now go on to make certain more concrete individual points on the future of Christian theology, though our choice of these points may seem somewhat arbitrary.

The biblical and historical (history of dogma) branches of theology as they exist today seem to me in a certain sense to have reached a crisis. Of course this applies to historical theology in an essentially higher degree than to biblical theology (obviously including exegesis). First with regard to historical theology, there will in fact always be a place and an important task for this, and not merely among those who have a justifiable and selfless interest in history as such, and to the extent that they have this – in other words among those seeking simply to know about past developments. Historical theology also has an important function for theology as a whole and as such. This is not only because theology must constantly be referring back to the authentic and binding pronouncements of the official Church of earlier ages which, since they still continue to remain a norm for the theology of today also, though on these grounds alone there must be a historical theology. But a further reason is that ultimately speaking the only way in which we can arrive at a sufficiently clear understanding of these official doctrinal pronouncements in their full bearing and significance, as also in their limitations, is to take account of their historical

[11] cf. the article cited above in n. 9.

[12] cf. K. Rahner, 'Pluralism in Theology and the Unity of the Creed in the Church', *Theological Investigations* XI (London and New York, 1974), pp. 3–23; *idem*, 'Zum Begriff der Unfehlbarkeit in der katholische Theologie', *Stimmen der Zeit* 186 (1970), pp. 18–31.

context as a whole. And for this, historical theology must provide a contact with the totality of theological thinking. In other words it must embrace the study of the history of dogma and theology throughout all the centuries.

1. *The History of Dogma*

But unless I am mistaken in my impressions, this historical theology as practised hitherto has been sustained by the expectation that over and above the officially defined and assured doctrines of the Church, there are still teachings to be discovered in the Fathers of the Church or the theologians of the Middle Ages – if only we study them closely enough – which belong to the faith of the Church as such. This kind of exaggerated pietism and fideism, based as it is on a false conception of tradition, is something that should explicitly be abandoned – and in fact even in its application to the earliest of the Fathers. We can indeed discover in their works a theology from which we of today can still learn much. But it is precisely *theology* and not *ipso facto* or of itself dogmatically binding theses, going beyond those already recognized and acknowledged as binding by the Church's teaching office. It is true that what we find in these past ages is not merely a history of theology but a history of dogma as well. But right from the earliest ages of the Fathers of the Church onwards this is not a history of individual theological dogmas, each of which has been handed down as an entity already fully matured and existing in its own right, such that we can still discover further statements of a similar kind within the volumes of Migne. On the contrary, this history of dogma constitutes that part of the history of theology (springing from very simple sources) which already begins in the New Testament itself, and has assumed the form of irreversible decisions or dogmas in the Church's conscious faith. This is not the place to treat of the question of why and how there can be any such discipline as a history of dogma in the true sense within the history of theology and emerging from it. Arising from what has been said, the point that is important for us here is that we cannot approach the history of theology in the manner of a prospector searching for metals (dogmas) still hidden beneath the rocks of the history of theology. Our way of studying it must involve, rather, two distinct approaches. (a) We must recognize both the meaning and the limitations of the dogmas actually formulated. Presumably these have reached a stage at which they are no longer susceptible of further explicitation and so of further extension through theological study, as a result of some datum purely of the history of theology or dogma coming to be discerned in them, which had hitherto only been implicit. This is, of course, not for one moment to deny the Church's right to exercise her official teaching authority in producing fresh definitions in the future. But she will arrive at such definitions in some other way. (b) Our approach to the history of theology must, as Bernhard Welte puts it,[13] take the form of 'a deductive investigation of the major historical stages' which have taken place in the history of dogma, to see 'what authority they carry, *and at the same time their limitations*'. This means that the historical approach to the study of theology today will involve not so much an explicitating theology, one, that is, which in a direct sense yields fresh material either consisting in dogmatically binding pronouncements or providing an immediate point of departure for some new statement of this kind.[14] In its historical approach modern theology will be, rather, a 'reductive' theology. It will not involve any false or exaggerated emphasis on the formal authority of the Church's official teachings in terms either of the material it investigates or its pedagogic approach (the Church's doctrinal authority is beyond dispute. But the material and concrete factors on which it is based are precisely *prior* to it, and it is necessary to make these clear ever afresh). But the new theology will have to be a 'reductive' theology in the sense of showing how all the manifold individual statements of the Church's faith derive from the simple and pristine kernel of the Christian faith (even while recognizing the historical mode in which this is mediated).

2. *Exegesis*

The conditions governing that department of historical theology which we call exegesis and biblical theology are similar, and yet in some respects different.[15] Something similar to what has been said would apply to this

[13] cf. B. Welte, 'Ein Vorschlag zur Methode der Theologie heute', *Auf der Spur des Ewigen* (Freiburg, 1965), pp. 410–426 (quoting from p. 420).

[14] When, for instance, the dogma of the Assumption of the Blessed Virgin Mary was due to be defined there was a reluctance to admit plainly and openly that it was not only impossible to adduce any proof that the doctrine had explicitly been believed all along as a truth of faith, but that any such proof that was adduced would certainly be false. For this reason attempts were made (e.g. by Otto Faller) to ascribe the earliest possible date to explicit witnesses to a pious belief of this kind. Alternatively its exponents sought to assemble all possible witnesses, and so to give the impression that it was explicitly attested by an existing dogmatic tradition even though 'for a lack of still available witnesses' it was no longer possible to trace the tradition right back to apostolic times.

[15] Without denying the unity of 'scripture' as constituted by the Old and New

department of historical theology to the extent that, in terms of time and content alike, not only the Old Testament but the New Testament too has a long history. And even in the New Testament several different theologies are to be discovered. If we take a dogma to mean some one specific individual statement, formulated as such by doctrinal authority, and reinforced with an anathema, then presumably it is no longer possible to discover any fresh dogmas of this kind even in the New Testament,[16] however true it may be that a 'history of dogma' in the specific sense in which it may continue to exist even in the future must constantly be proceeding from, and returning to, the New Testament. The conditions applying to exegesis and biblical theology are different to the extent that the New Testament as a whole will always remain the norm by which theology is judged, and not simply (as with the later history of theology) something from which elements, entire theologies, or trends of development can be set aside as illegitimate. (This does not, of course, mean that one particular question is thereby settled: the question, which is in fact in a true sense obvious, of the 'canon within the canon'; of whether a 'hierarchy of truths' is to be found even in the New Testament; of whether different *niveaux* are to be found even in the New Testament. Even for Catholics these are open questions, and Catholic theologians should be far bolder in their way of tackling them than they have been in other contexts. This is the question which has, in effect, been recognized all along under the formal heading of the *analogia fidei*. The only remaining point

---

Testaments, we are confining ourselves to one observation on the New Testament, because it is impossible to say more at this point, and because even within this unity of Scripture, the Old Testament is, after all, very clearly distinguishable from the New Testament as a whole in its function and significance for Christian theology.

[16] What we are referring to is the appearance of constant 'new' individual propositions such that, as new, they would belong more or less unambiguously to Scripture itself and (after sufficiently preparing the ground by exegesis) could then be defined by the Church in virtue of the fact that they were 'revealed'. In putting forward these considerations we may possibly be beating upon an open door. Yet I do have the impression that right down to our own times the old-fashioned conservative type of Catholic theology has worked with this assumption. The work of biblical theology will not become any less important once this tacit assumption is abandoned. But then the question which the exegete and biblical theologian will ask is whether he can show his own theology faithfully to reproduce the message of Scripture, whether Scripture has some fresh message for his theology, or throws new light in some way upon it. But he must pursue this line of enquiry within a pluralism of theologies which he already encounters in Scripture itself, and *a fortiori* in the contemporary scene, without being able fully to integrate it, in any positive sense, within any one single theological system.

to be made for the Catholic biblical scholar of the future is surely this; he has certainly the right and the duty to avail himself of all the methods of historical science in his task, and so, for instance, of those of form-criticism, redaction history, etc. He can also be far more critical than formerly in drawing a bold and explicit distinction between the truths which he can deduce from scripture working purely as a historian and fundamental theologian on the one hand, and those which he finds in it when he is working as a believing dogmatic theologian within the context of that understanding of the faith which belongs to the Church as a whole on the other. For precisely on a Catholic understanding of what faith means, a distinction has to be drawn between these two approaches. In respect of their purview, their certainty, and the kind of certainty involved in them, these two approaches do not lead simply to one and the same con-clusions. And the exegete has the right to make these differences clear. But the exegete is also as such not simply a secular student of the history of religions, but a theologian who has to take responsibility for the whole of theology, and who also has a function·in fundamental theology, one which he cannot shift to any fundamental theologian who is not a special-ist in exegesis (and in most cases is incapable of being so). Admittedly a point which calls for more explicit reflection than has formerly been accorded to it is where precisely the task of the exegete in fundamental theology reaches its limits. What, in real terms, can or cannot be demanded of the exegete by fundamental theology or dogmatics?[17]

3. 'Ecumenical Theology'

There are, perhaps, some points also to be made with regard to the 'ecu-menical theology' of the future. So long as there are Christians (and, of course, among them officials too) who feel convinced in conscience by their reading of the truth of the gospel that they cannot give their adher-ence to this or that community of Christian believers without betraying the truth of the gospel and so forfeiting their salvation, so long will there be confessional theologies orientated each towards its own particular specific Church community. (There is a further and different question which cannot be treated of here, the question namely of how it comes about that the vast majority of contemporary Christians do not really have any confessional awareness in the theological sense whatsoever, but belong to one specific confession solely for historical and social reasons.) So long as

[17] On this cf. K. Rahner, 'Remarks on the Importance of the History of Jesus for Catholic Dogmatics', in the present volume, pp. 201–212.

theologies of this kind exist, differing from one another in a sense that is (theologically speaking) confessional, there must also be an 'ecumenical theology' in the individual Church communities. The reason for this is simply that the Christians of different confessions have the Christian duty of being concerned about one another, and must strive for the unity of the Church. What form this ecumenical theology will take in the concrete is another question. It may be suggested that all the major institutes of theological study should, with the necessary provisos (and with intelligent concentrations of resources), set up special chairs of ecumenical theology. But almost more important than this is the requirement that there should be an 'ecumenical' element in the study of all the theological disciplines, each according to its own special approach. Nowadays this is already fairly obvious so far as exegesis is concerned. But for many other disciplines it is still more or less a demand for the future. It is necessary for each separate discipline to include such ecumenism as an intrinsic element, if only for the reason that any theology of the future must be mystagogic and missionary, and this means that the hearers who must be envisaged in such a theology can in concrete practice never again be solely, or even primarily, the theologian's own co-religionists.[18] But we have still not so much as touched upon what is surely the true problem for the ecumenical theology of the future. Future Catholic theology will have to reckon with a very considerable degree of pluralism within itself. In these circumstances it will be far from easy to establish, and give expression to, that unity of the creed which has to be preserved in the midst of this pluralism (for without every possible help from theology this will be quite impossible). Again there is an unmistakable trend for contemporary and future theological opinions, in establishing their frontiers, to cut across established confessional divisions among the Churches.[19] And a point which cannot be gainsaid is that a consensus either has already been achieved, or is perfectly capable of being achieved, on many questions on which the Churches were formerly divided in the answers they gave. At any rate it is often the

[18] Even if in theory someone did not hold this opinion, he would have to remind himself that today (the very climate of ideas dominating human relationships everywhere makes every thinker akin to every other, and this situation in itself is enough to justify us in the point we are making) even in every Catholic, regarded from a 'psychological' aspect, a potential Protestant and an atheistic unbeliever lies concealed. If we bear this in mind, then we shall recognize that the requirement mentioned above is justified in practice at any rate.

[19] Because the current problems in theology are no longer in any sense the ancient themes of the Reformation on which the differences between the sects were based, or at least are not these in any direct sense.

case that the answer given, even to a question of this kind within a particular Church, is no longer regarded as inseparably bound up with some confessionally binding doctrine. And if all this is true, then, after all, a position might be achieved in the theology of the future in which the theologies of the various confessions are no longer really confessional in any sense at all. Instead many of them, as pursued in the various confessions, while taking a clear stand against those who deny the real and basic substance of Christianity, have come to a legitimate understanding among themselves as having a unity in the midst of pluralism. Now on this showing a position might be arrived at in which the individual Church institutions, together with their official representatives, while recognizing the divisions among themselves, could actually regard themselves as having eliminated the theological grounds for their state of separation, and could recognize that the only real factor causing them still to remain separated was the hold that past history and sociological circumstances had upon them. What then? Will the leaders of the Churches appoint the sort of theologians (for there both are, and will be such) who will make a 'bona fide' use of their theological acumen to develop still more doctrinal differences, possibly leading to still more declared divisions between the Churches (differences in which each theologian persists in identifying his own theological opinion with the binding teachings of his Church, and declares that anyone deviating from it is merely tolerated, and does not possess the true spirit of that Church)? Or alternatively will the leaders of the Churches have the heroic courage to draw the institutional consequences from any such possible theological situation, and to allow *one single* Church to emerge, which will maintain and recognize a great pluralism of Church life within itself? But let us return to those factors which constitute the prior conditions for such possibilities!

For instance we have nowadays reached a point at which it is no longer possible, in any really serious sense, to regard the doctrine of justification as a ground for division between the Churches, at least not in the sense that each of the separated Churches has its own distinct theology of justification uniformly accepted by all of its members.[20] We must maintain a version of the institution of the sacraments by Christ, and of the distinction between them, which is, in the fullest sense, possible for Catholics to hold. We must maintain a theology of the word which is fully possible for Catholics. And we must sincerely accept[21] the third canon of the seventh

[20] We have only to think, for instance, of H. Küng's study on Barth's teaching on justification and the foreword to this study written by Barth himself.

[21] In this connection, on any serious evaluation, the history of the Catholic

session of the Council of Trent (DS 1603). But even while recognizing all this, the difference between the various sacramental doctrines must not be regarded as insuperable. A similar situation prevails today for the theology of established authority in the Church, even though here we do seem to have somewhat further still to travel. What we have said applies, of course, solely to the doctrines which became matters of official controversy between the confessions at the Reformation period. In addition to these, the various Protestant theologies do, of course, include opinions which, while they are not objected to by the authorities of those Churches, can nevertheless have no place in a Catholic theology. But this is, once more, a quite different question, in itself and in its consequences for ecumenism. We have to begin, in fact, by finding the answer to the first question, which, even from a theological point of view, has a different bearing, the question, namely, of what the situation is, in terms of theology, in which the various confessions as they *de facto* exist now find themselves, seeing that those doctrines which, as a matter of history, have been responsible for the separation between the Churches, no longer constitute unambiguous grounds for such separation. (With regard to the second question of the ecumenical relevance to be attached to other differences of doctrine which, though they do *de facto* exist, are not those of the official Churches, surely all that needs to be said here is that in any case it would be illusory to suppose that the various Church congregations, together with their theologians, would simply follow their ecclesiastical representatives into the unity of the Church the moment that point in the future was arrived at when these had achieved unity at the theological and institutional level between their Churches. It would be an illusion to suppose that the members of the various Churches would do this merely because these representatives of their Churches claim and exercise a certain general doctrinal authority.)

To all these considerations it would of course be possible to reply that even today the doctrine of papal authority as interpreted by the First, or even the Second Vatican Council is still – and, moreover, in its theological aspects – a doctrine that divides the Churches, and one which banishes all the hopes of a theological unity between the Churches to an unforeseeable future. This remains true whether this doctrine is viewed in itself or in the assumptions on which it is based (e.g. in respect of the concept of truth as such or of the structure of the Church in general, with regard to the pro-

---

theology of the sacraments in the Middle Ages justifies us in developing a far more flexible theology of the sacraments than is recognized in post-Tridentine theology.

cesses by which the Church seeks to discover the truth, the relationship which one particular proposition of faith, taken in itself, bears to the Christian faith as a single whole). But even in this question do not misunderstandings still exist with regard both to the content of this doctrine and to the ways in which it is put into practice – misunderstandings such as the Catholic ecumenist might be able to overcome not only so far as non-Catholics are concerned, but also in his own mind and the minds of his own co-religionists? In any case, as I see it, the most notable obstacles to the progress of the ecumenical movement come not from the side of theology but from the weight of traditional and institutional factors (and sometimes factors belonging merely to the realm of folklore). Ecumenical theology, therefore, would also have the task of working out conceptual models for the leaders of the various Churches which would be comprehensible to them and acceptable to their theological conscience, aiming at a rapprochement between the confessions which can be achieved at the institutional level as well. Among other advantages it will also have the effect of throwing light on the question of what policy the authorities of the various Churches should adopt towards those Christians who find it simply impossible in the concrete conditions in which they *de facto* live so to understand and to realize the existing doctrinal differences (including the doctrine of papal authority) in all the seriousness which should still perhaps be attached to such differences, that, so far as their own consciences are concérned, these differences amount to confessional divisions at the level of theology, and not merely of ecclesiastical sociology. Since the various denominations are no longer confined to particular regions, or cut off from one another by territorial boundaries, such a question would have the highest urgency. The impression may possibly be given that at least among us Catholics it has not yet seriously been posed, because individuals baptized as Catholics are presumed to be Catholic Christians in a theological sense too until the opposite is proved in the individual case, whereas the real position is that despite Catholic religious instruction, the majority of them are Catholic only at the level of the sociology of religion, and very often the kind of Christianity which they 'draw' from their Church is more or less simply that which is common to all Christians. This is certainly not enough to provide any adequate account of the nature and task of the ecumenical theology of the future. But for further details we must refer our readers to the literature which has appeared on this.[22]

---

[22] Here we may simply refer to the number of 'Concilium' devoted to ecumenism, which has appeared every year since 1965, and in which these questions are treated of. On this cf. K. Rahner, 'Zur Theologie des ökumenischen Gesprächs', *Festgabe für*

4. 'Political Theology'

Let us attempt at this stage to make a few brief observations on the question of 'political theology' as well.[23] They will be offered with the proviso that what the idea of a 'political theology' precisely means has probably not yet been established beyond all possible ambiguity, and that I myself am not really sure in my own mind whether I understand what is properly meant by it. What is certain is that 'political theology' has nothing to do with any political activity of the Church or her clergy. On the contrary it recognizes the existence and the legitimacy of a secular world on theological grounds. Hence it does not in any sense run counter to that 'withdrawal' of the Church from 'politics' which has been progressively taking place in the last few decades, and which has been hastened by the Second Vatican Council. The Church cannot influence politics even 'indirectly' by invoking the natural law which it has to uphold (a temptation, not wholly overcome even today, to which those so-called 'Christian social sciences' are subject which in many cases have established themselves in the theological faculties as a theological discipline). The reason is that on any truly thought-out view of the natural law, in which its own historicity is correctly taken into account, it is impossible to deduce from it an unambiguous model for the politics of society even from the point of view of a particular historical and social situation. If we take 'political theology' to mean simply that which explicitly gives value to the relevance of all theological statements for society, then of course there must be a political theology. It will be not so much a regional theology as a formal point of view inherent throughout in all subjects for theological investigation. For on a right understanding (and without falling into any false theological anthropocentricity) all theological statements say something about man. And when we view man as a member of society we are not, in the last analysis, considering factors which are realized merely in particular individuals and in particular regions. These factors, rather, apply at all times to mankind as a whole from one particular point of view. Again the converse is also true: society is never merely the sum total of the individuals of which it is constituted. In this sense at least there is an urgent need today for a 'political theology', because traditional theology betrays

---

Bischof Volk, O. Semmelroth *et al.* edd. (Mainz, 1968), pp. 163–199; J. B. Metz, *Reform und Gegenreformation heute. Zwei Thesen zur ökumenischen Situation der Kirchen* (Mainz/Munich, 1969).

[23] For a description of Catholic 'political theology' cf. H. Peukert ed., *Diskussion zur 'politischen Theologie'* (Mainz/Munich, 1969); also J. B. Metz, J. Moltmann, W. Oelmüller, *Aspekte einer neuen 'politischen Theologie'* (Mainz, 1970).

certain tendencies to circumscribe Christianity and to regard it as applying merely to the private life or the interior salvation of the individual man. And a further reason is that the theology of hope has likewise been conceived of at the exclusively individual level, while the earthly task of man as endowed with creativity has been regarded too little as that of communicating his eschatological hope and his love to his neighbour. Furthermore 'political theology' can be regarded as the special task of theology in maintaining a constant critical reappraisal and calling in question of the social system prevailing at any given time, seeing that there is a constant temptation to make an idol of this, and to establish it as absolute by unjust oppression. It is true that we are not forced to regard 'political theology' as a mere partial discipline (more or less subordinate to, or leading up to, moral theology or the Christian social sciences, which are themselves regarded as partial disciplines), but however true this may be, it would surely also be wrong to regard political theology simply as *the* theology of the future, which, in virtue of the new social situation, does away with all previous theologies. The real situation is that the significance of man is not fully apprehended even at the social level by considering him in his place in society, the influence of society upon him, or his function in society. Hence I find myself unable to see how on this showing a transcendental theology and a political one necessarily exclude one another or do away with one another. The very statement that man is a social being, and must therefore develop his theology as a political theology, is in itself a transcendental statement, which has to be based on transcendental grounds. Otherwise it may lose its validity in the future, and might be rejected even today. And this in itself is enough to show that transcendental and political theology are not mutually exclusive. This is an age in which the social sciences have come to the fore, side by side with philosophy, the traditional speculative disciplines, and the modern natural sciences, as on an equal footing with them and to be regarded as autonomous disciplines in their own right in their bearing upon man's understanding of his own nature and shaping of his own course. And obviously in such an age, and arising from this essential change in its situation, theology must and will take these into account in the future far more than it has done up to now. The social sciences themselves will have a part to play in theology of the kind which up to now has at most been accorded to philosophy and, in recent times, to the scientific study of history. This means that it will also be an essential task of 'political theology' to examine more closely the precise connection between 'politology' (in the broadest sense of the term) and theology. A question which may be left open is whether much which has hitherto been studied under the heading of the sociology of religion or pastoral sociology will in material terms be included as an integral part of 'political theology'. Wherever a tendency arises to erect the social sciences into ideologies, or an attempt is made (whether explicity or in practice) to give them an absolute status as basic and all-dominating sciences, a 'political theology' should precisely serve as a corrective to such false claims.

In conclusion attention may be drawn, in quite brief and simple terms, to a few still more particular points. From what has been said concerning mystagogic and missionary theology and transcendental theology we may surely conclude, without any prolonged discussion, that a far closer unity should be forged between fundamental theology and dogmatics than is, or has been, customary in the study of theology up to the present. Hence it would be perfectly conceivable to assign fundamental theology in its explicit form a place at the conclusion of dogmatics where it could serve as a further critical reappraisal of, and reflection upon, the responsibility which our faith and our hope lays upon us. On any showing it is true that whatever the point in dogmatics at which we attempt to achieve a transcendental understanding of the basic statements of our faith, there we shall be embarking upon a part of fundamental theology which will thereby emerge from that formal void in which it is usually studied (especially in the treatises, 'De Deo Revelante' and 'De Christo Legato Divino'). With regard to the methodological and didactic aspects, and above all with regard to the question raised at the Second Vatican Council as to the essential character of a 'basic course' in theology, I must refer to observations published elsewhere.[24] The same applies to a fundamental and formal theology (which is not to be confused with fundamental theology!).[25]

In this survey much is certainly lacking of what might justifiably be expected in the way of answers to the relevant questions. Perhaps we should have included a section more explicitly devoted to theology considered as the hermeneutics of the Christian message, and to the necessity and limits of a theology of this kind. Certainly we have said too little about the question of the freedom of theology, the question of how, in technical terms, the theology of the future will be organized, the questions (primarily concerning the internal policies of the Catholic Church) of theology and priestly formation, of a theology for layfolk, etc. The ques-

[24] cf. K. Rahner, *Zur Reform des Theologiestudiums,* Quaestiones Disputatae 41 (Freiburg, 1969).

[25] cf. K. Rahner, 'Formale und fundamentale Theologie', *L.T.K.* IV, 2nd ed. (1960), cols. 205–206.

tion of the connection between theology and the natural sciences has not been treated of as a distinct subject in its own right, but who is there who would dare to prophesy, or is even in a position to prophesy, on all these matters?

Has theology still a future before it? It is not only 'heathens' who raise this question only to answer it in the negative. It is being asked by Christians and theologians too who have been thrown into uncertainty when faced with this question. If there is to continue to be any theology in the future, then this theology will certainly not be of the kind which is set up, right from the outset, simply as a world apart, side by side with, or above the ordinary world. It must not regard itself as a distinct department of life in its own right – not even by invoking the factor of divine revelation. First because this factor of revelation and gracious self-bestowal on God's part has entered into the midst of this world, and hence does not exist apart from, or above it, on any right view of the world and revelation alike. But this also has a bearing on the secularized perspectives of the thinking of modern man, in cases in which these have been accorded an absolute value, and developed into an ideological system. Even when modern man is prepared to allow these ideas of his to be called in question, he still has the impression that unless revelation actually *enters into* his own contemporary world, it is totally unintelligible. There is, of course, the scandal of the Cross, and we are prone to appeal to this whenever we have an inexcusably old-fashioned theology to put forward. But even taking this into account, in facing up to the question so anxiously pondered among theologians of whether there is still any future for theology, we shall still have to say that this can be answered in the affirmative only on condition that theology learns to speak about God in the language of this world. To speak about *God* of course, and not about that world which a primitive empiricist might envisage. Such a one might suppose that the world contains nothing except those things the reality of which not even the most stupid or superficial observers would dare to contest, or which might be 'demonstrated' by electric light, drugs, or atom bombs. But theology must speak about God as he is present in the midst of the world, recognizing that it is precisely in *this* form that the gospel bears witness to him as the salvation precisely of this world. Nowhere are any prognoses of the future justified which can deprive man of the boldness to hope against all hope. This also applies to theology. The future which we theologians are fighting for on behalf of our theology is not one in which we have to embark on anxious calculations to see whether it has any future at all. We create this future when – if need be against all the probabilities –

we engage in the study of theology, doing so because we love man, for whom this theology of ours is intended to act as a light, and also because we seek to serve God, who has set us upon the course which we must follow in our study of theology, so that thereby we may perhaps discover God himself.

4

ON THE CURRENT RELATIONSHIP
BETWEEN PHILOSOPHY AND THEOLOGY

THE task I have set myself is a difficult one: to give some reasonable opinion on the relationship between philosophy and theology, and on the significance which philosophy has for and in theology.[1] On these questions one has to seek calm and consolation again and again by reminding oneself simply that theology and (surely too) philosophy exist and are facts, and that, in the face of such facts, one must have the respect which is due even if one cannot work out any wholly adequate justification for the fact by an interpretation of its nature which, in the nature of things, can only be human and finite.

We may perhaps come somewhat closer to a positive answer to the question we have set ourselves if we try to achieve a clear view of the difficulties inherent in it.

I. THE UNIVERSALITY OF THEOLOGY

The very concept of theology is in itself difficult and obscure. For our present purposes, it is true, we shall be quite satisfied with the statement that theology consists in a process of human reflection upon the revelation of God in Jesus Christ and, arising from this, upon the faith of the Church. It also includes the process by which this faith reflects upon its own nature as a factor inevitably entailed in any such faith. Yet this description, while it does bring us enlightenment on some aspects of theology, leaves us in darkness with regard to others. Let me draw attention to one single point, which is, nevertheless, of the utmost importance for our particular question. On any genuine interpretation of the nature of Christian faith,

---

[1] A lecture delivered on 13 November 1971 on the occasion of the ceremonial opening of the 'School of Philosophical Studies at Munich'. On the same subject cf. K. Rahner, 'Philosophy and Theology', *Theological Investigations* VI (London and Baltimore, 1969), pp. 71–81; 'Philosophy and Philosophizing in Theology', *Theological Investigations* IX (London and Baltimore, 1972), pp. 46–63.

at least as currently conceived of, whether we think of it as a given fact or as ecclesiastically and theologically possible, there is such a thing as a genuine revelation of God co-extensive with the history of the world and of ideas, and in that sense universal. The first point to be recognized about this is that it is not identical with the revelation of the Old and New Testaments, for this is confined to a particular area of human life and limited in space and time. Ultimately speaking, however, it does bear a relationship to revelation in this sense, a relationship which is capable of precise definition, though we shall not enlarge any further at this point on its particular characteristics.

The revelation we are speaking of, then, is universal. And though for the most part we do not reflect upon it, we should understand it as a transcendental determination of man, constituted by that which we call grace and self-bestowal on God's part – in other words his Pneuma. It may be present in a form in which it is either reflected upon or not, in a form in which it is either freely accepted or freely refused. And here again, under certain circumstances this refusal need not be at the explicit and conscious level. Nevertheless this revelation is constantly present, because otherwise it is not really conceivable how there can be any universal will to save on God's part, or any possibility of salvation which is perpetual and extended to all. For the reasons given grace (Pneuma), seeing that it is always present at least in the sense of always being offered to man, cannot be conceived of as one particular event in human life, making its impact only intermittently. Rather it is a transcendental determination of human life, albeit one that is freely bestowed by God, and even when it is never objectified or conceived of at the level of explicit consciousness at all. In fact it is, perhaps, quite impossible so to conceive of it without further factors being brought to bear in any process of individual reflection upon the conditions within which the concrete human spirit can operate and exercise its freedom. This is why revelation is always a phenomenon which has precisely those properties ascribed to it by Christianity in its faith and theology. It is of course, impossible at this stage or in this context to define more precisely why, how, or in what ways it is given to man, in the particular concrete circumstances of his life, freely to determine his attitude towards this grace-given and transcendental determination of his being. And this fact makes it still clearer why we both can and must understand this universal self-bestowal of God, considered as a transcendental determination of man, as also constituting revelation.

What we have just said has hardly ever found any clear expression in the usual textbook theology right down to the present day. Nevertheless, if it is correct, then there cannot be any pure philosophy whatever as something produced by man himself in his concrete life. In his thinking man as philosopher is in fact constantly subject to a theological *a priori*, namely that transcendental determination which orientates him towards the immediate presence of God. And this determination is something of which he is fully aware, even though it does not *ipso facto* follow from this that he can reflect upon it. There are, therefore, no pure philosophers – not even at the level of their conscious thinking. Nor is there any such thing as a pure philosophy, if we understand by this the self-perfection of the man who engages in philosophy as he exists in the concrete. This is all the more true because philosophy, when it is really true to its own nature, enquires into *all* and each within the totality; into man as such, and not into one predetermined or merely regional factor present in man or affecting human living. The process of philosophical reflection (whether in principle or as it *de facto* exists – this is a question which we must abstract from here) will rarely if ever succeed in objectifying and reducing to human terms this gracious determination of man in his transcendentality which brings him into immediate contact with God. This applies at least to the individual philosopher in his individual studies. Nevertheless this still does not alter the following fact: that the only way in which man can, in his reflections, successfully penetrate to the very *basis* of his own real existence (and, after all, this is something which he can never really exclude from the outset from his philosophy) is in practice (at the initial stage in his process of reflection) through that which we call revelation history, defining it in terms which assign it to a particular place in the total context of human living as belonging to the official life of the Old Testament and of Christianity. In other words the limitations of philosophical reflection which we have been speaking of make no difference to the fact that the primary and most radical history of philosophy is the history of Old and New Testament revelation. This remains true however shocking it may sound.

We must recognize that philosophy can *never* exclude *anything* from the outset as a subject which is *a priori* alien to it; that that transcendental determination of man is a factor present in virtue of the self-bestowal of God, and, moreover, present always and everywhere (at least in the sense of being offered); finally, as something that follows from this, that in principle there is no so-called philosophy such that it can exclude the process of reflecting upon this. What we are saying, then, is that philosophy in this sense, in the very process of reflecting, penetrates to the dimension of grace inherent in its subject as freely worked upon by God. It might then be said that at this point it should no longer be called philosophy, but rather theology, inasmuch as in this process of reflection it becomes conscious of the fact that the initial process of reflection, which is conscious of having achieved its goal, and which, therefore, is also the norm for all secondary 'philosophizing', is called Christian revelation. But if all this is true, then philosophy as such, or conceived of as 'pure', can only mean that the individual engaging in philosophy methodically abstracts from this factor of grace as a transcendental dimension of his very being, and from the historical manifestation of this, even though this objectification has initially been achieved in faith, which has then in turn been reflected upon in theology. But what philosophy in this sense cannot mean is a discipline which can justifiably and successfully abstract from the ultimate orientation of the human spirit and its freedom to the immediate presence of God, as an objective factor already given and recognized prior to its own speculations, and present through grace rather than as the outcome of any reflective process. This statement that there is a theological element inescapably present in every philosophy is, of course, first and foremost a theological statement. But the theologian will precisely have in mind this further statement: that he views the philosopher as constantly subject to that *a priori* truth which he makes explicit in his theology through a process of historical reflection upon the transcendental process by which grace is bestowed upon man, the process which is called the revelation history of the Old and New Testaments. For the theologian there lies concealed in every philosophy right from the first a theology which is either unreflectingly accepted or rejected in a manner which is (at least materially speaking) culpable. Indeed theology is so present in every philosophy not merely in the sense that the content of the philosophical propositions involve an objective reference to the realities of faith, or are open to them as that which ultimately fulfils and transcends these propositions, but rather in the sense that the very process of philosophizing, in the unity between *noesis* and *noema* inherent in it (if we may so express it), involves, of its very nature, a hidden element of grace, and thereby of theology. The theologian, therefore, discerns in every philosopher a counterpart of himself; or better, he discerns his own theology in a situation involving either salvation or sin, present in that hidden manner in which God, the true God who is no mere 'this-worldly' idol, is present in the world as that which is most interior to it, most hidden within it, as its future.

Philosophy, then, is the partner of theology in the sense that theology is its forerunner, and yet at the same time constantly retains its justified place in every one of its developments, not merely when it is engaged in evolving a 'natural theodicy', not merely when it explicitly comes into confrontation, either in a positive or a negative sense, with the statements of faith. From this point of view philosophy is properly speaking a theology that has not yet arrived at the fulness of its own nature. Now this process of arriving at the fulness of its own nature with regard to its individual themes does not always take place at the same stage. Conversely, theology too is still in process of development. And because of all this it is possible for philosophy, if we can still call it so, actually to have reached (albeit unreflectingly) a stage beyond that at which theology in its present state has arrived. Indeed under certain circumstances (after the pattern of the so-called pagan religions) it can do this not only with regard to the so-called natural assumptions or implications of theological statements, but even with regard to theological data properly so called, though unconsciously and not precisely *as* data of Christian revelation. In the light of this it can be seen that not very much is to be made of the well-known saying that philosophy is the handmaid of theology, even though, on any right understanding, this axiom is not necessarily false in every respect. We may remind ourselves, for instance, of I Corinthians 2:15, where we are told that all things, and so the wisdom of this world too, are subject to the judgement of the spiritual man. But there is one point which the theologian, in reminding himself of this saying, must not forget: that it is precisely not merely his own theology that confronts him from the world in a situation leading to salvation or sin, but the Spirit of God too who fulfils all, and has not appointed any administrator to act as his sole representative or regard this Spirit as his exclusive domain, not even the theologians. The theologian must not suppose that the only context in which theology is a living force (regarding it as the process by which we come to know of God, who, in a hidden manner, fulfils all and bestows himself) is in books in which citations from Scripture are adduced or references given to numbers in Denzinger.

In judging of a philosophy, therefore, the theologian will not, in any primary sense, take as his criterion the question of whether everything contained in that philosophy is correct. This is all the more true since there is an ultimate incommensurability of the two disciplines such that the question can be raised whether, in those cases in which theology disputes the truth of philosophical statements, this does not really and ultimately amount to the fact that the theologian is laying down in a negative sense that the given philosophical statement is not to be accepted as reconcilable with the propositions of faith, and should not, therefore, be put forward in the Church. If, then, what we have just said is correct, then, when theology exercises a critical judgement upon philosophy, it is attempting first and foremost to lay bare the hidden sinfulness or the hidden state of having grace bestowed upon it by the Spirit, inherent in all philosophy, even though philosophy itself does not recognize either of these states at the level of conscious reflection. The relationship between philosophy and theology, therefore, is in itself extremely obscure and complex. To see this we have only to ask what in more precise terms we really take theology to signify.

II. THE PROBLEMS ENTAILED BY PHILOSOPHY

This relationship becomes even more problematical when we ask ourselves in more precise terms what we should, and *de facto* do, take philosophy to signify.

We have already alluded to a possible sinfulness in philosophy. Could not philosophy itself too reflect upon this? After all, it should without difficulty be able to recognize that the philosopher, engaged as he is with *a priori* principles, is all along working from prior assumptions which he never reflects upon or is capable of reflecting upon in any adequate sense at all. He is working from absolute decisions taken prior to any conscious reflection, so that the field of his activities only seems to have a greater serenity and objectivity than life itself or history, with its cruelties, its delusions, and stupidities – in brief with that state of sinfulness which the theologian (resisting the attempt to explain it) seeks to keep clearly in view and to submit to the mystery of God's compassion. The philosopher, on the other hand, despite all his proud speeches in defence of freedom, is, after all, in constant temptation of explaining this factor away and precisely in doing so falls into one of those sins which are committed in philosophy. Why has no one written a hamartiology of philosophy and of the history of philosophy? Admittedly the failure to do so could be excused on one particular ground: that we must not judge, and that even when man created a real, and not merely an apparent, darkness for himself, still the light of God devours it. But let us leave this point.

In order to throw light upon the problems with which philosophy is faced (admittedly primarily from a standpoint which is of interest to the theologian) I may take as my starting-point that evaluation of philosophy which was put forward at the First Vatican Council. Although this Council has been so much derided by many of our contemporaries, if we

understand it rightly it was a great Council despite all the antiquated outlooks which so dominated the conciliar fathers of the time, obviously
frightened as they were by what was taking place in their own age. These
fathers, it is true, would much rather have returned to the ages prior to
the Enlightenment and the French Revolution. Yet for all this it was a
great Council. Why? Because it declared that it was possible to arrive at
a natural knowledge of God through the light of reason alone. In this
pronouncement let us set aside the terms 'reason', 'proof', 'knowledge',
'natural' etc.

All this is not the main point or the essential element in the declaration.
The heart and centre of it is this: man cannot escape from having to do
with God, and even at a stage prior to any Christian revelation conceived
of in explicit or institutional terms. This is inescapable and is something
he encounters before any particular prophets or pastors have reached him.
And if we fail to recognize this clearly, if modern man does not explicitly
assert it and the pastors cannot draw attention to it nowadays, then – if
the view of the Council is to prevail, and it will prevail – this inescapable
factor of God's intervention in human existence must precisely be taking
place in forms, and through experiences, and giving rise to forms of expression, which are unknown or unfamiliar to us And then it is for us
precisely to discover these, and not straightway to fall into lamentations
over the atheism of the present age. Our task is to convey to man where,
within the totality of his existence in all its breadth and depth, he is making
– even though he does not recognize it – experiences of God even while
the explicit statements about God among Christians may perhaps not
contain very much of God within themselves. What is astonishing about
the First Vatican Council, in other words, is the fact that it recognizes
something that takes place in man which is significant for his salvation
(if we want to put it in theological terms) and yet which is, independently
of Christianity or the Church, present inescapably and always. The famous
distinction which Paschal drew between the God of the philosophers and
the God of Abraham, Isaac, and Jacob, the God of Jesus Christ, is precisely
not made here, seeing that the God who is recognized by the light of reason is precisely he who appears as the God of salvation in fundamental
theology and theology. And this is all the more true seeing that it should,
after all, appear obvious that if there can be any such thing at all as a
knowledge of God through the light of natural reason, this cannot have
that liability to error which is entailed, for instance, in what man does or
does not know about Australia. Whether this inescapable reference to
God is 'natural', and whether this 'naturalness' is present in every case

autonomously and in its own right – this is a question that does not concern us here. What is exciting in this conciliar declaration is the assertion that there is a factor of decisive importance for human existence apart from faith in revelation at the biblical and ecclesiastical level, a factor which is of radical significance for Christian faith despite the fact that it is said to have its basis within itself. Whether this does, or does not mean that a 'pure' philosophy emerges as of equal rank with revelation theology, or indeed whether it means that ultimately speaking it is quite incapable of achieving such a position – this is a question which is, for the moment, not important. But what is utterly astonishing is that the faith of the official Church, of its own volition, ascribes so fundamental a significance to a factor which lies outside the Church's own conscious faith in revelation.

Now if we call this knowledge (however we should conceive of it in closer detail) philosophy (however this should be understood on any closer investigation of it), then what is being said at the First Vatican Council is that basically speaking philosophy has a similar significance (or perhaps better an equally important significance) as revelation. Textbook theology will, of course, cry out at this and say that this is not what the Council fathers meant at the time; that they did actually defend the autonomy of theology and its dominance over philosophy. In a certain sense all that is quite true. Yet in the Council's eyes there is precisely a certain autonomous knowledge which is of decisive importance for the sphere of theology, and which, nevertheless, is not revelation theology, something which is prior to any experience of revelation taking place at any particular time or in any particular region, as that which is universal.

The Council regards this knowledge, which is 'secular' and yet is one of the very roots from which theology springs, as having its unity only in God, the source of all truth, and not, properly speaking, in any earthly authority presiding over the two kinds of knowledge and subsuming both within a synthesis that is truly higher and in which each kind contributes to the other. Of course according to the Council in any case of conflict between theology and philosophy this faith constitutes the higher norm for the believer. But this applies so far as faith in itself is concerned. Nowhere is it said that in the case of an apparent conflict between faith and worldly knowledge faith will always prevail, or that it would be impossible for someone to believe that his faith was overthrown by some piece of secular knowledge, provided always that it was not really some *fault* on his part that gave rise to his false judgement in favour of secular knowledge and against faith. And above all: nowhere is there any promise for the believer of a kind of synthesis between faith and knowledge which is attainable immediately and in every instance. In other words in this time of pilgrimage he will actually have to live in circumstances of a gnoseological pluralism, and will never be able fully to achieve that gnoseological integrity which would overcome this unresolved pluralism. He will not even be able to achieve this in the area of those kinds of knowledge which are in some sense significant for salvation, for even in this area pluralism still prevails. What we have, then, is a knowledge of subjects which are important for salvation which, however it is to be conceived of in more precise detail, is different from the knowledge of revelation of the official Church. Now if we apply the term philosophy to this kind of knowledge, then the First Vatican Council has declared that a pluralism in gnoseology exists, in the concrete conditions of human living, between philosophy and theology. It is true that right down to the Second Vatican Council a cultural and social homogeneity in the sphere of knowledge which really belonged to earlier ages still survived for certain good Christians and Catholics in markedly ghetto-like conditions. But only this kind of outlook could fail to feel this pluralism, which in principle had been recognized by the First Vatican Council, as hard and dangerous. Only those affected by a cultural and social homogeneity of this kind could suppose instead that so far as Christians are concerned everything can easily and positively be brought into harmony in this sphere of knowledge. In other words, there is no need for any very peaceful or harmonious relationship to prevail everywhere and at all times between theology and philosophy. The conflicts which may possibly arise are not only such as the philosophical theologian or the religious-minded philosopher will have solved right from the outset, or which as conflicts arise only from the techniques of presentation in the textbooks. There will be many occasions on which there really are no positive solutions to such conflicts. We may perhaps have to allow them to continue unresolved in the conviction that we cannot do without either of the two kinds of knowledge involved in the conflict, even though they seem to us in all sincerity to be totally irreconcilable. We have really to endure under the pain of this gnoseological pluralism and this kind of concupiscence or yearning to achieve harmony. Paul's 'infelix ego homo' (Rom 7:24) has its place in this context too. Whereas the Council of Trent was the Council of a pluralism yearning for harmony in the dimension of moral decision, the First Vatican Council was the Council of a pluralism yearning for harmony in the dimension of the theoretical reason wherever this exists in concrete human life. In this area we are still constantly prone to refuse really to admit this state of a concupiscent pluralism or a pluralism yearning for harmony. We recognize that faith and secular reasoning should not be opposed as contradictory sources of knowledge, and that the integration of the several different kinds of knowledge is the goal which we must constantly be striving towards, albeit asymptotically. And because of all this we regard the situations of conflict which arise between philosophy and theology as from the very outset being sinful, and believe that we should force integration in the sense we have been speaking of upon them even when in practice this can only be done at the cost of intellectual honesty. And so we lose our attitude of sensitivity and alertness for the differences between the various languages in which these different departments of knowledge can and must find expression. From this point of view alone, and abstracting from all others, it becomes clear that the history of the relationship between theology and philosophy constantly gives rise to factors that are, in a genuine sense, new and *unexpected*: it is the history of two realities and the history of the relationship which each bears to the other, and there is no higher sphere within this world common to them both and transcending all the differences between them in which they can meet and be reconciled. It is, therefore, a history which cannot be planned, but remains open and subject to that freedom which itself has to survive in and in virtue of a number of different and unintegrated factors.

a. *Pluralism in Philosophy*

We have attempted to achieve a view of the problems entailed in the relationship between theology and philosophy precisely from the point of view of philosophy itself. We have tried to see how theology in itself, and according to its own principles, has to regard this. Now let us turn our attention directly to philosophy itself. In this connection we may draw attention to a quite simple fact, yet one which is of the utmost importance for theology. There are many philosophies. And theology is involved with many philosophies, and thereby is itself in turn divided into many theologies.

It is worthwhile to ponder this statement a little. When I was young I was devoted to the study of philosophy through thick and thin. And at that time our whole attitude was coloured by a belief in *one single* philosophy. Obviously we were aware (as men always have been) of the fact that in practice there were many philosophies. Indeed we studied the history of philosophy and there came to know of a whole range of the most varied systems and theories. And in systematic philosophy we took up a critical attitude towards these systems, deciding what to accept and what to reject in them. But in all this we were, after all, constantly, albeit tacitly, taking as our starting-point the belief that in adopting this approach we were touching more or less upon everything in the philosophy of the past and present alike which was of real philosophical importance; that we could and did draw from it into our own system everything that was true and valuable; finally that we were fully justified in rejecting the rest. All this is intended as a broad and general view of our principles and our approach.

Now I believe that the situation today is radically and insuperably different. Prior to the question of truth proper (I emphasize – *prior* to this!) the modern philosopher is confronted with a pluralism of philosophies which no one individual is any longer capable of mastering, and we are aware of this fact. Formerly there was a total unawareness of anything which could neither be integrated into, nor rejected from one's own personal philosophy. Today we are aware that there is much in the philosophies which we can neither reject nor particularly welcome precisely because we are unfamiliar with it. But we do know that we are not really sufficiently familiar with it either to welcome it or to reject it of our own resources and on our own responsibility. The means of communication of the present age have the effect of making us know that we do not know. And in fact this also applies to the realm of philosophy. I at least would regard it as both naïve and presumptuous if nowadays a philosopher were still to behave as though he could know and did know all the essential answers in philosophy as it is *de facto* being studied. Philosophy *as a whole* has grown to enormous dimensions. It has become planet-wide. It is no longer the prerogative merely of one particular culture, and precisely for this reason a whole range of philosophies has emerged, too many to be brought together in one mind, even though all possible efforts still can be, and are, brought to bear in this direction.

Now it is true that there is no such thing as a theology which does not unquestioningly include an element of philosophy within it, or which either can or would reflect upon the Christian faith without the help of philosophy in general or of one particular philosophical system. Perhaps the neo-scholasticism in the theology of the last 150 years constituted the final attempt to use *one single* homogeneous philosophy in the study of theology. But this is something that is simply not possible any longer, and contemporary theology also shows that it no longer in practice makes the slightest attempt to achieve this. What the implications of this are for the

Church's teaching authority, its methods and its effectiveness, is a question which cannot be entered into here. For our present purposes we have simply to recognize this: the fact that, prior to any question of truth properly so called, we have to recognize a pluralism of philosophies too great for us to master or control, compels us of today to recognize a pluralism of theologies prior to the question of theological truth, and without prejudice to a general orientation of all such theologies towards the original message of faith and the single teaching authority of the Church. The destiny of philosophy is today becoming, in a quite new sense, the destiny of theology too. Obviously we do not mean by this, in the case either of theology or of philosophy, that the relationship between these manifold systems is that of so many individual monads standing 'over against' each other. Obviously the boundaries between the individual philosophies and the individual theologies are in principle not such as can be precisely drawn. Obviously it is always possible to judge of the question of truth in terms of each such scientific discipline and in terms of its own individual findings.

But all this does not for one moment alter the situation that we find today, namely that as a result of the modern pluralism of philosophies our task is no longer simply to bring to light a series of theologies which speak with different tongues, i.e. use different philosophical systems. This fact has not yet sufficiently been recognized. The Church's teaching authorities have not yet taken due cognizance of it. No principles and methods have yet been developed for coping – indirectly if need be – with this fact without destroying the unity of the Church or of the Christian creed.

b. *Philosophy as it Affects the Specialist in Modern Scientific Disciplines*

In reflecting upon the relationship between philosophy and theology we have to evaluate the situation of philosophy from yet another point of view. Formerly philosophy was *the* representative embodying secular knowledge in its bearing upon the ultimate meaning and values of human life, and as significant for salvation. The prior equipment in terms of secular knowledge which the theologian had to have in order to be a sound and effective theologian he learned in philosophy, because in the concrete conditions of human living at the time this alone constituted the meaningful integration of knowledge as such. To the extent that a particular branch of knowledge was non-philosophical, to that extent it was also irrelevant for any theology in the true sense. This is shown by the very fact that formerly whatever affinity theology may in itself have had with history, there was no such thing as a science of history in the true sense to act as a partner to theology. In fact it was not really until the documents of the Second Vatican Council were produced on ecclesiastical studies that any real recognition emerged of the necessity for a partnership between theology and the science of history which could be methodologically effective. Previously scientific history had never been included as an integral element in the 'systematic' theology of neo-scholasticism. At most it had been tolerated as an unavoidable preliminary course leading up to the study of theology and apologetics. Admittedly this state of affairs was in reality an anachronism at least from the 19th century onwards, and here and there it was of course recognized as such – for instance in the Tübingen school. Today, however, the whole situation has been radically altered.

The sciences which exist side by side with philosophy include not only the speculative disciplines but the natural sciences and social sciences as well. And there are two points to be recognized about these: first, they regard themselves not as subalternate sciences, depending upon philosophy for their justification and the defining of their tasks, or having their methodological approach and their sphere of investigation determined for them by philosophy. On the contrary, these sciences are regarded as autonomous in origin and as self-authenticating. They are constantly liable to the temptation of regarding philosophy as a mythical prefiguration of themselves, or of thinking of philosophy as at most playing a supplementary role in reflecting upon and summing up precisely *those* methodological approaches which are developed within the sciences as of their own right. And the second point is that it cannot be said that these secular sciences, which have emancipated themselves from philosophy, have no relevance to our faith or our theological understanding of revelation in their bearing upon our view of the world and the concrete modes of human existence. It is true that on many individual questions an interchange of ideas has gradually been achieved between theology on the one hand and these individual sciences in their findings on the other over the last fifty years, quite apart from philosophy. Apparent conflicts between the two sides have been shown to be due to misunderstandings and so resolved. Yet at the same time the present age is dominated by a radical and all-embracing mental outlook conditioned by the natural sciences, and this continues to be something with which theology is constantly, directly, and uniformly confronted, or should feel itself confronted, and, moreover, this confrontation is not something which theology can simply delegate to an old-fashioned type of metaphysic to deal with as its particular concern.[2] The following grounds alone are sufficient to justify us in saying this: that in practice these natural sciences,. as practised today, are more ready to enter into serious dialogue with theology than with philosophy (whether they are justified or not in this attitude, it makes no difference to the facts). The reason is that in the positions which theology tends to adopt they are more ready to recognize points of reconciliation in which they can still remain detached and allow for differences between them, yet which, in the concrete conditions of human life, have a significance even for the practitioner of the natural sciences as such.

These natural sciences, then, regard themselves as autonomous. Yet they do have a certain radical significance, and one which applies to the whole of human life. All this is something which can no longer be denied at the present day And from this it follows that theology has to recognize as her partner in dialogue no longer philosophy alone, regarded as the sole mediator and interpreter of man's experience of himself as such in its most radical form On the contrary, theology has itself directly to turn its attention to the natural sciences, enquiring into their basic outlook and their autonomy, and allowing itself to be conditioned by them. *Mutatis mutandis*, the same must be said about the relationship between the social sciences and theology. Here too theology has acquired a new partner, one who refuses any longer to accept that the only way of communicating with theology is through the medium of philosophy. Hence theology must take due cognizance of this refusal as an actual existing fact. This remains true even if it is possible to say that theology has a duty *ex officio* to remind the social sciences of their theological implications. For the very act of doing this will in itself awaken a metaphysical conscience in these social sciences. Precisely in these social sciences it becomes manifest that the distinction in man between his metaphysical nature and his concrete, historically conditioned nature is far less easy to draw than was formerly supposed; indeed that it is in principle quite impossible to draw it in any full or adequate sense. Now if theology has to deal with man as a whole, seeing that it is in his wholeness that he is meant to enter upon salvation and that this salvation depends upon him in his wholeness, then it follows that it is quite impossible for theology to avoid turning its attention to the social sciences, with their *a posteriori* and historical level

[2] On this cf. the following two articles in the present volume, 'Theology as Engaged in an Interdisciplinary Dialogue with the Sciences', pp. 80–93, and 'On the Relationship between Theology and the Contemporary Sciences', pp. 94–102.

of experience, and to allow itself to be influenced in its lines of enquiry and its methods by these and not merely by philosophy as such. Presumably this process is still hardly in its incipient stages.

III. ASPECTS OF THE FUTURE PARTNERSHIP BETWEEN PHILOSOPHY AND THEOLOGY

Certainly it is a tenable position that metaphysics cannot possibly die so long as man has not degenerated into a clever animal or finally destroyed his own nature. But the destiny of metaphysics is, after all, precisely a destiny the future paths of which cannot be foreseen. And when it is predicted that something will bring metaphysics to an end, or asserted that it is already ended, this may itself once more be based on a wrong diagnosis. Even so, however, it is not simply a mere empty spectre, or an occasion of groundless alarm. Now on this showing it is obvious that the task of theology cannot be first and foremost to keep metaphysics alive or flourishing, even though there is inevitably a certain task to be fulfilled in this direction. Rather theology will keep its attention fixed upon man in the conditions of life in which he actually lives in the present, even though man himself may suppose that he is living in a post-metaphysical age. Theology will recognize (at least as a primary task) that it has to make man as he exists today aware of the blind spot in the vision of a post-metaphysical neo-positivism, the social sciences connected with it, and the interpretation of language which it puts forward. And theology must straightway attempt to supply a theological interpretation of this and not concern itself so much with working out, in any explicit or exclusive sense, the metaphysical implications involved in this positivism, by which modern man's whole mentality is almost totally conditioned.

In any case: with regard to explicit philosophy in the traditional sense, the theology of today cannot do this the favour of regarding it alone as its partner in its dealings with the world. To use a figure of speech that might seem almost malicious, this state of monogamy is over. Theology can no longer allow its connections with the secular and *a posteriori* sciences to take place solely through the medium of philosophy. Instead it has direct and autonomous connections with these. That the task of theology is not made any lighter thereby is obvious. For after all, in the sphere of Western civilization philosophy has all along been recognized as such as the sister to theology, so that in a true sense it was a simple matter for it to continue in partnership with theology. For while a dispute between relations may grow very bitter, it is much less dangerous than that situation of almost mortal peril which can emerge between those who are quite unaware of what they may have to do with one another at all.

Is it the case, therefore, that the marriage between theology and philosophy, now almost two thousand years old, is at an end? Or (*sit venia verbo!*) has it been transformed into a strange kind of 'love triangle', in which the sciences in the modern sense are also involved as of their own right? This is a question which properly speaking it is the task of philosophy and the sciences themselves to resolve rather than theology. For it is for philosophy and the sciences to determine their mutual relationship in principle and as it has *de facto* developed in history. It is of concern to theology that as positive a relationship as possible should be established between philosophy and the sciences, but theology itself cannot establish this relationship of its own power, even though it would suit it best. For otherwise it would itself have to engage in philosophy in pursuit of this aim. Certainly it can *de facto* do this, and is not prohibited from doing so, but in that case it would precisely be engaging in philosophy, and, moreover, however necessary it might consider its findings here, it would in practice be one particular philosophy, not excluding the possibility of others existing beside it, and a philosophy which was conditioned by practical historical realities. However this is surely something which theology can hardly take it upon itself to engage in of its own resources in any effective manner or one which can influence the course of history.

However this may be, nothing that we have said represents any threat to the true relationship which exists between theology and philosophy. Theology necessarily entails thinking, and thinking takes place outside the realm of theology. And provided this thinking is at a radical level, provided it touches upon man in his wholeness, provided it reaches to the level of mystery and faces up to it, provided it considers itself and not merely the things about us, it can be called a philosophy of confidence, and this prior to the question of what further developments may take place in the traditional forms of philosophy handed down through history, and how this radical self-realization on man's part may find expression in the future. Thinking of this kind must be engaged in within theology itself. First because for a Catholic theology man is the recipient of a revelation which is objectified and institutionalized in the Church as a historical phenomenon, and as such he is precisely not a *tabula rasa*, not some *materia prima* having nothing of its own to contribute to this revelation. In the very process of making this revelation his own he must recognize in himself that he is, from the outset, bringing something positive of his own to bear upon this revelation. This recognition of the part he himself plays may be 'secular' in character if not actually outside the realm of grace altogether, but man must still recognize his own subjective contribution, however true it may be that this is itself transformed in a historical process in and through this encounter of his with revelation. Regarded as a discipline designed to achieve a reflexive and critical understanding of the Church's revelation, therefore, theology includes, as an intrinsic element and not merely as an external prior condition, man's secular understanding of himself, and it is only in relation to this, and as confronted with this, that faith becomes theology. This is not to say that for the believing theologian all philosophy should, or even so much as could, be pursued only within the sphere presided over by theology.

It was Thomas Aquinas who first recognized philosophy as an autonomous discipline, and its secularization, its emancipation, constitutes the first step in the legitimate process by which the world is allowed to become 'worldly', a process which, ultimately speaking, is willed and has been set in motion by Christianity itself. Theology must, of its own nature, will that man shall freely, independently, and on his own responsibility, achieve an understanding of himself. It must will to have philosophy concomitant to, and independent of itself. Only in this way can philosophy be, in any effective sense, a *partner* to theology (of course in saying this we are not pre-judging the issue of whether the roles of philosopher and theologian can be united in the personality of a single individual, either in a positive or a negative sense). But to the extent that, as a matter of historical necessity, a 'worldly' world is the appropriate milieu for a theology that meets the demands of the true Christian faith, to that extent an autonomous and secular philosophy will also be right as the true partner in the dialogue with theology, provided only that we take philosophy to signify that understanding of himself on man's part which considers man as one and whole, and provided that the revelation of God, as truly objectified and achieving due recognition of its own nature in the Christian Church, is not from the outset introduced as the subject of this reflection and as the norm which governs it. Of course this does not entail any clear-cut distinction between man's understanding of himself on the one hand, and the revelation of God in its *a priori* form, as a grace that inescapably permeates all, on the other. But this is a point which we have already made at the beginning of these considerations.

Now this secular understanding of himself on man's part, which we have called philosophy in the sense described, will not, in its contemporary form, be controlled simply and exclusively by philosophy alone. Rather it remains subject to historical conditioning and dependent upon *a posteriori* experiences as institutionalized in the sciences. This means that theology must maintain a direct dialogue with these sciences as well, because the bearing which these have on man's understanding of himself is direct, and not merely mediated through philosophy. But this again is a point which we have already made.

What finally emerges, therefore, is a dialogue in which it is quite impossible to draw precise distinctions even between the roles which the partners to the dialogue should play. The theologian hears a philosopher who, ultimately speaking, bases himself from the outset on the theology of sin and grace, whether he is aware of it or not. The philosopher hears a theologian who – again from the outset (and again whether consciously or not) – has developed his theology with the help of philosophy; in other words one who, right from the outset, encounters him as a philosopher, so that, being this kind of theologian, he needs to have the problems of his philosophy set forth by a philosopher. Both, theologians and philosophers alike, are engaged in dialogue with the modern scientist who (whether consciously or not) has from the outset overstepped his boundaries and entered the spheres of philosophy and theology, thereby speaking to the theologian of matters of which the philosopher as such and taken in isolation cannot speak to him, and yet which are of crucial importance for a theologian, obliged as he is to take man in the concrete into his considerations. These are matters some at least of which it is quite impossible to reflect upon adequately from a philosophical point of view, and yet which cannot be left out of consideration in theology.

The scientist, who neither can nor should make the foolish attempt to monopolize his science and reserve it to his own official clique, may perhaps hear from non-specialists the kind of message which, however dilettante the form in which it is expressed, can still have a revolutionary, or at any rate a crucial, significance for his own science. And he hears explicitly the message involved in that tacit overstepping of boundaries on which he is forced unscientifically to depend in order to keep his own science vital, if only because the study of the particular science he is engaged in is always subject to norms which wholly transcend the material content of that science. If, therefore, the partners to the dialogue speak to one another, each in turn will be transformed, and their respective roles will be exchanged. And this transforming dialogue is an element in the true history of man, incalculable as it is, in which all branches of knowledge are constantly open from the first to the ultimate Mystery, ineffable and yet invoked, in which all science, theology, and philosophy alike, are comprehended. The label by which society assigns a particular calling to the individual, and the personal decision by which that individual chooses this or that secular calling in the world of ideas in preference to others – these are, ultimately speaking, provisional factors, and little more than a welcome or unwelcome deception. There is an ultimate *basis* at which each is constantly engaged with all. And this basis has still to be revealed. Only if we have engaged in all branches at this ultimate level, are we saved. Admittedly this state of being saved requires also the modesty of confining ourselves to our own proper sphere, and leaving other spheres to other thinkers. It is only for this reason and in this sense that we can nowadays open a philosophical faculty. The theologian welcomes it because everything human belongs to God, and only so is truly appropriated to man, and because in the midst of all philosophy the theologian discerns God revealing himself in his grace.

5

THEOLOGY AS ENGAGED IN AN
INTERDISCIPLINARY DIALOGUE
WITH THE SCIENCES

BEFORE we can embark upon any discussion of the possible participation and the task of theology in the interdisciplinary dialogue
between the sciences[1] we must first have found an answer to the
question of what interdisciplinary discussion is in itself. It is only when
we have found an answer to this question that we can then go on to
enquire *whether* theology has any part to play in it, and *what* that part is.
Yet I am not aware of any real answer having been found even to the first
question.

The fact that men speak with one another may be obvious, although
even in simple discussions so many mysteries lie concealed, the moment
they extend beyond the level of the sort of language which is necessary
for the most basic human communication.[2] The fact that the specialists in
the particular sciences speak with one another may also be obvious on the
assumption that as human beings their interest also extends to matters
which lie outside their own specialist fields, where their principal and pro-
fessional interests lie. But the question becomes obscure the moment we
seek to discern precisely what one partner to such discussions communicates to the other. For the question then arises of whether this is some-

[1] Certain ideas on the present subject have been published by a collaborator of the
author's under the same title: Fr. Mann, 'Die Theologie im interdisziplinären
Gespräch der Wissenschaften', *StdZ* 186 (1970), pp. 109–116.

[2] This fact has also been made particularly clear from a scientific point of view as
a consequence of the development of modern cybernetics and research into communication. Hence these have also given rise to a whole series of particular problems in
relation to theology. Literature is available on this subject, though here we may confine ourselves to a few passing references for the assistance of those who wish to
pursue the question further: H. R. Rapp, *Mensch, Gott und Zahl. Kybernetik im
Horizont der Theologie* (Hamburg, 1967); H. D. Bastian, 'Anfangsprobleme im
Gespräch zwischen Kybernetik und Theologie', *Theologia Practica* 3 (1968), pp.
33–42; D. O. Scumalstieg, 'Kybernetik – Theologie – Gesellschaft. Möglichkeiten
interdisziplinärer Theorie', *Internat. Dialog. Zeitschrift* 4 (1971), pp. 130–133.

thing which interests the other scientist precisely *to the extent that* he has further interests beyond the sphere of his own particular science. For in that case what is taking place is, basically speaking, not an interdisciplinary dialogue at all.

THE PROBLEMS ENTAILED IN AN INTERDISCIPLINARY DIALOGUE

Let us suppose that one scientist communicates to another a piece of information which is of interest to him precisely as a scientist. It seems that the only cases in which this can take place are those in which the particular specialist sciences overlap with one another in their subject-matter. In other words all that the first scientist is communicating to the second is something which as a scientist, he could also have come to know, or discover by his own researches. Properly speaking, therefore, what is taking place here cannot, except in a very broad sense, be called an interdisciplinary dialogue, for the specialist in a particular science *de facto* always knows less than he really ought to know as a specialist in his own particular discipline. I cannot really see how we can escape from this difficulty. It is, of course, possible to say that while the particular sciences are indeed concerned with their respective areas of subject-matter from particular aspects or with particular formal objects in view, in many cases these areas of subject-matter are themselves materially speaking identical. This, then, would explain why the result of one science concerned with one particular subject might be of interest to another, and would make an interdisciplinary discussion between them meaningful. But in response to this it might presumably be objected that even when two sciences are concerned with the same material object, the findings of one science are arrived at by considering a distinctive formal object in it from a distinctive viewpoint. Hence the only way in which the findings of one such science could be of interest to another is for the one to be subalternate to the other, to be a subordinate branch of the other science. And in such a case any dialogue between them would not, properly speaking, be an interdisciplinary dialogue, a discussion, in other words, between two sciences which are regarded as autonomous, and not as already subsumed under a single supreme science which has subsequently branched out into particular areas, and is arrived at by considering a basic conception that is common to all the sciences. We must take into consideration, therefore, something which is nowadays surely taken as established, namely an original pluralism of the sciences. We must not recognize any one science as occupying a position of supremacy or transcendence over the rest, or as assigning the individual sciences their place or their task (as in earlier times philosophy was called the ultimate science), and we must ask ourselves whether there is any such thing as a scientific doctrine prior to the individual disciplines, instead of being merely subsequently educed from the methods employed in these and arrived at by reducing what is common to them all to formal and systematic terms. And it is precisely when we adopt this approach that the interdisciplinary dialogue seems to be reduced to a dialogue between men as such – men, in other words who, while they are engaged in various branches of science, still fortunately take an interest in other matters outside their own particular science. Of course it would be possible to attack the initial postulate on which this finding is based, namely that pluralism between the sciences in virtue of which each is autonomous in its own right and from its very origins. It would be possible to postulate instead a basic science imposing its influence bindingly upon all *a priori*, and to call this logic, metaphysics, *a priori* scientific doctrine at an ontological level, or any other name we may choose. But in that case we would merely be setting up a postulate which *de facto* the individual representatives of the various sciences would find it quite impossible to accept, so that in the concrete it would have nothing to contribute in throwing light upon the nature and special characteristics of interdisciplinary dialogue. In reaction against this we might console ourselves with the assurance that even though the scientists assert their respective autonomies each in his own branch of science, they would still tacitly disavow this autonomy of theirs if they consented to engage in an interdisciplinary dialogue as such, and in the strict sense. Yet this is, after all, only a very slight consolation in view of the blind alley into which we have been led by the problems entailed in the idea of an interdisciplinary dialogue. For even if we are willing to accept this consolation as legitimate, we still have to concede that even if these scientists are willing to forego their own autonomy, which they claim each for his own particular science (anti-metaphysical in outlook as they in fact are nowadays), they do so precisely as *men*, though admittedly they show themselves wiser and more reasonable in this role than they would if they remained precisely scientists and nothing more.

INTERDISCIPLINARY DIALOGUE AS A FACT

Of course we can take as our starting-point the sheer fact that an interdisciplinary dialogue exists, at least to a modest extent, and, furthermore, even before it is recognized what, on any precise view, the participants are committing themselves to. We might be prepared to acknowledge that this fact has the same significance and the same justification as the individual sciences. After all, these too already exist and are actively engaged in even before they know precisely what the outcome of their activities will be. For while they do indeed know the subject-matter with which they are concerned, they do not know themselves. Their position is similar to that of a man who is already questing about in his everyday life even before he has arrived at any conscious reflection of what his precise purpose is in doing so, or why he ever commits himself to this totally unsystematic everyday life of his, and that too when it leads him in several different directions. Before coming to my real argument, I would like to supplement what I have said with regard to the problems entailed in an interdisciplinary dialogue at least from one further aspect. I believe that any interdisciplinary dialogue will in practice entail something like aggression in the actions and reactions of each particular discipline in its relations with the others. The individual scientist may personally be extremely modest, and have extremely modest ideas about his own science and the particular place it occupies within the total spectrum of human life and of the knowledge which mankind needs. Yet in practice he is secretly, and for the most part unconsciously, impelled by an awareness that he has something to say to all other men which is important for them and, moreover, precisely as the representatives of some other science. His attitude is that one has only to step out boldly enough and far enough from the starting-point of one's own science, to penetrate, in the long run, to all departments of human life while yet remaining within one's own science. Any science, at least as practised in the concrete by the individual scientist, has a tendency to monopolize. Every scientist, therefore, has the tendency to instruct the other sciences and scientists, and is prone to the temptation of failing to listen to the others, or being willing to hear from them only what is confirmed for him in his own science. Hence the strange attitude of aggression which prevails among scientists even when it is concealed by a mask of conventional politeness. But this is still not enough to explain the real grounds for this attitude of aggression on the part of particular sciences, causing them to seek to dominate all departments. Ultimately speaking these grounds are to be found in the paradox that every science as such regards itself as autonomous, and yet, in view of the unity of human knowledge, is secretly convinced of the fact that man has only to pursue his own scientific investigations at a sufficiently radical level to be able to identify them with the totality of human knowledge.

This attitude of aggression, therefore, secretly draws its vitality from an awareness that, despite the pluralism of the sciences, each of which regards itself as autonomous, a principle prevails, unacknowledged and yet necessary for the very life of each particular science, that impels it towards the totality of human knowledge; a principle, in other words, which belongs to it and yet is not subject to it and cannot be controlled by the science itself. Each particular science, therefore, taken in itself, is in a state of self-alienation, and that too in a positive sense, and it is this, so I believe, which constitutes the grounds for the positive side of the attitude of aggression towards one another which we find among the sciences, and which usually manifests itself with extreme intensity in interdisciplinary dialogue. One is not aggressive towards that which is totally alien. When one is aggressive one is asserting a difference on the surface and yet revealing the presence, albeit unacknowledged, of a hidden relationship with that which one opposes. This interior principle, present within the individual science yet never consciously reflected upon or brought under control by it, is the factor which secretly sustains its attitude of aggression towards the other sciences. And it also manifests itself in the fact that even when a science is intended to be effective in the modern sense of the term, it still always has to allow for the possibility that it not only fastens upon fresh subject-matter at the material level and makes it explicitly subject to its own laws, but also may call its own principles in question, break through its own perspectives and change them. Such a science may, in fact, of its own power, transform itself in its basic understanding of its own nature. Now a process of self-questioning of this kind is, after all, only possible provided that in every science a principle prevails which is not subject to the control of that science, a principle which the science concerned cannot bring into harmony with itself and which, nevertheless, is not subject to it either. And it is precisely this that seems to be the basis for the love-hatred between the disciplines, and for the possibility, necessity, and at the same time difficulty of an interdisciplinary dialogue.

THE HUMAN FACTOR AND SCIENCE

Of course it might be said that in all this we have simply been pointing, and that in very general terms, to the common human factor. Right at the beginning of these considerations of ours we said that it was this that sustained the interdisciplinary dialogue, and at the same time made it a dialogue to which the name of 'interdisciplinary dialogue' could be applied only in a very improper sense, seeing that, in the last analysis, it is not the scientific specialists as such, but the individuals who happen to be scientific specialists, who speak to one another in it. All this remains true. But what is the situation now that some indications have been given, however weak they may appear, pointing to the fact that this human factor as such may belong to each particular science *as such*, albeit only in a quite peculiar sense of the term 'belonging', such that it is at the same time not under the control of that science. Of course in saying this we also recognize that it belongs to each particular science in a manner quite specific to itself. It is true that in former times this factor common to all sciences which we have pointed to so obscurely, which contributes to their life-force without itself being susceptible to control by them, was called the metaphysical factor, the transcendental factor etc., which was the special concern of philosophy. Now we may seek to explain away this common factor as non-existent on the grounds that, at least to all appearances, philosophy and metaphysics in the derived sense have reached their end, or at any rate are incapable of treating of this factor common to all the sciences in a credible manner, even though it is this that sustains the interdisciplinary dialogue. Here again we may assign two grounds for this: either that it is something which in principle is not susceptible of scientific consideration, or that it cannot be upheld by any philosophy concretely enough or decisively enough to make this common factor a basis for an interdisciplinary dialogue in such a way that in that dialogue we can expect not merely openness and freedom, or in the end, at a secondary level, a mutual interchange of information, but conflict, decision, and the achieving of some genuine common ground as well. But can we really maintain this position? In present conditions will this common factor be sustained by some other 'science' or whatever name we may wish to give to the upholder of this common factor?[3]

THE STANDPOINT OF CHRISTIAN THEOLOGY

At this point we must begin by interpolating a few remarks. We are speaking of Christian theology. Here no distinction is being drawn between Catholic or Protestant theology. We may therefore pass over the problem of whether the two theologies do not differ to some extent in the way in which they regard themselves, and whether this would not also be a conditioning factor, causing each of these two theologies to place a different interpretation upon its particular powers and qualities as contributing to the interdisciplinary dialogue. A further question which we

[3] cf. W. Pannenberg, *Was ist der Mensch? Die Anthropologie der Gegenwart im Lichte der Theologie* (Göttingen, 1962).

are leaving on one side is whether theology can or should regard itself as a science which can take its place in the interdisciplinary dialogue as one particular science, or alternatively whether, even if it is something quite different, it should nevertheless hold firmly that it has a right to intervene at least at specific points in this dialogue, even though it is not intended to be a science. On this showing, therefore, the interdisciplinary dialogue would become something more, and would be less restricted to the science alone. This is a question which we can leave open, even though in doing so we are in no sense questioning the fact that from the practical and technical point of view theology cannot renounce its task of organizing something which at first sight appears like the systematic investigation of a science in the true sense, and even if we are convinced of the fact that this scientific or quasi-scientific enquiry on the part of theology (whatever interpretation may be placed upon it either by the theologians themselves or by others) both can and should be engaged in within the framework of a university. One third point: provided theology has not tacitly surrendered its role, does not allow its understanding of its own nature or awareness of its own task to depend upon the question of whether it is given a place in an interdisciplinary dialogue, or whether the other sciences have the impression that theology has something to tell them which is of concern or value to them, it is in a position to lead the discussion. Obviously theology too, like any other science, can act as an ancillary science to other disciplines. But if theology were to make its understanding of its own nature dependent upon the question of whether it was welcomed in the symposium of the sciences, if the only way in which theology could establish its position would be through the contribution it makes to the interdisciplinary dialogue (and this seems to me to be approximately the opinion of many of the younger theologians), then at basis theology would already have given up its true role, and would also have to be silent in the interdisciplinary dialogue, because it would then have nothing to say.[4]

THEOLOGY AND THE HUMAN FACTOR

Some may hold the view that in the interdisciplinary dialogue of today theology's role is to take over the defence of that mysterious human factor which is constantly present in the other disciplines, constantly making its

[4] See the symposium volume, *Recherche interdisciplinaire et théologie* (Paris, 1970), with articles by F. Houtart, H. E. Tödt, G. Palmade, J. Ladrière, M. D. Chenu, A. Astier and M. Faessier.

impact even when unacknowledged, and prompting these disciplines to transcend their own limits and, going beyond the explicitly methodological concept which they *ex professo* uphold, to submit themselves to the most radical questioning. Now if we ascribe a role of this kind to theology, critical and at the same time supra-disciplinary, then obviously we are placing it in an extremely hostile and unhappy position. This is not so much because the same role might, and in former times actually has been, ascribed to some philosophical system. If the philosophy of today is still willing to play this part, and is recognized as having this function by the other sciences, even though these are reluctant to allow philosophy to tell them anything, then certainly theology will not from the outset deny this role to philosophy. Instead, presumably, it will try to achieve agreement with philosophy in a more private discussion on the question of how philosophy and theology, each in its own way, and as the outcome of a decision arrived at only with difficulty, can together take over this task in the interdisciplinary dialogue. Moreover the difficulty which such a role involves consists surely not in the question of whether the other sciences will admit theology to their discussion, and then allow it to make that contribution which it believes it has to make in this dialogue in virtue of its very nature as it understands this. If the other sciences were unwilling to admit theology to their discussion the questions would have to be raised of what right they had *a priori* to exclude theology as a partner to their discussion, of whether in that case they knew what theology was and whence they derived their knowledge of it, whether it was from their own scientific findings or from some other source, whether this other source *ipso facto* constituted a criterion so sure that they could undertake to exclude theology in this way with a good conscience. And further questions which we would have to put to these other sciences are these: since their decision to exclude theology in this way would be *ex supposito* unanimous and common to them all, whether they recognized some authority among themselves common to them all and binding upon them all, and what this was (for instance whether after all it was once more philosophy *as such* or some system of philosophy). Again the fear of not being admitted to the dialogue at all rules out any possible risk that may be entailed in the part theology plays in the interdisciplinary dialogue. Finally the point to be taken into account in considering what such participation may entail is not the objection which might possibly be raised that every participant in such a dialogue must be personally responsible for bearing in mind the human factor as providing the basis and the ultimate perspective for the dialogue itself. For not only is every individual an upholder of this human factor, and responsible for upholding it, but in addition the human factor itself constitutes a hidden element intrinsic to every science and calling every science in question, compelling it to reach beyond its own limits and impelling it to make contact with all other sciences.[5] Obviously every partner to the dialogue must take responsibility for taking due cognizance of this mysterious human factor. But precisely theology proceeds from the assumption that basically speaking it is quite impossible for any individual to escape from being a theologian, at least implicitly, provided that by theology we understand the consideration of human life as a whole and in itself, over and above all the more restricted outlooks of science, and in its orientation towards the absolute Mystery. But precisely on this account the theologian will say that it is both good and necessary to have, among the participants in the interdisciplinary dialogue, one who has not any other part to play in it than to draw attention to that factor which all the participants have a duty to pay heed to, one who has no special interest in upholding any particular science, but rather has a responsibility to all in common.

THE TASK FOR THEOLOGY

But it is precisely this point that brings us immediately face to face with one particular element in this function of theology and of the theologian in the interdisciplinary dialogue which calls for the most careful consideration. We have seen that the special task of the theologian is not restricted to any one particular aspect of science, and hence, if we like to put it in this way, is not scientific at all. Yet even apart from the dialogue itself, the theologian exercises this function of his in the same way that the practitioner of one particular branch of science would, with all the imperviousness of the specialist, the egoism of the specialist, the attitude of aggression, the impulse to suppress all other considerations, which are actually characteristic of a recognized science. With regard to the mysterious human factor of which we have been speaking, therefore, the Mystery in the absolute which alone renders all science truly human, the theologian must begin by submitting his own science to the most searching criticism in the light of this. And whenever he has only a very imperfect recognition of this task of his, he is forced to be the upholder of this human factor from an attitude of critical detachment and superiority in relation to all other sciences. The theologian cannot be surprised, therefore, if the other

[5] From this point of view cf. K. Beck, ' "Kritische Theorie" und Theologie', *Theol. Prakt. Quartalschrift* 119 (1971), pp. 212–220.

sciences adopt an attitude of reserve and mistrust towards him in admitting him to this dialogue. The only way in which he can make this task of his acceptable to them is by acting as one who recognizes that even a factor which cannot clearly be discussed still has to be spoken of: that a rational account has to be given even of that Mystery which represents a continuous and radical threat to our rationality, because this does in fact belong to human life, and we do not get rid of a situation by simply refusing to trouble ourselves with it on the grounds that it is too much for us. At the same time it is clear that theology must take an extremely modest attitude in this dialogue, and be ready rather to listen than to speak; in fact that it cannot make any special material contribution of its own to knowledge in the way that the other particular sciences do in interchanging ideas among themselves. At least theology cannot do this so long as it is acting strictly as such and not merely as a science whose stock of knowledge inevitably exceeds that which belongs to it strictly as theology. In this dialogue it will, whenever necessary, prefer to appeal to that element of theology which is already present and active albeit implicitly and, perhaps, actually being repressed, in the other partner to the dialogue. It will gently and modestly put the question to the other partner, whether there is not here and there a blind spot in the eye of this particular science or this particular scientist, which needs to be taken into account, and which the other scientist too can discover, given some degree of methodological skill and some good will, seeing that by a paradox he and his science always constitute something more than that which explicitly characterizes them and distinguishes them from other scientists and other sciences. To this end theology must (provided always that it makes its message authentic and credible by the attitude it adopts towards itself) be the upholder of self-criticism on the part of the sciences. It must persuade them to be modest in outlook, to be aware of their provisional nature and their limited perspective, which they can never wholly overcome, whatever extrapolations, sometimes justified and sometimes not, any given science may inevitably and habitually undertake. In this way theology will become the defender of any given science against any other. As the upholder of the inconceivable Mystery which is uncontrollably but nonetheless really present, and which must be respected as such by every science, it will ward off the temptation to which every science is liable of setting itself up as wholly autonomous and totalitarian in character, and so to subsume all other sciences as subordinate to itself and to submit them to its yoke.[6] It is theology which defends a pluralism among the sciences

[6] On this cf. W. Weidlich, 'Zum Begriff Gottes im Felde zwischen Theologie,

which is wholly incalculable and incapable of systematization, against a danger which even today, in the age of the so-called end of metaphysics, has still not been banished. For in place of philosophy other individual sciences are beginning to claim a monopoly of authority over the rest.

A SITUATION OF 'GNOSEOLOGICAL CONCUPISCENCE'

In the old theology 'concupiscence' was a key term. It stood for the idea that man, despite the unity of his knowledge, and despite his unity as a being endowed with freedom, is not in any position to regard himself as a single integrated system capable of being controlled and carried through to its consummation from one single point within itself. Thus it is mortally dangerous for him to attempt to grasp to himself this ideal, so lofty as it seems, of radically systematizing his own existence, with all its impulses and instincts. In the same way we might say that theology is the guardian and defender of the situation of 'gnoseological concupiscence' in the sphere of the sciences, defending it against that mortal danger, inherent in every science, of according itself an absolute value and of supposing that the key which it carries within itself will fit every door. In those cases in which a science is already relatively mature and, moreover, has undergone a history of bitter disappointments and failures, the danger of over-valuing itself may not be so very great. In such cases the science concerned is satisfied so long as it is allowed to survive and continue. In fact, however, the inevitable situation is that further and new sciences are constantly emerging, and in their case this danger is present, the danger, namely that even though they are only idols, they will claim the adoration of all. Obviously the only way in which theology can fulfil this task of upholding the situation of 'gnoseological concupiscence' is for it itself, while indeed keeping the totality of knowledge in view, still for all that never, even tacitly, to fall into the trap of claiming a universality of scientific knowledge for itself, or of regarding all other sciences merely as its handmaids or as branches springing from its own roots. Certainly it is true that in the course of history theology has sinned often enough against this law, and precisely in doing so has demonstrated that even it is not in itself the immaculate representative of God, presiding over all human affairs. Yet we never rid ourselves of our faults merely by rejecting the very task against which we have sinned. And as I see it in the interdisciplinary dialogue theology too will have to undertake that basic task

Philosophie und Naturwissenschaft', *Zeitschrift für Theologie und Kirche* 68 (1971), pp. 381–394.

which we have just ascribed to it. And the less it is recognized as belonging to it in a formal and explicit sense, the better it will have to perform it.[7]

POSSIBLE FACTORS DERIVING FROM THE DIALOGUE WITH
THE INTELLECTUAL DISCIPLINES, NATURAL SCIENCES, AND
SOCIAL SCIENCES, WHICH MAY BE OF FURTHER ASSISTANCE

Obviously what we have said should not be taken as implying that in the interdisciplinary dialogue theology has no further task or no further possibilities whatever beyond those which we have just mentioned. Theology can again and again offer valuable assistance to all those intellectual disciplines which inevitably have to take historical facts into account in their work. For at least in the West the history of ideas has all along also been a history of theology, and precisely in those areas in which it has not been presented as such in any explicit sense at all. This means that if we are ever to achieve knowledge of the history of ideas belonging to us we must first understand something about theology and the history of theology. It is no disgrace for a non-theologian, working in the field of the intellectual disciplines, to recognize and admit that in certain circumstances he knows too little of theology and the history of theology for him to be able adequately to cope with his own subject-matter even taken in itself, and for him on this account to accept advice from theologians. Now both sides come to recognize that it is both necessary and possible for them to achieve a mutual interchange of information only when they take an interest in one another without any intention of gaining an advantage over one another. In the light of this, therefore, it is in the interests of each party, the intellectual disciplines and theology alike, to embark upon the interdisciplinary dialogue which is so necessary without any idea of gaining advantages over one another. Obviously this also applies to theology itself. The only way in which it can achieve an understanding of its own history is for it to accept instruction on the history of ideas in general – indeed actually on economic and social history in general. For it is within this that the history of the Church and of theology too has been enacted.

The dialogue between theology and the natural sciences[8] (regarding

[7] On this see, from the other point of view, U. Mann, 'Wahrheit in Wissenschaft, Theologie und Religion', *Zeitwende* (*Die neue Furche*) 42 (1971), pp. 247–255.

[8] An experiment from the side of natural science which is of interest for this dialogue is to be found in the small volumes by G. Ewald entitled *Wirklichkeit, Wissenschaft, Glaube, Die Frage der Wirklichkeit in exakter Wissenschaft und in christlichen*

this as extending beyond that basic function which theology has in the interdisciplinary dialogue which we have been chiefly concerned with in what we have previously said) will be possible, but will differ, in certain very notable respects, from the dialogue between theology and the intellectual disciplines. Certainly the history of the 19th century was chequered with a whole series of conflicts between the natural sciences and theology on particular material questions which had a theological relevance. But surely these conflicts have, in the majority of cases, been resolved. But this does not mean that the task of theology in relation to the natural sciences has been fulfilled, the task, namely, of allowing itself to be instructed by them on their own terms. This is a task, rather, which can only now really be embarked upon. For within theology (which, after all, must be concerned with man as one and whole) it is only gradually that a view is being achieved of man as portrayed by the rationalism of the natural sciences rather than by traditional humanism. After all theology, precisely in those areas in which it is, and is resolved to remain, an ecclesiastical discipline, is to a large extent conditioned by a type of humanism deriving from the early Fathers. And it is still far from having achieved a really adequate knowledge of him to whom its present and future message must be addressed. In this sense it still has a long time to spend in listening to the natural scientists. But conversely it too can and must draw the attention of the particular natural science to certain factors. For these too always and inevitably have a certain anthropological relevance. And to the extent that any given natural science has this, it may have allowed some undue foreshortening to appear in its portrayal of man, which represents a danger from the point of view of the natural science itself. And where this is the case theology can and must remind the scientists concerned of the human responsibility entailed in every finding of natural science. This surely is also an obvious contribution which theology can and must make to the natural sciences, yet one which must be realized ever afresh. In this connection it is also obvious that the task which both the natural sciences and theology have to discharge each for the other can only really be recognized in its true light by both sides if each takes an interest in the other without seeking to gain any advantage over it. And a further obvious point is that such a policy of taking mutual cognizance of one another's findings represents a problem, in view of the methodological difficulties and the material incommensurability of every modern science, a problem

---

Glauben (Wuppertal, 2nd ed. 1965), and G. Ewald, *Naturgesetz und Schöpfung. Zum Verhältnis von Naturwissenschaft und Theologie* (Wuppertal, 1966).

such as never existed formerly and which can be coped with only indirectly if at all. But this is a question which cannot be treated of in the
present context.

That the modern social sciences and theology can and should enter into
discussion with one another is obvious. The history of society has always
constituted one of the prior conditions and causes of the history of the
Church and of theology. And the converse has likewise always been true,
even though this relationship of mutual interdependence has never been
reducible to a single system by means of a methodological monism such
that the origin of the relationship could be ascribed exclusively to one of
the two sides. With regard to the social sciences, these both empirically
establish and provide possible models for society, and in some cases
these become normative. And it likewise seems to me to be obvious that
in respect of both these functions the social sciences must submit to a
critical enquiry by theology with regard to the image of man which determines their outlook. The converse is also true, namely that the relevance
of theology's own content as constituting a critique of society must also
be considered, and this is impossible without the help of the secular social
sciences. This point becomes clear the moment we remind ourselves that
contemporary theology is beginning to understand itself as 'political
theology'[9] (regardless of how in more precise terms we should understand
this concept), provided we are really to achieve a right understanding of
this 'political theology' and of the nature of theology as such. Finally I
believe that the scientific disciplines of today (including theology too
among these) must achieve a *rapprochement* both in order to enquire into
the question of which sciences should perhaps exist which do not yet
exist in any explicit sense, and also in order to investigate the question of
what kind of organizational and institutional footing an interdisciplinary
dialogue of this sort should be placed upon so that it does not remain a
pious wish or an edifying remark included in devotional Sunday discourses.

[9] On this subject cf. the survey by J. B. Metz, 'Political Theology', *Sacramentum
Mundi* V (New York and London, 1970), pp. 34–38.

6

ON THE RELATIONSHIP BETWEEN THEOLOGY AND THE CONTEMPORARY SCIENCES

WE have here certain observations to offer on the relationship between theology and the sciences, especially the natural sciences, which are intended to bring out as clearly as possible the difference and the autonomy both of theology and of the sciences. But before this certain basic points need to be established.[1]

We shall here be emphasizing the basic and original distinction between theology and the present-day sciences. But this does not mean that the differences between them amount to a total disparity such as to admit of no contact between them, and thereby capable of giving rise to situations of conflict. This is not what we mean if only because, for all the pluralism in human knowledge, there is a certain unity in it, and because theology, albeit in a manner quite peculiar to itself, makes assertions the subject of which belongs (still more directly) to that sphere in which the subjects of the natural sciences and the historical sciences too are to be found.

For our present purposes we shall pass over the question of the relationship between theology and philosophy,[2] and the question of the relationship between philosophy and the contemporary sciences. This chiefly because the following problems cannot be treated of or solved within the present context: the question of a transcendental metaphysics in relation to religions which are neutral in character; the question of the relationship between those sciences which nowadays regard themselves as autonomous and are unwilling to accept a position of subalternation to ontology on the one hand and a philosophy on the other which consti-

---

[1] On the question in general cf. the author's study, 'The Unity of Spirit and Matter in the Christian Understanding of Faith', *Theological Investigations* VI (London and Baltimore, 1969), pp. 153–177; also O. Spülbeck, *Zur Begegnung von Naturwissenschaft und Theologie* (Einsiedeln, 1969), and H. Schwarz, 'Das Verhältnis von Theologie und Naturwissenschaft als systematisch-theologisches Problem', *Neue Zeitschrift für sytemat. Theol. u. Religionsphilos.* 11 (1969), pp. 139–153.

[2] On this cf. in the present volume, 'On the Current Relationship between Philosophy and Theology', pp. 61–79.

tutes something more than a mere theory of science which is supplementary to the sciences themselves; finally the question of a pluralism of philosophies which we are nowadays no longer in a position to transcend (and which we still have to recognize even if we assume that these philosophies are not so opposed as to contradict one another).

Likewise, without any exhaustive discussion, we are assuming that the problem of a 'gnoseological concupiscence'[3] is something which still awaits solution after we have dealt with the relationship between theology and the sciences, and therefore something that must be thought out in its own right in order to cope in a more penetrating manner with the problem which we have now to discuss. By the term 'gnoseological concupiscence' I mean the fact that in human awareness there is a pluralism between the various branches of knowledge such that we can never achieve a full or comprehensive view of them all together, and that they can never be integrated in a unified system by man in a way which makes them fully controllable or comprehensible to him. This remains true even though no one branch of knowledge can be regarded as a matter of indifference when it comes to rightly interpreting another. The reason I call this pluralism, which can never fully be transcended, 'gnoseological concupiscence' is in order to show that problems arising in the sphere of knowledge are at least analogously the same as those which, in the traditional theology, are accorded close examination merely in the field of voluntary impulses.

THE CONTRAST BETWEEN THEOLOGY AND THE SCIENCES

We are assuming that every science is *per definitionem* a particular branch of human knowledge, but that this does not apply to divine revelation and theology, at least so long as these do not betray their own true nature, and finally that this fundamental difference must have a decisive influence upon the relationship between theology and the sciences. We must now explain in somewhat greater detail what we mean by this statement.

Every science constitutes, on a contemporary view, a particular branch or category of knowledge. It assembles particular phenomena, which are, and are assumed to be, different from one another. What the connection is

---

[3] On this cf. K. Rahner, 'Wandelbares und Unwandelbares in der Kirche' and 'Der Glaube des Christen und die Lehre der Kirche', *Schriften zur Theologie* X (Einsiedeln, 1972), pp. 241–261 and 262–285 (to be translated in *Theological Investigations* XIV with provisional titles 'Change and Constancy in the Church' and 'The Faith of Christ and the Teaching of the Church').

between these various phenomena, and what the purpose is of assembling them in this way, is irrelevant to our immediate purpose. In any case, however, a science does not consider the single subjectivity of the scientist as the condition which enables him to take it as axiomatic that the subject-matter he has to consider falls within one particular category. The science as such does not take into consideration the subjectivity of the knowing subject. It does not think about thinking – not even in the case of empirical psychology. For this invariably confines itself simply to establishing a connection between various individual pieces of data so as to constitute a category. Nor do the sciences as such consider that original unity of reality which is prior to the *a posteriori* experience of individual objects, which never constitutes the mere sum total of individual empirical data, any more than it constitutes a subsequent extrapolation of experience, extending it to fresh possible particular objects which, while they are not yet present, are nevertheless capable of becoming so. For our present question it makes no difference whether or not these sciences are investigating the real roots and essential natures of the individual objects and phenomena falling within their respective fields.

The area with which theological statements are concerned is the transcendence of man as such, that transcendence which is a special characteristic of knowledge and freedom, of the theoretical and practical reason, and to that extent is, once more, realized in the relationship between the two faculties mentioned, and, as an experience of transcendence, implicit in the inalienable difference and unity between them. There is a transcendental experience to the extent that the experience of that prior awareness which comes before any individual object of the two faculties we have mentioned constitutes an inalienable *a priori* condition of the knowledge of objects assignable to particular categories, and to the extent that the knowledge of these involves, at least implicitly, this prior awareness.[4] This transcendental experience is orientated towards that absolute Mystery (i.e. one which in principle cannot in its turn be apprehended by us) which we call 'God', and which constitutes the true 'subject' of theological statements. It makes no difference to our present argument whether the very process of recognizing this transcendental experience as a subject in its own right, and thereby postulating an explicit relationship to God, *ipso facto* assumes that relationship of God to man which in Christian terminology we call 'grace', 'the supernatural elevation of man', the 'self-bestowal of God', or whether this process of explicitating the relationship to this Mystery, sustaining and opening up this transcendentality of man,

4 On this cf. in the present volume 'Thomas Aquinas on Truth', pp. 13–31.

constitutes an *a priori* condition of human knowledge in the absolute, which in theological terms would be called philosophical in character. This question can be left open, not only for theological reasons which there is no need for us to develop here, but also because at that stage of human reflection which is demanded as necessary by the philosophy of today, and therefore too at the level of the theoretical reason as such, the pluralism of philosophies may perhaps be such that we can no longer transcend or control it, with the result that it surely becomes an extremely difficult question how to make God the subject of any purely philosophical or theoretical investigation. In passing it may be pointed out that this proviso does not involve any conflict with the declaration of the First Vatican Council concerning the possibility of knowing God at the philosophical level. But this too is something which cannot be considered any further at this point.

THE HEART AND CENTRE OF THEOLOGY

Now properly speaking the statements which Christianity makes about this absolute Mystery (called God) are only fairly few in number. But they are of fundamental importance for its dogmatic theology.[5]

We cannot avoid having to concern ourselves with this mystery, whether we explicitly objectify it to ourselves or not, whether we use our freedom to accept it or to reject and suppress it. What Christianity asserts is that its message is concerned precisely with that about which no 'clear' message can be conveyed inasmuch as *per definitionem* it neither has, nor is capable of having, any one particular place firmly assignable to it within the frame of reference constituted by human knowledge and human freedom. Theological statements, therefore, are, in the sense described above, different from scientific statements in respect both of their quality and their source. Hence theological statements, as thematic and verbal in character (and it is only as such that they constitute 'statements' at all) invariably point, despite the rational structure manifestly belonging to them (for without this they would, once more, not be statements at all), to the original pre-thematic and transcendental experience, and it is only on this condition that they are really comprehensible. Otherwise they would be mere rationalizing statements which would be very quickly unmasked and shown to be meaningless by the modern sciences (formal logic, the philosophy of language etc.).

[5] On this cf. the author's article, 'Mitte des Glaubens', *Hilfe zum Glauben*, Theol. Meditationen 27, A. Exeler, J. B. Metz, K. Rahner edd. (Einsiedeln, 1971), pp. 39–56.

Concerning this mystery which is made present in the transcendental experience as absolute, Christianity asserts that it is something more than merely the goal, remaining forever remote and asymptotic, towards which the human spirit moves in knowledge and freedom, in theory and practice. Also, and more than this, it has actually bestowed itself as absolute Mystery upon man so as to be the innermost consummation of the movement of his being and a goal to be immediately possesssd. This relationship which the absolute Mystery bears to man is a fundamental element in his transcendental experience, albeit not necessarily an element in his reflection upon, and interpretation of, this. To that extent every theological statement concerning that which we are accustomed to call grace, justification etc. has its place in a theological statement at the transcendental level. What we are accustomed to call, in Christian terms, the history of revelation is nothing else than the developing process, taking place within history, by which man reflects upon this transcendental experience of the self-bestowal of God, a reflection which, of course, in its process of historical development, cannot be achieved by the individual as such taken in isolation, but is rather sustained by the history of reflexive thought discernible within the history of mankind as a whole right from its origins, and is reflected upon anew at a merely secondary level in that discipline which we call theology. There is a further question, the question, namely, of how the revelation history of the Old and New Testaments has its special place within this more general revelation history, co-extensive with the history of human ideas as a whole. But this cannot be set forth in the present context. The element in all this which is absolutely indispensable for an understanding of theology will probably be made clear in the statements which follow.

This experience of the absolute self-utterance of God given in the transcendental experience of man achieves its supreme point in Jesus of Nazareth. He is the eschatological climax of the self-utterance of God to mankind, and of the primary history of reflection upon this self-utterance (primary because taking place not at one remove, at the level of theological reflection, but rather in the concrete conditions of human living and in the unity of action, passion, and word) inasmuch as it is in Jesus that this offering of God's self-bestowal becomes something more than a sheer offering. Rather, through the deed of God, it takes place and is revealed as *de facto* victorious and irreversible. This historical manifestation of the eschatological victoriousness and irreversibility of the self-utterance of God, which is in itself transcendent, does not remove the transcendental character inherent in all theological statements. For first, every transcendental experience as it takes place is invariably accompanied by an element of reflexive thought expressed in verbal form, which does not remove the transcendentality of this experience so long as it is aware of being at once orientated towards, and different from this transcendentality, or so long as – to adopt Anselm's way of expressing the matter – it is aware of the fact that here what is beyond human reason is conceived of as really present and inevitably rational. And there is a further reason why the transcendental character inherent in theological statements, and thereby setting them apart from scientific knowledge of concrete 'this-worldly' realities, is not removed in the case of Christian statements by the fact that they refer to the concrete 'this-worldly' reality of Jesus. In such statements about Jesus the relationship to him which it is intended to express and to make possible is precisely that which we have with him as having died. In other words the relationship with him is in that real event in which absolute transcendence in theory and practice is achieved, bringing us to the absolute mystery in the event which we are accustomed to call death. The statement of faith that Jesus has risen from the dead is merely the justified expression of the fact that our transcendental experience of the self-bestowal of God is attached to the historical event of Jesus, and it is in this that it achieves the fulness of its reality and manifests itself as victorious. And the same statement of faith expresses the truth that the event taking place in the death of Jesus, the event in which an individual man achieves radical transcendence and is brought into the incomprehensibility of the divine Mystery, has in concrete fact achieved its goal. The fact that the statements of Christian theology refer to the concrete 'this-worldly' reality of Jesus does not remove the transcendental character inherent in them as theological statements in virtue of the fact that in these Christian statements a concrete 'this-worldly' historical reality is being touched upon only to the extent that it is precisely the event of absolute transcendentality. In concrete fact the transcendentality belonging to us always takes place as a historical event, and the fact that this does not destroy this dimension of transcendentality is shown by our own experience in which transcendentality is invariably achieved in a specific historical situation without being destroyed as transcendentality thereby. We say that the Christian experience of the victory of transcendentality leading to the mystery of God achieves its full realization precisely in the experience of Jesus. Now this statement obviously involves a fundamental trust in the powers and significance of unique historical events which, in this unaccountable uniqueness of theirs, do not as such constitute subjects falling within the purview of the sciences as understood today, not even that of the historical sciences. For even historical events, considered as subject-matter for the historical sciences, are viewed by these, certainly in their *de facto* contingency, but not in their character as absolute and as posited 'once and for all', a character which they both bear within themselves and can also impose upon another subject. Nevertheless historical events as such, and as freely posited, have the character of being absolute and posited 'once and for all' in this sense, even though this cannot ever be authenticated by science, concerned as it is with objectifying concrete 'this-worldly' realities. Rather this character inherent in historical events vanishes the moment we seek to make it a subject for investigation by such sciences.

THEOLOGY AND THE SCIENCES IN THEIR RELATIONSHIP WITH ONE ANOTHER

In the light of what we have said we should now determine the relationship which exists between theology and the modern sciences as they nowadays understand themselves to be. However, in the present context it is possible only to provide a few pointers, somewhat arbitrarily selected.

Before we can undertake to define this relationship, we should of course consider more precisely the connection between the following two factors: on the one hand the original, grace-bestowing experience of transcendence (faith) and the concrete expression of this, and on the other human reflection upon this, and the further process of reflection at the theoretical level (= theology). For obviously the relationship between the sciences and faith on the one hand and between these sciences and theology on the other, is not simply one and the same.

The difference between concrete 'this-worldly' experience and transcendental experience does indeed imply a fundamental and justified distinction between that which ultimately constitutes the subject-matter of theology, and that which is the subject-matter of the sciences. It is, therefore, in principle legitimate to regard these two entities, theology and the sciences, as irreducibly distinct from one another, and as caught up in the state of gnoseological pluralism, together with the 'concupiscence' which this involves, in the total context of human knowledge. But this does not imply any absolute disparity between theology and the sciences. First, theology itself has in its turn a concrete 'this-worldly' history of its own, in which it can be made the subject of historical science in the secular sense, albeit from a point of view which reduces all history to the same level and concentrates upon its common factors. But also, and more than this, in its assertion that an event of absolute transcendence has taken place, theology postulates the historicity of Jesus and of his interpretation of himself (whatever more detailed description we may give of this), and thereby achieves an established point of contact with the historical sciences. Theology neither can nor should, therefore, regard itself from the outset as of such a nature that cases of conflict between it and these historical sciences are totally inconceivable. It belongs to the very nature of theology to accept that such cases of conflict are possible, even while it hopes, once more at the eschatological level, that no such case of conflict will be regarded as so radical and so positively insurmountable that the only remaining course is for either theology or the sciences to surrender and submit. Nevertheless any such ultimate reconciliation between theology and the sciences is not a state of affairs actually established once and for all, but rather a subject of eschatological hope, and one which can be conceived of and made real anew stage by stage only as this hope moves towards its ultimate goal.

The sciences can have a certain significance for the investigation of mystagogy into the transcendental experience, in virtue of the fact that these sciences do communicate something like the first intimation of transcendental experience. For these sciences conduct a critique of themselves, and involve a pluralism of methods which can never fully be eliminated or overcome in a higher synthesis. And from this arises a relativism of the methods they employ. Again human life in its totality constitutes a threat to them from without which can never fully be removed, and for all these reasons they themselves impart something like a first intimation of an experience of transcendence.

Theology and the sciences also come into contact with one another (in both a positive and a negative sense) to the extent that the sciences have *per definitionem* a tendency to achieve the greatest possible rationalization of human life, but in doing this always come up against the freedom, uniqueness, and sheer factualness of life as it exists within the wider sphere of the possible. Thereby, in their rationally conceived demands for the future of man, they encounter the eschatological limits imposed by theology in the name of faith in the incomprehensible God of freedom and of the future alike.

So far as the role of theology in the interdisciplinary dialogue between the sciences is concerned, I may refer to observations which I have offered elsewhere.[6]

---

[6] On this cf. 'Theology as Engaged in an Interdisciplinary Dialogue with the Sciences' in the present volume, pp. 80–93.

Faith and theology are related to the sciences as to all other concrete 'this-worldly' realities in human life. These are already there even before faith and theology realize their own natures. These human realities of a concrete 'this-worldly' kind, and so too the sciences, have their own special meaning for man, a meaning which does not and should not vanish in that insuperable pluralism in human awareness which is necessary for faith even when man himself begins explicitly to orientate himself towards the absolute Mystery as that which is near and all-embracing. For the eschatological integration of all reality in God, and in his knowledge and love, is the deed of God himself, a deed which takes place precisely at the point at which, and in virtue of the fact that, man endures the pluralism of his world, and so too of his knowledge, and does not suppose that he is standing at a point at which all reality, and the knowledge of it, is one. For at this point stands only God himself.

PART TWO

Anthropology

7

INSTITUTION AND FREEDOM

Has the theologian as such any contribution to make on the subject of 'institution and freedom',[1] without *ipso facto* arrogating to himself the role of a social scientist or an authority on jurisprudence? It must be said that the theologian is concerned with this subject as such, and will from the outset seek for an answer to the question as posed in one specific direction. This will surely be clear in the light of the following consideration: in the history of ideas of the last few decades a phenomenon which appears again and again is an atheism that is postulated in the name of human freedom. Whatever terms it may be expressed in, what it says is that God is to be thought of as nothing else than the great architect of the world, the ultimate principle of order and law, the great institutionalizer. And this being so, he neither can exist, nor should be allowed to exist, if their either should be, or is in fact, such a thing as freedom. Whether freedom and institution are ultimately speaking and in the absolute reconcilable, therefore, is manifestly a theological question right from the first, one which is of immediate concern to the theologian as such, and not merely as a man.

'INSTITUTION AND FREEDOM' AS A QUESTION FOR THE THEOLOGIAN

When we open the pages of the New Testament or study Pauline theology then we perceive that freedom is a key concept occupying a central position in the Christian understanding of human life.[2] For Paul the real gift

---

[1] On this theme cf. also the author's *Freiheit und Manipulation in Gesellschaft und Kirche*, Münchener Akademie Schriften 53 (Munich, 1970).

[2] On the concept of 'freedom' see K. Rahner, 'Freedom III. Theological' *Sacramentum Mundi* II (New York and London, 1968), pp. 361–362, with further bibliography, and also M. Müller and J. B. Hirschmann, 'Freiheit', *Staatslexikon* III (Freiburg, 1959), cols. 528–548; J. B. Metz, 'Freiheit III. Theologisch', *HbThGB* I (Munich, 1962), cols. 403–414.

of God in his Spirit, the fruit of saving history for mankind and for the individual alike, regarded as something which both has already taken place and is to achieve its fulness in the future, is freedom. Certainly this freedom of the redeemed children of God, regarded as a gift of the Spirit in faith and hope, is not *ipso facto* identical with that freedom which constitutes an ideal of social politics and is engaged in a constant struggle with self-alienation, enslavement, the lack of freedom, as constituting a constantly renewed threat to man emerging from the concrete forms of history. But while the *former* kind of freedom, namely the religious one, and the *latter* kind, namely the social one, are not simply identical, still they are in a very essential sense connected with one another, although this is a point which cannot be developed in detail in the present context. The only way in which we can achieve a spirit of faith and hope in ultimate freedom as a gift of God in his Spirit, and as the content of his kingdom, is for us in principle to opt for social freedom and to play our part in striving to make it real. In just the same way there can be no love of God without love of neighbour, and the will to achieve a world worthy of mankind or a better future is intrinsic to the will that hopes for the final coming of the kingdom of God, the will which we call faith.

The real blessing of salvation, then, which Christianity proclaims as the goal of its hope as expressed in concrete action, is that freedom in the theological sense which has an intrinsic connection with social freedom. And this means that this social freedom too must be considered if we are to arrive at true and Christian ideas about God. Now the significance of this can be expressed as follows:

We may think of God as the great architect of the world, as the operator of a universal cybernetics, as the law-giver, as the ultimate guarantor for all structures and orders in reality which we directly experience (all these conceptual models, as applied to that which we call God, are meaningful only provided that we retain our overall awareness that God is the absolute Mystery, and one which we can still never incorporate within some higher system). At the same time we may, by contrast, regard freedom not merely as any kind of factor making itself felt within this world which belongs to God, but as constituting the central blessing of salvation itself. Now if all this is true, then God, as the author of all structures and orders in the world, can be conceived of simply as the provider and the content of this freedom regarded as a blessing of salvation, seeing that all orders and structures of which he is author can themselves be conceived of as the condition making *freedom* itself possible, and providing it with its context. The point can be expressed in different terms by saying that God can be thought of in this way provided that all orders and structures are themselves ultimately thought of not as opposed to freedom, but as an intrinsic element in it. Only on this showing can we say that a positive option for freedom does not entail any demand for atheism. Only on this showing can God be conceived of as the absolute, single, and original source of freedom *and* structure and order at the same time.

Now it is undoubtedly true that all institutional factors constitute, in a social sense, the outer periphery and the utterly secondary (although not inessential) realization and concretization of that which is called structure and order in the world, the more so since these institutional factors are to a large extent dependent, in their concrete forms, on the free will of man himself, and so much more liable to change than that which pertains to the structures investigated by the natural sciences and intellectual disciplines inasmuch as these are concerned with what is permanent and enduring. But despite this fact, the institutional factor at the social level still belongs in its own way to those structures and orders of the world which are unavoidable, if only because the institutional factor in the concrete can be brought to an end only by introducing some other institutional factor, though perhaps a better one, and not by simply obliterating it. Now if the institutional factor at the social level is in this sense to be numbered among the enduring structures and orders of the world, at least to the extent that it is a world of man, then it is clear from the outset that the institutional factors in the world of man are of concern to the theologian as such as well. The theologian may indeed say that this institutional factor at the social level, as it exists in concrete reality, belongs only to this world of man as transitory, and that one day this will be dissolved and give way to the kingdom of God as the kingdom of freedom. The theologian may regard precisely this human institutional factor as in an especially pressing sense subject to man's decision, undertaken in hope, to change the world. For man himself strives for the dominion of perfect freedom. And yet the theologian, with his belief in God as the source of all freedom, and as the source of all structural factors as well, can only concern himself with this world of the institutional – inasmuch as it is the institutional factors that constitute the enabling condition for freedom – if he also includes under this heading the institutional factors at the social level as well.

I hope that I have given some indication of why this theme of 'institution and freedom' should be of concern to a theologian, and what the direction is in which his ultimate and basic positions will lead him to turn for an answer to the question to which this theme gives rise. If, therefore, little more seems to be said on the subject of theology in what follows, the subject being treated of is, nevertheless, one which a theologian may treat of without being accused of going beyond his brief in an amateurish manner. Admittedly in doing so he will be obliged to confine himself to observations remaining at a relatively general level, since his starting-point must be his own particular discipline.

FREEDOM AS A SLOGAN: A KEY FACTOR IN MODERN LIFE

Every age has its own great and dominant ideals, its slogans (using this term in a wholly positive, or at least a neutral sense) in which it sums up its hopes and its desires. A dominant idea of the kind we have in mind, in which everything is drawn into a synthesis, may on this account be very imprecise, if only because – to put it briefly – man cannot arrive at a definition of the whole when he does not himself stand outside it, or assign what is an *ultimate* practical goal to a place in a system of co-ordinates which is different from, and higher than, itself. Such slogans, key concepts, and all-epitomizing ideals belonging to a particular age may undergo changes. For a man whose awareness is safeguarded against falling into a mere pluralism of totally disparate realities they are both necessary and justified. Slogans of this kind should not be blamed on the grounds that they are not susceptible of any full analysis or exact definition, even though of course this fact again should not wrongly be exploited as a blank cheque to justify us in producing mere phrases where exact answers and precise reflexive thought are possible. Man is in fact a being such that his reflections upon himself and his understanding of his own existence are invariably only approximate, if only because the reflexive thought itself as it develops is subject to intellectual perspectives and motivations which are incapable of being in their turn objectified, reflected upon, or subjected to critical analysis. In this situation slogans play their part. They are intended to sum up the awareness and the aims of a given epoch, without thereby standing for a process of reflection which is total and all-embracing, or capable of being analyzed down to the last detail. A given epoch – it may be precisely the present one – can have several such slogans and dominant ideas. In the present age the term 'freedom' certainly constitutes one such. It is true that for at least two hundred years it has been included among the ideals of all movements in social politics, but even so it has still not lost its power of attraction. It has become a watchword throughout the world, and peoples of very widely differing stages of economic and cultural development have fastened upon it.

Precisely on this account it is, of course, almost inevitable that the word 'freedom' has come to stand for an entity which is almost indescribable, and in fact is unknown. The social scientist, with his rational and empiricist approach, would therefore be justified in saying that freedom has become, to such an extent, an indeterminate entity, something which bears a different meaning for every individual, every nation, and every social group, that any social politics capable of giving an account of itself in rational terms will find this concept totally intractable. But even the practitioner of this science of social politics should at any rate concede that such a slogan *exists*, that it makes its impact in the minds and hearts of individuals, and that therefore, whether it is welcome or not, it does on any showing make itself felt as a force in the field of social politics. We can also understand that the reason why this term should already have made so strong an impact for so long, and should still be making it today, is that freedom has still not become something that can be taken for granted, something no longer capable of stimulating any movement. Presumably it would indeed be perfectly possible for us in all sincerity to uphold the position that at least in the Western industrial countries the degree of social freedom already achieved is greater in relation to the broad mass of men than has been achieved in any previous age. But even though this fact can presumably be adduced, it still does not make freedom something that can be taken for granted, something which, since it already exists for many individuals and in a notable degree, is no longer of concern and no longer capable of serving as a slogan to express the expectations and demands for social change in the future. For in the sphere of society freedom is always a relative concept, related to the sum total of what men value as capable of achievement within a foreseeable space of time. For the men of a particular age, or at least according to their opinion, whether true or false, the sum total of these physical, medical, economic, and social changes which they demand may be very great. And in these circumstances, when these physical, medical, etc. factors in practice remain stable, they feel that their freedom is needlessly restricted by this lack of change, when in principle change is possible. And they feel this even though materially speaking the freedom they enjoy is far greater than that of the men of some former age, who must have regarded the restrictions upon their freedom as in practice more or less unalterable.

Now the situation today is that the sum total of economic, social, etc. changes which, at least in the opinion of individuals, might be introduced, is immense, regardless of whether this opinion is altogether correct, or whether further distinctions would have to be drawn in order to make it so. And for this reason the men of today are far from feeling that they enjoy a particular freedom, especially in the case of those who no longer recognize their existing situation as the outcome of free and creative activity on the part of those who overcame conditions of economic and cultural chaos so as to bring it about, and hence regarded it as manifestly praiseworthy. Today many, especially younger men, are reacting against the contemporary social situation by aggressively demanding more freedom. But I believe that we should view this in the way that we have indicated above. Presumably it would not be very meaningful if we sought to explain this aggressive demand simply by saying that in a technological and industrial age and, in conditions in which the population has increased enormously by comparison with earlier ages, the economic, social, political, and legal conditions in which men have to live have become so complex and so difficult to change that even when they are regarded as inevitable, they are still felt to restrict the freedom of the individual in the highest degree. In a certain sense this may be justified. But as an explanation of the aggressive demand for more freedom it is straightway open to the objection that in former ages man, living as he did in simpler situations of life and social conditions, did not in any sense enjoy any more freedom, either for the shaping of his own life, for going where he liked, for choosing his own philosophy of life, forming the sort of social groups he wanted, choosing the goods he thought best, etc. The sole difference between this and former ages is simply this: that the compulsions of former ages, which allowed man less freedom, were felt to be more or less unalterable, and therefore the demand for more freedom could not be regarded as capable of fulfilment in any effective sense. But this brings us back once more to the explanation we have adumbrated at an earlier stage as to why there is so aggressive a demand for greater freedom today, even though, objectively speaking, there has never been more freedom than there is today. Now this enables us to give a certain description of what is meant by freedom as such at the level of social living. On this showing freedom would be a condition in which it is possible to get rid of a situation which is regarded as undesirable and capable of being abolished. In arriving at the judgement that a given social situation is undesirable it is possible that another situation, the one that replaces the previous one, is regarded as desirable. And this view in turn may be justified or unjustified, or may be arrived at with or without the agreement of the majority of one's contemporaries, with or without appealing to this. But it may also be the case that in struggling against the existing situation we do not make any attempt to consider in detail the future situation which is intended to replace it. In other words that it is a matter of indifference to those advocating the change whether they fall out of the frying-pan into the fire. The characterization of freedom in the social sense which we have given is, of course, at a very formal level. But surely the reason for this is to be found in the fact that it actually *does* take very different forms at the material level as well, this freedom which individuals and groups desire when they put forward their demands for more freedom. We could of course draw a distinction between genuine and merely supposed freedom, and say that a greater freedom is to be found in those cases in which an individual, without being hindered by external factors, can direct his own human and individual nature in general, and the value attached to it, and in which he has greater scope for this in terms of the possibilities and the means at his command. But while in itself such a definition of the nature of social freedom would be justified so far as metaphysical anthropology is concerned, it too would fail to bring us any closer to the answer we are seeking because precisely on this point, of how we should rightly understand the nature of man and his dignity, very different ideas are put forward, and any description of freedom, if it is to be effective at the level of social politics, must take into account the pluralism of anthropologies which exist today and come to terms with it.

REALITY AND INSTITUTION

What then is to be said about the relationship between institution and freedom? Before we attempt to give an answer to this (to the extent that a theologian can give an opinion upon the matter at all), one further word remains to be said as to what is meant by institutions in this context.[3] As with the term 'freedom', so in this respect too, we must remain at a very general level. Presumably we shall not meet with any contradiction if we say that by 'institutions' in the sphere of human society we mean only those realities which, at least in some sense, are capable of being changed by the exercise of human freedom. Compulsions which are contrary to freedom may derive from those natural laws which fall totally outside the sphere of human freedom, and are to that extent unalterable by it. Certainly no one will want to subsume these under the heading of institutions.

[3] On this cf. G. Gundlach, Cl. Bauer, A. Bellebaum, 'Institution', *Staatslexikon* IV (Freiburg, 1959), cols. 324–334; G.Sta venhagen, 'Institutionalismus', *Staatslexikon* IV (Freiburg, 1959), cols. 334–338; K. Rahner, 'Institutionalismus', *LTK* V (Freiburg, 1960), cols 714–715.

Conversely, however, we can, for our present purposes, include under this heading all those realities in the social sphere which are subject to change, and which impose certain compulsions upon human freedom, in other words not merely human laws bearing upon various departments of human life and having juridical effects, but also dominant ideas, customs, taboos (as we are accustomed to call them nowadays), and other realities in such society, which do in fact exist but are capable of being changed. So far as human freedom and decision are concerned these constitute pre-existing conditions which exercise a prior influence upon such decisions, canalize them, make them advisable or unwelcome by the attaching of social sanctions of either a positive or a negative kind to them, etc. All this can surely be included in the *present* context and for our present consideration under the heading 'institution', so long as we also remain aware that from many points of view we are expanding the concept to a not inconsiderable extent. For I am, of course, fully aware of the fact that among sociologists the term 'institution' has a narrower and (if one likes to express it so) a more precise meaning inasmuch as in these circles the only cases in which the term 'institution' is used are those in which a specific system of rules is being put forward and applied by means of some specific equipment operated by a specific personnel.

COMPULSIONS AND CHANGES

Now with regard to the relationship between freedom and institution in the second sense mentioned above, it is correct, first of all, to say that freedom is, and can be felt to be, opposed to institution. All the institutional factors in our lives also imply a certain restriction of our freedom, because in manifold ways they debar us from possible courses which would remain open to us, and could be acted upon, if our freedom were absolute. For the most part we do not feel these compulsions upon us at all. We are accustomed to them. They actually bring us advantages which we are unwilling to forego, and they seem to us to a large extent obvious and unchangeable. In other cases, however, institutional factors of this kind in our lives may be regarded and felt as capable of being changed. At the same time we may regard them as preventing us from acting upon one of the possibilities which freedom entails. And in cases such as these we begin as free creatures to react against them. We feel that our freedom is in some sense oppressed and enslaved, restricted and frustrated by these institutional factors. Obviously this applies chiefly to those cases in which the possibility which freedom offers, and which is then withdrawn by an institutional factor of this kind, seems clearly the more favourable one by comparison with the institution itself, at least as actually applied to the freedom of the particular individual concerned. In this sense there cannot be any doubt that the incalculable multiplicity and complexity of present-day institutions must strike us, to a terrible extent, as restricting and (if we wish so to express it) frustrating. The present age and state of society, with its discoveries and techniques, opens up before our eyes an almost infinite range of real possibilities, which are now brought almost within the grasp of our freedom as such. And at the same time they are withdrawn from us by the institutions of our age and society, institutions which, since they now exist within the wider context of many other real possibilities, strike us as themselves capable of being changed, and so precisely cause us to feel that our freedom is being curtailed. We have already said that this experience of frustrated freedom must manifest itself chiefly, and with the greatest acuteness, precisely in the case of those whose memories are shorter, for these are no longer in the position of having experienced present-day institutions of all kinds in society as they actually emerged, or at a time when they were felt as liberating men from conditions which undoubtedly entailed still more restrictions and frustrations of freedom.

In connection with this experience of freedom being restricted by an already existing institutionalization of society, the following point too must not be overlooked, so as to enable us to arrive at a right judgement on the conflict between the generations which has arisen in this area. The attitude of some who demand freedom is such that change is felt to be desirable for its own sake and precisely as a full exercise of freedom, regardless of whether or not the innovations which it brings can *ipso facto* be recognized as improvements. Things are different from what they formerly were, and this in itself is very often enough to give a sense of freedom. This is especially the case when this feeling that freedom is to be found in change as such is not counterbalanced by a sense of familiarity with conditions as they have been hitherto. For in the case of the old their anxiety when faced with the unfamiliar and untried elements in the new conditions can give rise to a state of tension which is in part justified and in part due to physiological factors. And this anxiety may take away any joy they might have had in change as such. We can recognize the phenomenon which we are seeking to describe in its plainest and most familiar form in the changes which take place in the so-called fashions, meaning by this not merely fashions in clothes and similar outward customs in everyday life, but also fashions in art or science, in the preference given to certain specific themes etc. All fashions are nothing else than changes made for their own sake, without regard to whether the innovations introduced are or are not improvements as well. They are changes which give rise to a sense of freedom – changes, therefore, which in terms of physiological factors and differences between generations are more acceptable to the young than the old. The former will always find innovations as such to be attractive, whereas in the latter the same innovations will arouse anxiety. The only way in which we can achieve a serious discussion between the young and the old as to the desirability of a given change is to pose the question of whether, taking all aspects into account, the innovation concerned, even by the standards of the younger generation, and on a realistic appraisal, turns out to be worse or better than that which it is intended to replace. Without a discussion of this kind the balance will be tipped in favour of what is new as such in the judgement of the young, and in favour of what is familiar as such in the judgement of the old. Each side will regard its choice as the better institution for ensuring freedom, and the only remaining question will then be whether it is to be the young or the old who have the power to make their judgement prevail and begin to act upon it. It cannot be denied, however, that what is new purely as such does in itself possess a certain value for freedom, and both is, and will continue to be, one of the sources of social change. If what is new is not notably worse than what is old the old too cannot seriously raise many objections against such fashions, but must endure them with the wisdom of those who know that changes are still welcomed even when they do not bring any convincing improvements with them.

After this brief digression (if in fact it is such), let us begin by recognizing the simple fact that institutions, just because they occur within the context of wider possibilities and are felt to be capable of change, are also held to be restrictions and obstacles to the freedom which men seek. So much is this the case, as we have said, that in some cases we do not even pause to ask, in our quest for freedom, whether our protest against the situations and institutions which curtail freedom actually have some possibility of improvement to offer. And when we refuse to answer this question, and are thereby impelled into an adventure the outcome of which can no longer be foreseen, then obviously our demand for freedom is shown by this refusal to be materially and morally capricious and reprehensible. At the same time, however, the fact that innovation as such does inevitably have a certain intrinsic rightness of its own becomes clear the moment we enquire into the basic reasons underlying such attitudes of capriciousness, and ask ourselves why the danger with which they constantly threaten us is so indefatigable.

THE AMBIVALENCE OF CREATIVE FREEDOM

We must concede, then, that there is a *prima facie* opposition between institution and freedom. But this must not be allowed to obscure a deeper unity existing between the two entities and a relationship in which each influences the other. Man, when he has the power, does in fact himself create these institutions of his freedom. They are objectifications of freedom. Indeed this should constitute an intrinsic element in our description of what institution means, distinguishing it from those compulsions which are present within the sphere in which freedom is exercised in virtue of the unchangeable laws of nature. In fact it is only by recognizing that institutions derive from free acts that we are able to see also that the compulsion which they bring to bear is in a real sense capable of being changed or abolished, and it is the recognition of this fact that provokes freedom's protest against the restrictions imposed upon it. We are here faced with the paradox that freedom is protesting against its own creations. Faced with this paradox, we feel it only a slight and partially valid consolation to say that the institution is the creation of *one* freedom, while it is *another* freedom that is protesting against it. For first, the freedom of the individual in individual life creates certain conditions, and then, having created them, it itself protests against them as imposing restrictions upon it. But more than this, insofar as it is possible to speak of a single society in a single age we must also say that this same society invokes the principle of freedom to protest against its own institutions, which it has created through its own freedom. In fact there is no lack of examples which we might analyze to show that the individual protests against institutional compulsions upon his freedom within his own society even when, from a different aspect, he freely assents to, and positively wills them. And yet he never notices this contradiction in his attitude. The situation is, in fact, that freedom creates its own compulsion within itself. It objectifies itself, and creates for itself the external conditions for its own fulfilment, shapes them and so opens out a sphere within which it can operate. And everything which freedom thus creates for itself, even though called forth by freedom, nevertheless achieves an autonomy and independence in relation to freedom both in the mind of the individual man and in the society he belongs to. We freely create customs within ourselves, and surround ourselves with institutions in order to be free, in order to disburden ourselves of compulsions which already exist by nature, and what we thereby create in freedom then confronts the subject endowed with freedom as autonomous and, as it were, alienated from him, in the form of a fresh compulsion. But this ambivalence and dialectical character inherent in the forms in which we objectify our freedom should precisely not blind us to the fact that these secondary compulsions are created primarily as objectifications of, and aids to freedom. We submit ourselves to traffic regulations so as to achieve more unhindered conditions of travel. We enact permanent laws which are binding upon us for the regulation of commerce in order to remain unimpeded by others in the disposal of our own property. We produce what are nowadays contemptuously called taboos in the public awareness, even though we may feel restricted by them, but our basic reason for doing so is simply to ensure a greater sphere of individual freedom – for example to guarantee a sphere of intimate privacy which is immediately available simply to oneself. In other words we would ultimately speaking have less freedom without such taboos than we have with them. (Of course this is not to deny that there are taboos of this kind which either are meaningless or have become so in the course of time, but precisely this fact too is merely the outcome of that ambivalence inherent in every form in which freedom is objectified, and which at once makes freedom possible and places limits upon it.) Now in view of this inescapable ambivalence inherent in all the institutions which arise from freedom, are intended to make freedom possible of achievement and to safeguard it, *and* at the same time restrict its scope and in certain senses frustrate it, there are two points to be made. First, any such objectification of freedom, or of the history of the freedom of the individual or of society, can be for better or for worse in its effect upon this freedom itself. Presumably man is to some extent justified in interpreting more or less everything which has appeared in the course of human history as developed from freedom in order to contribute to freedom. Not only will more or less everything which takes place in society in the course of history actually be *presented* as a contribution to freedom, to a certain extent it actually *is* so. Let us consider, for example, the institution of absolute monarchy or of the most totalitarian régime. On close examination it appears that these invariably leave a certain scope for freedom unaffected. The reason is that a society simply cannot exist which is constructed and controlled totally and all-embracingly from one single point. The more so, since the absolute tyrant, in order to be absolutely uninfluenced by anyone else, would have to die in his own state of absolute isolation. But more than this, such systems do in fact, by comparison with other social orders, create elements providing fresh scope for freedom. This factor, which it is impossible to deny, does in fact provide propaganda for the most absurd and tyrannical social systems always and inevitably to have some appearance of justification. And among older individuals it is a factor which has led often enough to the sceptical conclusion that all social orders are at basis equally bad, and that the only difference between them is to be found in the different holders of power and the different ideologies on which they are based. At basis the same old situation remains, it is alleged, despite all these variations, especially since for the majority there is from the outset no prospect of gaining power for themselves within a given society.

But however strong an element of truth lies concealed in all this, the fact still remains that in relation to freedom some institutions are better and some worse, according as they limit and frustrate the legitimate freedom of the many in a greater or lesser degree. And hence there is a genuine history of freedom, a struggle for greater freedom that is genuine and not merely apparent; a legitimate protest against social institutions that unjustifiably restrict freedom, a protest which has a greater significance than a mere selfish clamour for a power hitherto possessed by others. In society institutions really do exist which, for all the ambivalence inherent in them too, serve the interests of freedom better, at least in cases where new and changed conditions have come to prevail affecting the numbers of the population, their level of education, the resources of communication, the quantity of goods which a given economy is now capable of producing, etc. Not all the forms, or even the institutions, in which freedom is objectified have the same restricting and frustrating effect upon freedom itself, quite apart from the fact that, as we have said, a certain preference can be given, with the necessary provisos, to new institutions as such over those which have been in force hitherto.

While we cannot enlarge upon this fact any further in the present context, we must recognize, then, that it makes it both right and necessary to maintain, and constantly renew, the struggle for greater freedom. But to this first factor a second and different one must now be added. It is true that the new and improved forms in which freedom is institutionalized serve the interests of this freedom better, and offer it a wider scope for its fulfilment. But even these new forms remain subject to that law of ambivalence which applies to all institutions, namely the inescapable law that they invariably both make freedom possible and frustrate it at the same time. It is at this point that the theologian raises the question of what the significance of this is. He asks himself whether, on this showing, man is able of his own resources to tolerate this ambivalence inherent in the situation of freedom. The question is whether man is not constantly exposed to the temptation and the danger of throwing off the oppressive frustrations to his freedom inherent in the situations in which he finds himself, even though they also contribute positively to his freedom. Again he may be tempted to throw them off in this way even though he actually needs these institutions as indispensable for his life, and the innovations which he is not yet willing to trouble himself about, so far from constituting improved forms in which to objectify his freedom, are actually harmful to it. He feels the oppression of the present existing institutions, the even more frustrating character of which weighs upon all except perhaps for a few of those actually holding power. This oppression stimulates his freedom to act against it. He does not yet feel the oppression and frustrations of the future institutions which he will perforce have to go on to create. He falls into a paroxysm of uncontrolled desire for a freedom which is quite unrealizable, destroys more than he can build, comes to a deadlock again and again in the course of history, and finally creates institutions which are not very dissimilar to those against which he was previously struggling. They may perhaps be *different*, but are only *better* – at least in certain respects – provided that all turns out well. In view of this question the theologian cannot hold that history as it *de facto* exists will ever be able to eliminate errors of this kind arising from the will to achieve freedom. They certainly belong to the very roots of history, which, viewed from the loftiest perspectives, are inescapable. But this sceptical view of past and future history as it *de facto* unfolds does not give the theologian any licence for holding that man has the right to give his support to such paroxysms and upheavals in the cause of a desire for freedom which is ultimately destructive, or to claim that he has a right to support such movements. The fact that world history as it develops always entails sin, error, and bias, does not mean that a morally responsible subject such as man is intended to be has any right to commit such acts as and when he sees that they are in prospect.

Now on this assumption the theologian will ask what sort of interior dispositions man must have in order to avoid being liable to the seduction of such a desire for freedom. And the theologian's reply will be this: ultimately speaking man is only immune to such diabolical temptations to freedom from freedom itself when he recognizes, and accepts in a spirit of hope, a dimension of freedom which transcends this ambivalence inherent in the forms in which freedom is objectified. We mean that dimension of freedom which is the kingdom of God. In this connection it makes little difference, ultimately speaking, whether an individual who in fact actually achieves, and lives by, this state of interior liberation of his freedom, which transcends the ambivalence of the forms in which that freedom is objectified, does in fact explicitate the theological interpretation of this state of liberation in conscious forms of words. Anyone who, having been set free for his freedom to be engaged in infinite hope, accepts the limitations imposed upon his freedom at the social level by all the institutions to which he is subject (and in fact, of course, without making this liberation of his grounds for an unjustifiable conservatism and social petrification), is living for God in a spirit of faith and hope. And this is what the theologian calls the freedom which has been liberated by grace from all earthly powers, and interprets as the true blessing of salvation, regardless of whether the individual concerned consciously recognizes it or not. In this sense the spirit of faith and hope in an absolute future is to be numbered among the prior conditions which alone prevent us from despairing of that freedom which is ever subject to institutional frustrations, and in our despair from destroying it.

THE INSTITUTION OF FREEDOM

In speaking of the relationship which exists between institution and freedom there is one further and special secondary kind of institution which calls for special mention. For there are institutions which are created with the special purpose of contributing to freedom by counteracting the effects of other institutions. In earlier ages, when human relationships were, in concrete practice, unalterable, this secondary kind of institution to which we refer, designed to counteract the curtailments of freedom imposed by other institutions, was confined almost exclusively to the sphere of law as such. In this field there were, and still are, officially appointed defending advocates, courts of appeal, and similar institutions. All these are, after all, institutions designed to uphold freedom which are something more than mere forms in which freedom is objectified. Rather they are precisely of a kind designed to defend freedom against other institutions. In other words in them the paradox achieves palpable and explicit form at a secondary level of an institution designed to give freedom. An institution is *ex professo* set up as a means of counteracting the effects of other institutions as inhibiting freedom. We cannot see why such a thing need necessarily be confined solely to the sphere of the administration of justice as such. Many institutions which do exist might perhaps be better understood in their nature, and improved and made more effective in their functioning, if they were consciously interpreted in the way we have indicated as institutions for safeguarding freedom against the restrictive effects of other institutions. I can only speak in very abstract terms here, but I believe that at the various levels of our society further and new institutions could be created of this kind, which would contribute to freedom in specific areas.

Only an absolute social system, integrating, organizing, and controlling everything within itself, something, therefore, which, in its extreme form would constitute a barefaced tyranny, could prevent legitimate claims to freedom as such from being raised against society itself by groups outside the institutionalized sections of society who felt particularly frustrated in their freedom. It is in these circumstances that the real seeds of a revolution are brought into being. And regardless of the forms in which such a revolution appears or the means which it uses (these may be very different from the ones known from former times), it brings about changes in society which were not previously catered for in it by the relevant institutions which were responsible for bringing such changes about merely by evolutionary methods. Only an absolute tyranny, subsuming and bringing everything under its control, could assert that within its sphere a revolution was from the outset unnecessary and impossible; that it itself constituted the permanent revolution. And because there cannot be any absolute tyranny, it also follows that in any reasonable society, which precisely on this account has never reduced to institutionalized form every conceivable or newly developed possibility for society, it is always possible in principle for a reasonable and justifiable revolution to take place. We older members of society should not in principle deny this merely in order to have the rest we have earned. But although it is impossible already in the here and now to forestall every kind of future claim to a justified revolution by devising institutions within society in its present form, this should not divert our attention from those still unrealized possibilities in a whole range of fields for creating institutions which as such, and as actually acknowledged here and now by society in its existing form, are designed to counteract the effects of other institutions within the same society, and to provide a greater scope for freedom. Such fresh institutions constitute an institutionalized element in social change as such, and thereby are capable of bringing about very much by way of evolution which otherwise would have to be forced upon society by revolution, with all the harm entailed in the use of uncontrollable force. Obviously such institutions, working as they do in favour of freedom to counteract the effects of other institutions, are, or would be, of a secondary order. They are also always liable to succumb to the law of obsolescence, to bureaucratization, to the danger of frustrating their own real purpose in the effort to maintain themselves, to Parkinson's law. And again, institutions of this kind will not bring the kingdom of infinite freedom upon this earth. But we should still ask ourselves where scope can yet be found for such institutions, working for freedom and counterbalancing the other institutions. The representatives and administrators of the primary institutions would be enquired of and appealed to in their wisdom and foresight not to feel that their authority was being limited or inhibited by such secondary institutions. In order to have such wisdom these officials will in turn have to have that spirit of detachment towards the ambivalence and authority of institutions which ultimately speaking is achieved only by that liberation of freedom which comes from God, and which we have sought to point to in what we have said.

8

EXPERIENCE OF SELF AND
EXPERIENCE OF GOD

IN view of the magnitude and difficulty of the theme under investigation, it is impossible, within the scope of a brief study such as the present one, to treat of more than a few particular aspects, which have been somewhat arbitrarily chosen. Experience of God and experience of the self each constitute themes in their own right, and in a real and fundamental sense they stand for the totality of human experience and human knowledge, albeit each in its own special way. For when man, the subject, experiences himself as such, he is recognizing himself to be that particular being which is '*quodammodo omnia*', not, that is to say, one particular subject among many others at the material level, but that inconceivable being in which the sum total of reality as such achieves realization of itself, so that the only way of fully understanding it would be to achieve an experience and understanding of reality itself. Metaphysical anthropology, therefore, is, on any right understanding of its nature, not one particular department or branch of science among others, but rather that philosophy which is concerned with *the* being as such, even though it is true that as anthropology this philosophy is attempting to understand the whole of reality from one specific point of departure, namely from that finite subject which is, nevertheless, open to the infinite. Presumably we do not need to justify in any greater detail the proposition that teaching about God does not constitute one particular department or branch of science, but, regarded as teaching about God at the philosophical level, constitutes an ontology as one and total, considered from one particular aspect. But if it is true that a metaphysical anthropology and a philosophical theology constitute, each in its own way, a universal science, then there are still stronger grounds for regarding the question of the mutual interconnection and underlying unity between them once more as a question involving an enquiry into reality in all its aspects.[1] Hence it is

[1] On this cf. the author's 'Reflexions upon Methodology in Theology', *Theological Investigations* XI (London and New York, 1974), pp. 68–114; also 'Theology

obvious that on such a theme, and within the scope of the present study, it is only possible to touch upon it in a few brief and inadequate remarks.

I

Let us begin by drawing attention to the terms in which the subject of this consideration has deliberately been defined: *experience* of self and *experience* of God. Thus we have avoided the terms 'knowledge of God' or 'knowledge of self'. This should be enough to indicate from the outset that what we are treating of is that kind of knowledge which is present in every man as belonging essentially to the very roots of cognition in him, and as constituting the starting-point and prior condition for all reflexive knowledge, and for all derived human knowledge in its function of combining and classifying. We are assuming, therefore, that there is such a thing as a passive experience of this kind as a matter of transcendental necessity, an experience so inescapable, in other words, that in its ultimate structures its reality is implicitly asserted in the very act of denying ir ot calling it in question. In accordance with this, it must be emphasized, with regard to man's experience of himself, that we are treating of this here in its initial stages as an unconscious factor in human life, one that is prior to any anthropology (at the philosophical level and as a particular department) in its reflexive and classifying functions, through both of which it exercises the further function of objectifying. Man's experience of himself sustains all such objectifying anthropology, and can never fully be grasped in man's findings as he reflects upon his own nature. Thus it would be justifiable to say that man always experiences more of himself at the non-thematic and non-reflexive levels in the ultimate and fundamental living of his life than he knows about himself by reflecting upon himself whether scientifically or (mainly in his private ideas) non-scientifically. The transcendental orientation of man to the incomprehensible and ineffable Mystery which constitutes the enabling condition for knowledge and freedom, and therefore for subjective life as such, in itself implies a real, albeit a non-thematic experience of God. With regard to this experience of God we must emphasize here above all that it can be so non-thematic, so different from any theology, whether popular or scholarly (whether philosophical or revelational in character) that on the one hand the experience really is present, yet on the other, under certain circumstances, the individual concerned may be ignorant of the very word God. An experience of God of

and Anthropology', *Theological Investigations* IX (London, 1972), pp. 28–45, and 'Transzendentaltheologie', *Sacramentum Mundi* IV (Freiburg, 1969), pp. 986–992.

this kind, therefore, is present from the outset in everyday life, even though the individual may be interested in everything else except God. It is also present, although it may be isolated or suppressed, in one who believes himself to be, or wills to be, an atheist. We have drawn a distinction between man's original and non-thematic experience of himself and of God on the one hand, and a knowledge about God and man in which this experience is objectified and interpreted on the other. Obviously in making this distinction we do not dispute that it is both important and inevitable that man must achieve a certain stage of reflexive knowledge (at least of himself as subject). Nor does man's interpretative knowledge of his own experience constitute in its turn an element in the history of man's experience in the concrete. Again when we speak of an experience of man and God we are inevitably using the very abstract term of 'experience', yet what we mean is that concrete developing history of experience in every individual man in his uniqueness and difference from all others, and in the whole length and breadth of an individual human life, different in every case, in which the struggle for conscious knowledge, objectified and explicitated in conscious terms, constitutes only a modest and secondary part of life. And let us further assume for our present purposes that every human experience, and so too that which we are concerned with here, contains within itself a transcendental and *a posteriori* element of historical development. In this sense it is both subjective and objective at the same time, so that the personal history of life in the concrete is, in virtue of this fact, precisely the personal history of the transcendentality of knowledge and freedom in the individual man. Conversely the only way in which this transcendentality can really achieve its true nature is for it boldly and freely to expose itself to the experience of the undeducible historical development in its *a posteriori* character, without attempting wholly to detach itself from this history belonging to it by a process of reflecting upon itself.[2]

II

If we are to speak of the experience of self *and* the experience of God, then the first point to be established is that they constitute a unity. Obviously what we mean by unity here is not simply an absolute identity. For when,

---

[2] On what follows cf. 'Reflections on the Experience of Grace', *Theological Investigations* III (London and New York, 1967), pp. 86–90, and, in a different connection, 'The Experience of God Today', *Theological Investigations* XI (London and New York), pp. 149–165.

in experiencing ourselves as subject, we see ourselves as 'transcendental', even then this 'transcendental' subject is absolutely different from that which we mean when we speak of 'God'. Even the most radical truth of self-experience recognizes that this subject which we are is finite, even though, precisely as such, and in its sheer transcendentality, it contains an absolute orientation towards the infinite and the inconceivable through which it is this without being identified with it. In other words, therefore, its nature is constituted by something, and experiences itself as so constituted, which it itself must perforce refuse to identify itself with. While, therefore, experience of God and experience of self are not simply identical, still both of them exist within a unity of such a kind that apart from this unity it is quite impossible for there to be any such experiences at all. Constantly both would be lost, each in its own way. This unity implies, of course, not only that every experience of God (like every other knowledge of God) as it exists in the subject is a process in which this subject is at the same time made present to itself and experiences itself. Taken by itself such a unity would in fact still not constitute any *characterization* of the experience of God as such, for in every spiritual act of knowledge or freedom, whatever it is concerned with, the subject is made present to itself. Or, to put it in Thomas' terms, a *'reditio completa subjecti in seipsum'* takes place. The unity between the experience of God and the experience of self is too ultimate and too all-embracing for it to consist solely in the simple fact that, as in every other 'subject' of human knowledge, so too in the knowledge of God, the subject experiences himself at the same time. This unity consists far more in the fact that the original and ultimate experience of *God* constitutes the enabling condition of, and an intrinsic element in, the experience of self in such a way that without this experience of God no experience of self is possible. In other words the personal history of the experience of God signifies, over and above itself, the personal history of the experience of the self. Of course the point could equally well be formulated the other way round. The experience of self is the condition which makes it possible to experience God. The reason is that an orientation to being in the absolute, and so to God, can be present only when the subject (precisely in the act of reaching out towards being in the absolute) is made present to himself as something distinct from his own act and as the subject of that act. In accordance with this we can then likewise go on to assert: the personal history of experience of the self is the personal history of the experience of God.

All this is certainly something which cannot be said of every 'subject' of experience. It is true that there is no experience of the self without the passive experience of subjects of some kind of an *a posteriori* character in the personal life of the individual concerned, subjects which are offered to the individual in the course of his life by his environment and his social milieu. To that extent the 'return' to the self necessarily also involves in all cases a 'projection' into the world outside. So much is this the case that true observation of the self at the level of explicit reflection upon oneself (whether scientific or non-scientific) constitutes only a very secondary and supplementary process in the totality of the human experience of the self. Nevertheless the knowledge of a particular individual subject within the world does not constitute the necessary condition enabling man to experience himself or the subject of that projection in which this experience is achieved. Yet without any experience of God, however non-thematic and non-reflexive in character, experience of the self is absolutely impossible. And hence it is, as we have said, that the personal development of experience of the self constitutes the personal development of the experience of God and *vice versa*.

The unity which exists between experience of God and experience of the self as here understood could of course be made clear in a process of transcendental reflection. Inevitably some of the factors involved in this have already been indicated in what we have said so far. The transcendentality of man in knowledge and freedom, as it reaches up to absolute being, the absolute future, the inconceivable mystery, the ultimate basis enabling absolute love and responsibility to exist, and so genuine fellowship (or whatever other presentation we may like to make in fuller detail of this transcendentality of man) is at the same time the condition which makes it possible for the subject strictly *as* such to experience himself and to have achieved an 'objectification' of himself in *this* sense all along. But this philosophical argument for the unity between experience of self and experience of God will not be pursued any further in the present context.[3]

In place of this, attention may be drawn to a theological consideration which shows that such apparently remote and abstract lines of thought have, after all, a concrete bearing upon life. The unity between the experience of God and the experience of self is the condition which makes it possible to achieve that unity which theological tradition recognizes as existing between love of God and love of neighbour, and which is of fundamental importance for any right understanding of Christianity.[4] In

---

[3] For a more detailed treatment this cf. 'The Concept of Mystery in Catholic Theology', *Theological Investigations* IV (London and Baltimore, 1966), pp. 36–73, and also *Worte ins Schweigen* (Innsbruck, 11th ed., 1972).

[4] On this cf. 'Reflections on the Unity of the Love of Neighbour and the Love of

order to achieve a clearer view of this a preliminary consideration must be included at this point. The only way in which man achieves self-realization is through encounters with his fellow man, a fellow who is rendered present to his experience in knowledge and love in the course of his personal life, one, therefore, who is not a thing or a matter, but a man. Of course an individual experience of self on the part of the subject, taken in isolation and abstracted from the totality of the course of a human life, is conceivable in connection with an individual piece of material 'subject-matter'. In that case '*I* come to know something' would be the formal structure of an experience of self of this kind in connection with a piece of 'subject-matter' which, following the custom of the philosophers of old, we conceive of, not without reason, as a material object. In reality, however, the situation is different. One's fellow man is not any 'piece of subject-matter', one of many in which the experience of self can be achieved. The true, living, and concrete experience of life which is identical with the experience of self in the concrete has, in relation to its 'pieces of subject-matter', a structure in which not every item has an equal value. Despite the ascendancy nowadays enjoyed by the sciences orientated towards material realities, and which also include man as one such material reality within their area of subject-matter, the experience of life is an experience of one's fellow men, one in which material objects are encountered as elements connected with, and surrounding concrete persons and not otherwise. Life in its full sense is in the concrete achieved in knowledge and freedom in which the 'I' is always related to a 'Thou', arising at the same moment in the 'Thou' as in the 'I', experiencing itself in all cases only in its encounter with the other person by recognizing itself to be different from that other person, and at the same time by identifying itself with that other person. The original objectivity of the experience of self necessarily takes place in the subjectivity of its encounters with other persons in dialogue, in trustful and loving encounter. Man experiences himself by experiencing the other *person* and not the other *thing*. Man could not achieve a self-withdrawal from a world consisting exclusively in material objects any more than he could from his own body, the concrete experience of which as it *de facto* exists also in fact presupposes an encounter with the physicality of other persons. Self-experience is achieved in the unity between it and the experience of other

God', *Theological Investigations* VI (London and Baltimore, 1969), pp. 231–249; 'The "Commandment" of Love in Relation to the Other Commandments', *Theological Investigations* V (London and Baltimore, 1966), pp. 439–459.

persons. When the latter is harmoniously achieved, the former succeeds as well. He who fails to discover his neighbour has not truly achieved realization of himself either. He is not in any true sense a concrete subject capable of identifying himself with himself, but at most an abstract philosophical subject, and a man who has lost himself. The subject's experience of himself and of the Thou who encounters him, is one and the same experience under two different aspects, and that too not merely in its abstract formal nature, but in its concrete reality as well, in the degree of success or failure with which it is achieved, in its moral quality as an encounter with the real self and with one's fellow in love or hatred. Thus the concrete relationship of the subject to himself is inextricably dependent upon the factor of how a subject encounters his fellow man. Now assuming all this (though this statement of ours constitutes only a cursory adumbration of it) we can now enquire into a further implication of it, one contained in the doctrine of the bible and the Church, namely that love of God and love of neighbour constitute a unity. In other words it follows from this Christian doctrine that in view of the fact that on the one hand the experience of God and the experience of self are one, and on the other that the experience of self and the encounter with our neighbour are one, that all these three experiences ultimately constitute a single reality with three aspects mutually conditioning one another. Now this also implies the converse, namely that the unity between love of God and love of neighbour is conceivable only on the assumption that the experience of God and the experience of self are one. The unity which exists between experience of self and experience of God, which at first seemed to be formulated and pointed to in purely philosophical terms, is also an implication of that principle, basic to Christianity, that love of God and love of neighbour are one. We must think of these three relationships of the subject to himself, to God, and to his neighbour, not simply as separate from, and existing side by side with one another like the relationships which a single subject bears to another contingent being which he chances to encounter, or to the subject-matter of *a posteriori* experience. These relationships, on the contrary, are present, as a matter of necessity, all at once, and as mutually conditioning one another, in every act of the subject endowed with intellect and freedom, whatever form this act may assume. Only if we recognize this can we say that the love of neighbour is the fulness of the Law, and that in it the destiny of man as a whole is decided. Only then can we say that man discovers himself or loses himself in his neighbour; that man has already discovered God, even though he may not have any explicit knowledge of it, if only he has truly reached out to his neighbour in an act of unconditional love, and in that neighbour reached out also to his own self. In brief, among many other reasons which might be adduced for the unity of this experience, but which cannot be developed here, there is a theological one too, namely the unity between love of God and love of neighbour. This statement can be maintained in its real and radical significance only if the relationship inherent in every act posited by the subject is extended to God and the neighbour also with the same transcendental necessity as it is to the subject himself, if God and his fellow man (his fellow man in principle and in general, even though this is then concentrated in the concrete other subject whom he encounters as a matter of irreducible contingency in the course of his personal life) constitute not particular factors confined to one area within the total scope of the experience, but are realities present as a matter of transcendental necessity opening up and sustaining the experience in its totality.[5]

III

A further point, following from what we have said, is that the personal history of the experience of self is in its total extent the history of the ultimate experience of God itself also. The history of knowledge of God at the consciously explicitated level is merely one particular and secondary element in this. But once we go beyond considering the unity of the experience of the self in formal and abstract terms and consider it is its concrete reality, it becomes in itself an anthropological problem of the utmost obscurity. For, in accordance with our basic thesis, it must also have its effect upon the history of the experience of God and its unity. The true and full unity of the history of the experience of self cannot consist

[5] On attempts to tackle the same question up to 1969 cf. 'Neue Versuche zum Verständnis der Gottesfrage', *Herder Korrespondenz* 23 (1969), pp. 184–189. The fact that this is a burning issue is shown by the copious literature on the question. Here we can give only a few random references, which, nevertheless, could lead to a work of far greater scope and depths: K. H. Weger, 'Gotteserfahrung in der Glaubensnot', *Geist und Leben* 39 (1966), pp. 343–354; Kl. Riesenhuber, *Existenzerfahrung und Religion* (Mainz, 1968); E. Kunz, 'Uberlegungen zur Gotteserkenntnis', *Geist und Leben* 41(1969), pp. 86–101; *idem*, 'Wie kann Gott vom Glaubenden erfahren werden?', *ibid.*, pp. 421–431; W. Kasper, 'Möglichkeiten der Gotteserfahrung heute', *ibid.*, pp. 329–349; R. Egenter, 'Praeambulum fidei. Eine Uberlegung zum christlichen Gotteserlebnis heute', *StdZ* 185 (1970), pp. 18–26; E. Kunz, *Christentum ohne Gott?* (Frankfurt, 1971); E. Coreth, 'Weltverständnis und Gottesverständnis', *Atheismus kritsch betrachtet*, E. Coreth and J. B. Lotz edd. (Freiburg and Munich, 1971).

merely in the fact that the subject endowed with spiritual faculties experiences himself at every moment in his self-realization as 'subject to time', i.e. as in the abstract orientated towards past and future in general. The unity of the concrete history of the experience of self to which we refer – in other words, therefore, the enduring possession of one's own personal history – cannot have its basis solely in what we call, in a popular and superficial sense, our memory. This cannot be the case seeing that then there would no longer be any abiding unity in the history of the experience of the self, any identity of the subject with his own past in relation to the earlier occurrences in his life. This remains true even though we do not overlook the fact that the potential memory as upheld by the material organism in man (the 'brain') is far greater than the total range of items which we can actualize from it at will. For only if this potential memory in man were present in every part of the material organism in itself alone (in a way similar to that in which the genetic code is present in every cell of the organism), something which it seems impossible to accept, could we think of the identity of the subject with his own past history of experience of the self, and thereby the unity of this history, as having its basis solely in this potential memory. This unity of the history of the experience of self, and the abiding identity of the subject with it, does not in any sense need in principle to be extended to all and every occurrence which has actually taken place in physical concrete fact in such a history. This is something which can never be demanded of a philosophy of the material as such, even abstracting from the question of whether a factor in the history of an individual can and must also have a permanence which cannot be lost even when it has never entered his awareness. A real state of belonging to the past is inherent in the material as such if it is regarded purely in itself, and to the extent that in viewing it in this way we really do see something which objectively belongs to it in itself. To that extent we can confidently conclude that there can be occurrences in man's history of experiencing himself too, which at least as such totally disappear, as such no longer exist, with the result that it would be totally impossible and meaningless to assert any abiding identity of the subject with them. There is a further question, namely, over and above what we have said, how the unity of the history of the experience of self, the abiding nature of this history, and the identification of the subject with his own history, should be thought of in further detail as *prior to* the freedom inherent in this history. But this is a question with which we shall not concern ourselves any further in the present context.

But there is a further and special question to which we must draw attention, that namely of how the unity of this history of the experience of self is to be conceived of if, and to the extent that, it constitutes a history of freedom, in other words of the free self-interpretation of man. For this question is of special importance in its bearing upon the unity of the history of the experience of God. The freedom in which the history of the experience of self is achieved cannot, it is true, eliminate the identity of man with his own past history, in other words a unity of the history of his experience of self which is not subject to man's own decision. In other words in the decree posited by human freedom man cannot so detach himself from his former history that this no longer affects him in any way whatsoever, even if this freedom of the past (in 'conversion', as repentance, or even as guilt) can undergo very real re-interpretations. Nevertheless freedom does introduce certain radical caesuras into the abiding unity of any such history of understanding of the self or experience of the self. So long as the single personal history of freedom belonging to the individual man endures, it is exposed, for all the unity and permanence inherent in it, to the constant possibility of fresh interpretation through the exercise of man's own freedom. At any moment in the here and now past history may be rendered present through the freedom of man in the form of a free identification of the subject with it, in the form of explicit rejection of it, in the form of unconscious yet free suppression of it, in the form of culpable and lying re-interpretation, and so on. This is all a line of argument that cannot be further developed here. But in the light of our basic thesis it is immediately clear that in saying this we are also saying something of decisive importance about the history of the ultimate and basic experience of God, when we conceive of this not at the abstract and formal level but in its concrete reality. The history of the experience of self, i.e. of man's interpretation of himself as achieved in freedom, is *eo ipso* the history of his experience of God as well, and *vice versa*. The destruction of false idols, the act of attaining, or failing to attain, a state of transcendence over all reality definable in terms of particular categories and also reality as the necessary starting-point for our knowledge of God, extending up to the Mystery which is beyond all our conceiving or achieving, man's surrender of himself, constant yet ever renewed, to the inconceivable God, or the refusal of such surrender in a lying self-sufficiency – these and many other episodes in the history of the experience of God are *eo ipso* events directly belonging to the history of the experience of the self as such as well and *vice versa*.

A complete and exact table might be drawn up of the correspondences between the one history and the other, because what is in question here is simply two aspects of one and the same history of experience. Such a table, which it is of course impossible to set forth here, would be very necessary precisely today. For in this way it might be possible for modern man, for whom all explicit statements about God fall all too easily under ideological distrust, to have it brought home to him that whether he wants it or not, in the changing history of his relationship with himself (whether in trustful acceptance of himself, in loss of identity, in hatred towards himself, in love for his fellow man, and only in this for himself, despite all his sceptical experience of the fragility and unreliability of finite man etc.) that he has all along been living through a history of his experience of God. With such a table it would be possible constantly to translate and describe an anthropology at the existential level and also in concrete human life, primarily in the form of teaching about the experience of God and *ipso facto* in this in a theology. It could be shown that in the history of experience of the self the experience of the loss of identity (to the extent and in the manner in which such a thing is possible, since in fact even that which is lost still always remains present in its own way) is also (in the same sense and with the same provisos) a loss of the experience of God or the refusal to accept the abiding experience of God.

9

DOES TRADITIONAL THEOLOGY REPRESENT GUILT AS INNOCUOUS AS A FACTOR IN HUMAN LIFE?

NOWADAYS an attempt is being made to unmask the problem of guilt, and to show that in reality it is an apparent, rather than a real, problem.[1] In the present context no attempt will be made either to set forth or to analyze the lines of argument for this process of unmasking the problem which are usually followed today. Again there is a question which in itself is of the utmost interest (and, moreover, one which has hardly been considered within theology itself), namely this: on the *hypothesis* that these unmasking processes are in fact justified, would it not be *quite impossible* for any such phenomenon as guilt to exist at all – in other words do not the arguments put forward in these attempts to show guilt to be an unreal problem prove simply *too much* about something that is a basic phenomenon of human life, and therefore is it not quite impossible for them to be correct, seeing that on any serious view they are wholly incapable of going on to explain how any such 'apparent problems' can arise at all? But the question which we are posing here is both

---

[1] The problem of evil, sin, and guilt has been approached in recent times from the most diverse aspects. The following bibliography is intended merely to give some indication of this multiplicity, and so at least provide some idea of the background against which the essay which follows has to be viewed. B. Welte, *Über das Böse*, Quaestiones Disputatae 6 (Freiburg, 1958); H. Boelaers, 'Ist jede schwere Sünde eine Todsünde?', *Theol. der Gegenwart* 3 (1963), pp. 142–148; K. Lorenz, *On Aggression* (trans. by M. Latzke, London, 1966); K. Rahner, 'Guilt and Its Remission: the Borderland Between Theology and Psychotherapy', *Theological Investigations* II (London, 1963), pp. 265–282; P. Schoonenberg, *Theologie der Sünde* (Einsiedeln, 1966); M. Adam, *Le sentiment du péché*, Etude de psychologie (Paris, 1967); B. Schüller, 'Todsünde – Sünde zum Tod?', *Theologie und Philosophie* 42 (1967), pp. 321–340; K. Hemmerle, 'Evil', *Sacramentum Mundi* II (London and New York, 1968), pp. 279–283 (with bibliography); K. E. O'Shea, 'The Reality of Sin; A Theological and Pastoral Critique', *Theol. Studies* 29 (1968), pp. 241–259; M. Oraison, *Was ist Sünde?* (Frankfurt, 1968); F. Böckle, 'Das Problem der Sünde', *Handbuch der Pastoraltheologie* IV (Freiburg, 1969), pp. 115–127.

different from, and far more unusual than these. It is a question of whether attempts at showing that guilt is in reality an innocuous phenomenon in this sense are not to be found within classic Christian theology as well, even though it itself is not fully aware of the fact.

At first sight the thesis does not seem a particularly reasonable one. In reply to it it might straightway be objected that it would be impossible for any such attempts seriously to be made within Christian theology. After all Christianity is a religion of Redemption, and is rooted in an event in which the real guilt incurred by man's acts, and from which he cannot escape, is removed by the deed of God alone. So true is it, in fact, that Christianity is the religion which views man as radically subject to guilt, to malice and not merely to evil, that it would have to abandon its own essential nature if it sought itself to deny the reality of malice or in any sense to unmask it as an apparent, rather than a real, problem. Yet the matter is not so simple, if only because of the following factor: there is always a difference between living practical devotion (which invariably includes some elements of which we are not fully aware), and a fully reflexive theology. And because of this difference even when theories are put forward by the upholders of this devotion tending to suggest that guilt is unreal, there is a stage at which such theories are not yet perceived to have this implication. Later, however (after a long period during which they have been at least tolerated by the Church's authorities), such theories can have a devastating effect in the concrete living practice, the devotion, and the life of the Church. In fact such theories have already been taking effect over a long period in contexts outside the Christianity of the Church (for secular heresies can be the logical and open outcome in radical form of heresies that secretly propagate themselves within the Church).

In this sense, therefore, the theme we have put forward may perhaps repay consideration after all. But our consideration of it will *not* proceed from the tacit assumption that such heretical views secretly propagating themselves, in which malice is regarded as apparent rather than real, certainly *do* exist in the theology of the Church. Throughout our investigation we shall fully be taking into account the possibility that the classical theology of the schoolmen may in itself turn out to be (in a positive sense) more penetrating than the average feeling of the 'devotees' in the Church, and may actually have undertaken a justified 'demythologizing' of ideas of guilt which, as they exist in the average practice of the Church, have never ceased to contain a strongly 'mythical' element. Obviously it is impossible, in brief considerations of this kind, to provide a record of the history of theology involved. All that we can do is to offer a few very basic reflections on what we actually find in the average outlook of the official theology of today.

It seems to me that any considerations we may put forward on the theme we have defined involve one basic difficulty: that the 'factor' being pointed to in the thesis we are seeking to defend is itself precisely lacking in clarity. What is guilt? Under what circumstances is guilt 'rendered innocuous'? Under what circumstances is its 'character as absolute' threatened or overlooked? It is relatively easy to counter any *modern* attempts to 'do away with' guilt by pointing out that once a relationship to that which is called God, freely entered into by man, is declared by the 'enlightened' to be a misconception (whether on positivist, sociological, existential, or any other grounds) it is evident that there is no such thing as 'guilt' in the sense upheld by Christianity and the Church. And conversely the fact that Christians do dispute this 'declaration by the enlightened' is itself an argument in support of the proposition that there is such a thing as guilt, something which actually *exists*, from which man does not liberate himself of his own resources (in the form either of enlightenment or progress), something which, on the contrary, if it can be removed from man *at all*, is removed by being forgiven him. Admittedly in any such argument in defence of the reality of guilt, in which we contest the assumption on which the opponent of guilt bases his case, we must not overlook the fact that in any intellectual position as it exists in the concrete the proposition we 'assume' as our basis is already conditioned by the conclusion we feel justified in drawing from it. To put it in concrete terms, we shall hardly be in a position to understand what is meant by God without freely accepting the attitude that guilt is possible.

But how are we to take the field against the outlook which we presume to exist *within Christianity itself*, and which regards guilt as unreal? Nowhere here do we find any denial either of God or of the existence of a possible guilt in his sight (which at least to this extent has a certain absolute character). What, therefore, is there to contest, apart, perhaps, from a few theologumena of the official theology which do not in any sense touch upon the Christian attitude to guilt as it really exists in the concrete? Admittedly the opposite might equally well be the case. The doctrine of guilt which, taken as a whole, is orthodox, might be the façade behind which lies concealed an attitude of unbelief towards guilt which, though unexplicitated, is nonetheless a real factor in 'concrete life'. (Who nowadays is still subject to the '*Angst*' of going to hell?) Is it perhaps possible that precisely *this* unbelief could betray itself through this or that detail in the orthodox teaching (if we were, so to say, to lay this teaching on the psychoanalyst's couch and pay rather closer attention to the remarks thrown up from time to time in what it then had to say)? Or again, this orthodox teaching might be subjected to questioning with regard to such details in it by those who feel a certain astonishment and doubt, and who would like to ask it why, as a matter of concrete living practice, it has become so ineffective nowadays, and whether the underlying reasons for this might not, after all, be discovered within itself.

Our line of investigation will be as follows: we shall draw elements from certain theories, the orthodoxy of which has either been recognized in officially accepted theology, or at any rate not disputed. With the help of these we shall attempt to present an argument against 'guilt feelings' or in support of the 'demythologizing' of guilt. Thus we shall produce an 'enlightened explanation' of guilt which (at least to all outward appearances) is drawn from within theology itself, yet which, when pressed to its radical conclusions, *must* be pronounced false when it is submitted to the judgement of the Christian conscience. In this way we shall be able to see what consequences follow (at least incipiently) from pressing a genuine theology of guilt to its radical conclusion in this way, or what context such a theology of guilt must be viewed in in order to find an interpretation for it such that we do not have to regard it as a false demythologizing of guilt.

The line of argument adopted in a Christian case for the defence of this kind, supporting the utmost possible exculpation of man, might run as follows: there is no guilt or, if this sounds too imprudent and heretical, guilt is a 'peripheral concept' in the sense that in practice it does not arise or (to put it still more prudently) not in any notable degree or one which is relevant to the world and history as a whole. Rather it is something which, for various reasons (of which we shall have to speak at a later stage) cannot totally be eliminated from human awareness as an idea, a threat, a stimulus, even though the 'poison' of this idea should be used for purposes of a psychological and social hygiene with the utmost prudence and (quite otherwise than in former times) in the very mildest doses. This is the basic thesis put forward in this case for the defence.

What we mean by 'guilt' here is an (*in se*) definitive state into which man enters of his own freedom, and of which he cannot rid himself of his own resources, yet which sets him in contradiction to his own nature as a whole and (thereby) to God and to the relationship which in itself he has decided to bear to man. This state of contradiction is such that it leads to the final and definitive 'perdition' of man as a whole (or alternatively actually *constitutes* this perdition). It is as a (fictitious) argument in support of this conception of guilt, therefore, that we have put forward the above thesis.

The first point: we are here assuming the existence of freedom (in a psychologically indeterminate sense), but such freedom is finite. This is a point which the theologian is least of all in a position to deny. But what this finitude of freedom implies in terms of content is becoming clearer today than it formerly was, and the moral theologian nowadays takes this factor freely into account. He recognizes the physiological, psychological, and social factors which condition the choice that is made within the scope of finite freedom. Man as he *de facto* exists is restricted in his knowledge by these conditioning factors, so that only a finite number of objects[2] is open to him to choose from. It is perfectly conceivable – indeed more that probable – that this limited number of options which it is open to him to know and freely to choose from, is in turn far more restricted by the following circumstance. It is very far from being the case that all the objects impinging in any way upon the awareness of the individual within the total scope of his conscious awareness are *ipso facto* so 'attractive' to him that they are capable in any real sense of constituting genuine objects of choice. Now in no concrete individual case (whether by the individual concerned reflecting upon himself or by external observation) is it possible to establish in the concrete with any certainty whether precisely in the *concrete* case this extremely restricted finite number of objects of choice available on any given occasion include among them that which constitutes the '*objective*' good (that which is willed by God). This is something which cannot naïvely be taken for granted without further ado. It is perfectly possible that in specific cases the objects of choice *de facto* available in the concrete include only those which are objectively bad. Even then the individual will regard one such object of choice as the 'better' one, i.e. as constituting the better choice in comparison with some other possible object from this or that point of view. Again, it is still possible to say in such a case that someone has the moral duty to choose the lesser evil in preference to the greater. But this does not alter the fact that in such cases something which, objectively speaking, does constitute an evil course will be taken in virtue of the fact that in the concrete the individual concerned has no real objective good within his purview. And again it is extremely questionable whether in such a case in

---

[2] Here of course we are speaking only of realities constituting the subject-matter of knowledge and freedom which – as capable of being freely realized – constitute 'options' to the subject endowed with freedom to choose and to decide upon.

the concrete that which constitutes the lesser evil is so distinctive and so important that a moral significance is to be attached to the act of preferring it to all other options. Now if this is so then is the individual really 'responsible' in such cases as these? Can something significant really be taking place here? And even supposing that an 'objective' good is recognized as possible (obviously this is the case in unnumerable instances) still in the concrete instance it remains open whether the individual can freely choose it or whether it is present merely as an object of a 'choice' which is already predetermined (from a physiological, psychological, or sociological aspect). The same applies *a fortiori* to something that is recognized as evil. In each concrete instance it remains open to question whether a particular option is present to the individual's awareness at all, whether it is present in its moral relevance precisely as *evil*, and whether as it exists in the concrete (as evil) it is present to the individual as a real object of free choice. It might be argued that after all the question of whether this or that specific object of choice is present to the individual's awareness, and is chosen by him in freedom, is something that can be established beyond doubt simply enough by a straightforward act of self-introspection. But to this we would have to reply that a free choice of one specific *individual* object at a level beyond all doubt, and as present to the subject's awareness as something actually *reflected* upon by him, is something that we precisely do *not* have. The individual act of freedom as such, and precisely as an *individual* act, is not a direct datum of the individual's awareness, if only for this reason: the fact that no determinative motive (object of choice) is present precisely *so far as* the subject's own objectifying and reflexive awareness is concerned is still not in itself any proof that no such motive exists. It may still be present and effective even though the subject has not objectified it to himself or reflected upon it. (The philosophically valid 'proof' of the existence of freedom can and must be established in a quite different way, and one which we shall not be entering into here. For this proof we do not need to rely upon the *individual* act of freedom as such, and as directly present to the subject's awareness as such. Hence in order to prove the existence of freedom we do not have to be able to assert that freedom, together with a specific moral value, is certainly present in any one *particular* act.) At basis all this is theologically clear. If it were indeed the case that by a simple process of self-reflection (subsequently and finally reinforced by the observations of another too) it were possible to establish the free character and (thereby) the moral quality of a given act with complete certainty, then we would likewise be able to achieve complete certainty about our relationship with

God in each concrete individual case with regard to our 'state' of justification or mortal sin (which, as we are told, we incur only when in possession of clear knowledge and full freedom). And a knowledge of this kind is precisely what we do not have. The genuine Christian attitude towards God forbids us to seek a completely sure and fully conscious knowledge of precisely *how* we stand in God's sight. It prescribes that we shall endure, in a spirit of hope and not otherwise, the uncertainty to which our reflections upon our interior state are subject, even as, in the non-reflective movement of the practical reason (despite the claims of the speculative reason to act as judge), we reach out in hope towards that future which is constituted by the 'compassion' of God. But then we ask precisely, Does not this make guilt an extremely questionable phenomenon? Now there is a certain transcendent awareness of freedom prior to the specific individual act of freedom – prior, that is, in a logical and existential sense, not in a temporal one or as immediately preceding it. But whatever the nature of this knowledge may be, and while recognizing that the question of guilt or lack of guilt is in all concrete cases insoluble, we do hold that *every* Christian must from the first, without 'judging' himself, flee from himself in a spirit of hope in God's compassion; in fact that *every* individual must capitulate before God as *simul justus et peccator* (a formula which retains its justification and its truth throughout the *whole* of Christendom and beyond all theological controversies and differences of opinion). Now if this is true then is not the question of guilt in the concrete individual case (guilt, let us note, in the theological, and not the' civil' sense), if not actually eliminated, at least left behind from the very outset? On this showing is not guilt reduced to a mere peripheral concept (again in a theological and not in a civil sense), seeing that *every individual* can and must take into account guilt of this kind at the unreflecting level, and *every individual* can and must hope for forgiveness to the extent that it really is guilt in God's sight that is in question and not some deed in which he had transgressed the laws of this world and can be called to account by the civil authorities?

Can we not go further and say that the biblical doctrine of the punishment of hell (as presented in the literary *genre* known as the 'threatening sayings') are *nowadays* so conceived of that, while they do indeed express a real *possibility*, they tell us nothing as to whether this final and definitive perdition will truly be realized as a matter of historical fact. It might of course be objected that regarded as a hope in the concrete conditions of human living rather than as a theoretical statement, this does not rule out the *de facto* incurring of grave guilt (but only its final and definitive outcome). But in reply we in turn might put the question of whether on this showing too such guilt is not rendered innocuous, seeing that it is 'in principle' denied that it will ever arrive at this definitive outcome (even though this is based on the universality of *hope* and not on any theological principles of the theoretical reason). The question might be raised of what kind of 'possibility' (of eternal loss) this really is, seeing that on the one hand it must be something seriously to be taken into account by man (with the seriousness due to something that affects his entire existence), and which he has to, and indeed must, resist with the no less total and radical resolution of his hope. Is not the situation really that this hope, which is asserted to be so radical and universal (and unless it is this can it be the theological virtue of hope?) has the function of unmasking the 'guilt' in the world (not at the theoretical level but in the concrete practice of life) as a mere façade[3] – something, precisely, which is invariably overcome by hope? Must it not be unmasked as an apparent hopelessness in which we suppose that we know for certain precisely *that* in many cases history does, despite all, end in the radical contradiction of perdition, a perdition which, nevertheless is, when viewed in the true light of hope, meaningless even in relation to God? For he certainly has no need of this in order to manifest his 'righteousness', as an officially approved seminary theology, prevalent in many Christian denominations, impertinently believes that it can recognize (though it cannot invoke the support of Scripture for this, seeing that for Scripture such a revelation is merely the means of revealing *grace*, and that in the case supposed it would cease to have this function). Nor yet should we say that freedom in relation to God can only exist if guilt also exists as really incurred in God's sight. This is in fact often asserted in a popular apologetics of God's 'right' to 'tolerate' guilt. But ultimately speaking it is in contradiction to the basic conviction of all theological schools in Christendom, all of which are convinced that God can, in all cases without exception, of himself predestine the goodness of the creature as *free*, if he wills it so, *without* thereby inhibiting the freedom and responsibility of the creature endowed with intellect and will. Now if this is correct, then it becomes difficult, to say the least, to understand what real (as distinct from merely verbal) distinction should then seriously be drawn between a mere 'tolerating' of freely committed evil (if we are to regard this as really existing!) on God's part and an actual

---

[3] What we mean here is a 'transcendental' appearance which is constantly there, and therefore has constantly to be overcome. But we do not mean a misunderstanding to be removed once and for all by explanations, so that it finally and definitely ceases as soon as we become a little more enlightened.

'willing' of moral goodness and of finite evil in the non-moral sense within the world. For must we not in all honesty say that to 'tolerate' something is actually to 'will' it if it is within one's power to prevent it, and that too without inhibiting the quality of freedom inherent in the action involved? Let us consider the various theories of the traditional theological schools with regard to the relationship between God and human freedom. Where here do we find any real distinction between tolerating and willing, seeing that the entire concrete reality of the human act is also actively brought about by God? Furthermore, let us consider the negative element in this positive and real act. Where do we find any room for a distinction between 'tolerating' and 'willing' here, seeing that the only way in which this negative element can exist is *in virtue of* the concrete causality of this positive element, seeing that the free act of the man willing this negative element, considered in its positivity as an act, also comes into being only in virtue of an active collaboration on God's part? And the question which then arises is whether the impossibility of this distinction between 'tolerating' and 'willing' which then imposes itself so strongly does not after all permit us to conclude that an evil presumed to be radical is in reality merely an evil which God is capable of willing in, and in collaboration with, a finite world.

But from other aspects too the question can be posed of whether traditional theology does not engage in something like an argument designed to deprive guilt of its force. What we mean is the doctrine that the formal evil of guilt is something 'privative', a privation of being. This is the principle which Augustine used successfully in order to overcome Manichaeism. And this thesis has continued to belong to the common stock of Catholic theology right down to the present day. But do the devout take this thesis seriously, and conversely, if this thesis is in fact taken seriously (i.e. not merely invoked when questions of theodicy arise, but rather accorded an integral place in our conception of guilt as a factor in our concrete lives), does guilt still continue to be guilt? There are certain questions which, though they are certainly not easy to answer, must be wholly set on one side here. The questions namely of what a 'privatio' really and precisely is in ontological and ontic terms, inasmuch as it is different from a simple state of non-being. And even if we recognize this distinction as valid beyond doubt, and take it with all due seriousness (the state of 'having been robbed' cannot as such simply be nothing), still there is a further question with regard to the thesis of the non-being of *malitia formalis*: whether its ostensible meaning does not conceal a further underlying intention with regard to God and his collaborating with the action of his creature. Since on any showing God does actively collaborate at that point at which the distinction between mere non-being and '*privatio*' is constituted as real, an explanation must be found, so it is felt, in which we do not have to attribute oɪ God and his 'active collaboration' with his creature in its action the causing of the evil which the creature commits. In any case, however, in order not to attribute this to God by upholding the thesis of the non-being of *malitia formalis*, we would have to raise a further question with regard to the real and positive action causing some deficiency which should not be the case to be produced from something which should be the case through something which has been brought about (whether an act or the outcome of an act). The question is, therefore, whether this real and positive action is nothing but good, or whether it itself is *ipso facto* morally evil because of what it brings about. In the first case the whole matter becomes totally incomprehensible. Something that is good and nothing more brings about something that is morally evil. In the second case the whole question recurs afresh unresolved. On this showing, then, two conclusions may be reached with regard to the thesis itself: It may be (a) an instance of a wrongly applied conceptual model. We recognize the possibility of something that is good in a pre-moral sense yet which might be better. It lacks some further goodness which we can imagine, but which does not belong to it as a reality, as 'existing', though this does not mean that even without it the thing concerned is evil. Now we apply this conceptual model to the question of moral evil. The 'deficiency' then seems to constitute a mere 'non-being' in this case also. But we are overlooking the fact that on this showing only two alternatives are open to us with regard to the moral evil: *either* it too is as innocuous as the lack of some further goodness in the original conceptual model, *or* the true evil lies in the objective origins of this deficiency and the question arises afresh. We may, however, take a *second* line of argument: (b) basically speaking, all that we intend to assert in this thesis is that when a free creature uses its freedom to act culpably it cannot on this account make God *ipso facto* responsible for its deed on the grounds that he sustains and causes all that exists. And this remains true even though this thesis does not *explain* why we cannot make God responsible for our faults in this way. With regard to this thesis, all that we are doing is (rightly) to maintain that God's effective activity is present all-pervasively throughout the whole of existence. But even if the thesis is taken in this sense, i.e. as having the function not of explaining evil but merely of maintaining its reality, a further question which can then be raised is whether there can still be any place for evil once we recognize this all-pervasive effectiveness of God's act which brings about everything that exists, and at the same time assigns everything its due limits and boundaries. The situation seems to be such that we must either hold a theism which reduces evil to unreality in view of the all-pervasiveness of God's effective activity, or (conversely) we are driven to a position of hypothetical atheism in order to maintain the reality of evil as a radical factor in existence. Evil seems no longer to be evil if it can be tolerated by a God of absolute moral perfection, even though he can prevent it and, moreover (a point which we have already made and which needs to be carefully noticed!), without withdrawing or diminishing creaturely freedom. For according to all Catholic theories of grace and freedom genuine freedom is both freedom in the fullest sense and at the same time absolutely under God's disposing power (whether through a *praemotio physica* or by way of *scientia media*). It might be rejoined that what has just been said means merely that God himself has a radical attitude towards evil proper to *him* alone, such that, if the creature were to claim it for himself, this would imply the absolute presumption of claiming to be God, and further that this distinction between the two attitudes (of God and of the creature) towards evil is simply a further explicitation, application, and radicalization of the absolute difference which prevails between God and the creature, between his and our attitudes to everything whatsoever (being, time, individual reality etc.). But to this we in turn might reply: precisely this statement in fact confirms that what we are stating about evil is stated with reference to *ourselves*, and not to God. In other words, evil is radically evil in this sense only because, and to the extent that it is related to ourselves, who are finite, whereas in its relation to God evil is precisely *not* as evil as this. But if this is true then who can really prevent the creature from knowing precisely this (it actually asserts it!), and thereby ascribing to evil a relative status in relation to itself as well, placing itself in the position of God (there is in fact some echo of this even in Rom. 6:1) first at the theoretical level and then at the practical level too. i.e. in practice how can we still be afraid when we know that through the evil which we do we are playing a part which fits perfectly into the total symphony which God conducts, at least from his point of view, and which at least to *his* ears sounds sweet? For does not traditional theology from Paul onwards maintain that God, at least so far as he is concerned, is able to use the evil to initiate something, e.g. he can use it as the prior condition for his grace, for the revelation of his righteousness etc.? With regard to the creature endowed with intellect and will who is able to make this assertion, how can he still be afraid for himself, seeing that after all it is actually asserted that through evil God has performed a kindness? How can evil still be evil in any effective sense?

To this line of argument Paul has only one reply: μὴ γένοιτο (Rom. 6:1). But we still do not find any arguments supporting this disclaimer in his writings. But what arguments can be found on which to base it? Is it enough to say this: Constituting as he does a finite spirit which is, nevertheless, open to the infinite, man is precisely such that he knows about God (and therefore too about that relationship to evil which is unique to himself) and nevertheless (nevertheless!) precisely as such man is *not* God (and so too does not have the same relationship to evil as God has)? Is this answer enough? Is it enough precisely in view of the fact that after all in traditional theology we regard our relationship to evil (if it is a correct one) precisely as a unilinear extension and reproduction of the relationship which God has to evil? If we have to say that we ourselves can have a less 'relativist' relationship to evil than God has (and this is really what is said by Paul and by traditional theology when it recognizes that God can tolerate evil in order to reveal his justice and his mercy), can we then still really maintain the reality of this knowledge if the state of affairs which is expressed here not only exists but is also precisely something of which we ourselves are aware? Does not the fact that we are aware of it at basis reduce evil to unreality? And when a man does evil is he not acting upon this ultimate reduction of evil to unreality when he – so it seems – does evil in the awareness that there is an ultimate reasonableness in so acting? It can still only have a good outcome.

The way in which traditional theology tends to represent evil as innocuous – of course always clean contrary to its own real intention – can be viewed from a completely different aspect. Has it ever occurred to the exponents of this theology to be surprised at the fact that they are ascribing to God the power of forgiving and removing evil? Should not the very first point to be recognized be that the very nature of human freedom is such that in all cases once a free agent takes a decision, if and to the extent that his freedom is fully exercised in arriving at it, the only way in which it can be rescinded is by himself, always provided that this process of a free decision rescinding a free decision is not itself in turn contrary to the very nature of human freedom as a finite created entity? Traditional theology finds an easy way of answering this question by saying that obviously the agent endowed with finite freedom must himself be converted and 'repent', otherwise any divine forgiveness is of its very nature impossible (incidentally even in this statement we can see that traditional theology is wavering in that to some extent it regards this proposition as valid merely at the *de facto* level, and not as something that necessarily follows from the very nature of freedom itself). But if the free agent himself must be converted in order to remove the evil he has done, why then is there any need for a distinct and separate act of divine forgiveness? Why can this conversion take place only during earthly life, before or at the moment of death? Can we find an answer to the first question by invoking the example of an injured party who must of his own initiative grant forgiveness even when the offender from his side decides not to continue his offence? For we can at least ask whether an offence against God still continues to be such, and therefore requires to be forgiven by him, when man, by his repentance, removes the offence which (*ex supposito*) he has committed against God. Those who wish to protest against this general line of argument must allow the question to be put to them of whether they are not falsely transferring from the conceptual model, and introducing into the theological consideration, a concept of time and certain social factors (unconnected with man's intrinsic make-up) which basically speaking either assert or tacitly assume that the offence against God is, as a free act of man, finally and definitively posited and so in itself definitive and irremovable in the sense that it can be removed only by God (precisely *as* God and not merely as any sort of injured party) for reasons which are quite beyond our conception (and through resources which belong only to God as God), and moreover precisely *in that* he extends to man the possibility of repentance. And the only way of avoiding an extremely anthropomorphic and decretorial way of thinking about God is to deepen our theology even of biological death, unless we are willing to accept the doctrine of the transmigration of souls as providing a conception of man's moral development and of the history of freedom leading to a final and definitive state as more in accordance with God's nature, the more so since in fact any transmigration of souls must be conceived of as a never-ending process. In the light of these two questions alone it seems that it is only with great difficulty that we can arrive at a position which really lies *between* asserting that every radical exercise of freedom is absolute and definitive on the one hand, and asserting that every particular fault is simply provisional and to be regarded as a stage which man both can and should pass beyond in his moral development on the other.

Whatever position may in fact be adopted on these two questions, which are far from easy to answer, a further question which must in any case be raised is whether God really can remove evil by an act of forgiveness. This is all too easily assumed to be obvious. Any genuine and radical phenomenology of the human awareness of guilt both can and must bring out clearly the experience of the radical inescapability of guilt. It can and must show how real guilt is experienced as that which can no longer be made good (once there has been any effective betrayal of love how can the former position be restored? etc.). God would, therefore, precisely *per definitionem*, have to be *postulated* as he who can in some sense remove an irremovable and inescapable guilt of this kind despite its irremovability. (We may conceive of him either as one who simply adds his forgiveness to the sinner's repentance or as one who alone can make such repentance possible.) In recognizing the phenomenon of guilt and in hoping that it can, in spite of all, be removed, we must not simply take God for granted, but reach out to him, rather, as the factor which makes it possible to have such hope at all. Can we not say that in this respect too traditional theology tends to render the phenomenon of guilt innocuous, seeing that it takes the possibility of its forgiveness far too much for granted?

Let us approach the problems indicated above of regarding evil as a '*privatio*' in a somewhat different form. For the same reasons as those which prompt it to conceive of evil as *privatio*, traditional theology lays down that evil can be willed only *sub ratione boni*. All evil-doing, therefore, in the concrete conditions of human life, takes place, according to this doctrine, as the outcome of a transcendental willing of the good as such and in general to the extent that the impulse of the human spirit towards good in general takes effect through the medium of the specific concrete exercise of knowledge and freedom (in the form of a concrete free decision), and is prompted by some finite (or conceived to be finite) particular good which precisely should not be aimed at here and now and in the particular circumstances in which it occurs, since to do so constitutes a denial of some higher concrete particular good which should be aimed at here and now, and thereby constitutes a voluntary denial of that good at the universal level and as a whole which we must constantly strive for as a matter of necessity. The will to the good, therefore, is present and active in all human actions, even those in which evil is done. And to the extent that this will to good in general and as a whole is still being exercised even in the free act which is directed towards some concrete particular good or evil (or one conceived of at this level), this will to the good in general and as a whole always still remains a free will. On this basis the evil is properly speaking only a certain misconception (if it exists at all) in the process taking place at the concrete particular level by which the free will to the good as such, for blessedness as such (considered in its formal structure) is mediated. If evil is conceived of somewhat along these lines is it so evil? On this showing is it not *ipso facto* constantly being corrected by the fact that further effects follow from man's striving in any given case through the necessary alterations in living situations necessarily imposed upon the individual, which make it quite impossible for him to hold firm to this or that particular good (which in the concrete circumstances is interpreted as evil)? Does not life gently withdraw from man that which he eagerly seeks to retain ('But only wait. . . .'), and does not man himself in the end (at latest in the moment of death) willingly relinquish that which is thus withdrawn from him, that which, if he either could or would cling fast to it and finally and definitively opt for, could be called evil? Of course we can put forward the postulate that even while ultimately and definitively protesting against something, a man can still use his freedon to cling onto it, and that it is precisely through this that he is brought to a final and definitive state of inner conflict in which he is torn between two goals, that which as free he clings onto obstinately, and that which constitutes his true good. But is it probable that this in fact often happens, in view of the infinitely powerful yet gentle pedagogy of death, regarded as man's farewell to every concrete particular good which he has really possessed? And is that particular good, so perversely clung onto in the individual act (so that it comes to be called evil), of such importance in the economy and history of the world when we compare it with the immense multitude of evils which are not the outcome of free acts, and which constitute the major part of human history? In fact we must not exaggerate the significance of guilt (so the argument might run) in order to eliminate such guilt as far as possible from the world, if only because, as it may be presumed, the total amount of evil *de facto* arising from such guilt in a world in which this metaphysical and theological interpretation applies will hardly be smaller than in a world which rejects such an interpretation. At least it will not be diminished within the sphere of actual human experience. The total amount of evil in the world arising from guilt seems to remain more or less constant throughout, in the course of history to vary in the forms it assumes rather than in its degree of intensity, and to be held in check by factors arising from the limited resources of human nature, factors, therefore, belonging to the physical and social, rather than to the moral order in any true sense of the term. On this showing, then, is not the concept of final and definitive evil reduced to a peripheral concept? Is that which we really call evil, and experience to be such, not merely a process in which we are temporarily captivated by some good which loses its hold upon us as we develop further, or which can and must voluntarily be subsumed within an integral order of good in the absolute existing at a higher level?

What then are we to suppose? Are we to say, 'Yes, we must press on in the process of "demythologizing" evil along the same lines as have been sketched out, at least incipiently, in traditional theology'? Are we to say what is in fact said by, or at least ascribed to Teilhard, namely that evil is, after all, the mere manifestation of frictions which arise in the process of cosmic development, which are inevitable and are only 'evil' when we cease to view them as a factor in a broader movement, a factor which is itself precisely overtaken by this movement and so eliminated? Are we to say (which would really amount to the same thing as has just been said, only expressed in theological terms) that the evil consisting in that which is willed by God, and conceived of with a good end in view as a good means of achieving it, is only evil in so far as it is viewed in isolation, and apart from this function which it has of being a means to an end. In God's eyes, however, it precisely does not have this absolute status in any sense, and therefore can perfectly well be willed by him, whereas we confine ourselves to saying that it is merely tolerated by him if and because we view it apart from this reference it has to an ultimate goal. Are we to say that evil is only apparent on the grounds that all creaturely good is finite, and, when willed by man as a promise of the infinite good, always carries with it that appearance of being more than it is in itself? Or conversely that to will it would imply over-valuing it in the sense of stopping short at the creaturely good in itself without recognizing its character as pointing on to something beyond itself? Are we to say this: that it is only within the course of the history of our personal freedom that we can (for the time being) falsely identify a particular good with the absolute good and so evoke the appearance of evil, whereas once we have attained the fulness of freedom in the moment of death, and all specific 'this-worldly' goods have passed away, it will be quite impossible for us any longer to will anything except the sheer good in the absolute, and in that sense we shall be liberated in any case from the apparent evil, the appearance of evil? The transcendental appearance of evil will necessarily vanish with death, in which the factors on which such appearance rests themselves disappear. And even if on other grounds we cannot affirm any theory with regard to this redemptive function of death (though as a participation in the death of Christ it need not contradict the doctrine of the Redemption by Christ), still would it not be perfectly possible to hope that death will have this effect at the practical level?

Or do we have to say this: given that it is at least possible to draw these conclusions, and in fact difficult to resist drawing them, from the traditional doctrine of guilt and evil, they show that some false or exaggerated factor must lie concealed in the traditional premises, for these conclusions do follow more or less from the premises concerned, and yet at the same time the Christian conscience, convinced as it is of the radical nature of evil, protests against these conclusions leading to a demythologization of it? But how are we to attack these premises when, after all, they are not only strongly traditional, but seem to be quite inescapable unless we are to make God the cause of guilt or to take the line of Manichaeism or some other dualistic system? Are we to develop an ontology in which the 'reality' of evil is made clearer without thereby falling into a Manichaean dualism or projecting evil into the dimension of God himself?

Presumably – not to develop these points any further – the solution to this entire question must be sought from some different direction, so that we do not have to decide between the two tendencies with which we have been concerned up to now. As a quite general principle is there not, in the individual man and his knowledge, a pluralism of views which is too much for him to overcome, views, therefore, which cannot be brought into harmony in a higher synthesis? In this connection is it actually the case that we cannot even reduce these manifold branches of knowledge of ours, incapable as they are of being synthesized, into a single dialectical synthesis, because even this would still constitute an attempt to overcome their pluralism? If we can give an affirmative answer to this question, then we can go a step further. There are in man two fundamental experiences which provide the basis for two kinds of knowledge, and both are, in a real sense, incapable of being reconciled in a higher synthesis: the experience of the innermost state of being threatened by sin, the experience of the possibility of guilt on the one hand, and the experience of hope in a reality (called God and his grace) which can and will remove this guilt whether as a possibility or as an actuality on the other. These two basic experiences give rise inevitably to different interpretations. But we should not suppose that they are simply to be unified and reduced to a harmony by dialectical methods. This is not possible because both experiences, so far from representing opposite poles within a single order, which still remain static entities, have their place, rather, in a developing personal history of freedom which cannot, in any full or comprehensive sense, be the subject of conscious reflexive examination. It is not the case that everyone has, at every moment in his personal history, the same causes for fear, for trembling, or for hope. The changes in the theory are the necessary consequences of the personal history of both experiences. In those cases in which these experiences are made within the believing community of the Church, they are, of course, in some sense brought into a unity and reconciled with one another in their verbal presentation as an impartial dialectical doctrine which avoids all radical one-sidedness. But the moment we look into the matter more closely and examine more closely the terms that are used, it appears precisely that we are far from being able to achieve here a 'reconciliation' of such a kind that now a positive and fully intelligible synthesis is achieved between fear for salvation and hope for salvation. It appears that the traditional theory of guilt is really (at least to a predominant extent) a theology of guilt formulated from the standpoint of guilt. This does not mean that, by a process of conscious separation, this awareness of guilt, based on the experience of hope, can precisely be distinguished from the theology of guilt based on the experience of guilt. This is something that we can precisely not do, even though we can recognize that in this traditional theology of guilt an element of salvific optimism must lie concealed which derives not from the knowledge of guilt in itself but from the experience of hope as instilled by grace. We shall even be able to say that the Church neither can nor should develop any other theology of guilt than one of such a kind that hope has a decisive influence upon it if the Church as a whole and as holy is sustained by this hope and must by no means depart from this situation brought about by God. To this extent too it is not surprising that we have never really succeeded in the least in what we have said above in developing a clear counter-position by any truly theological process of reflection to the classic doctrine of guilt, a position which consists in something more than merely dumbly pointing to the experience of guilt itself and as inescapable. Only the classic theology of guilt must always remain aware of the fact that it cannot be an 'objectively' neutral theology of guilt. Rather it itself *ipso facto* includes the idea of Redemption from guilt by God even when it seems to be speaking only of guilt as such. And it must constantly remain aware of the fact that it speaks from this basis, and that it only remains valid provided it retains its openness to that desolation and darkness of guilt of which man too must still remain aware when, in a spirit of hope, he turns from it (as he must) so as to understand guilt in *that particular* light in which it stands when it is viewed in its relation to *God* and not in its relation to man. In guilt a reality is present which can be understood only on the basis of living practice, in which man hopes for something more than that which his theoretic reason can tell him about it. We should affirm the traditional doctrine of guilt in this sense and in no other, namely that, sustained by the grace of God that arises out of guilt, man lives in hope. Otherwise this traditional doctrine would indeed have the effect of representing guilt as innocuous. Otherwise we would be setting ourselves up wickedly and in mortally sinful arrogance so as to adopt the standpoint of God (whereas it is only the hope created by God, and this only in view of the very real existence of guilt, that enables us to adopt this standpoint). The only two courses open to us are either to live in that hope of forgiveness which we accept in freedom, *or* in the despair, freely admitted, to which guilt gives rise (even though we may not consciously advert either to the one attitude or to the other, as in fact we are *incapable* of consciously reflecting upon them in any full sense). We live, then, by either the one or the other basic decision upon which we can never consciously reflect in any full sense. For this reason too we cannot lay bare and examine every possible aspect of it in our theological calculations. And because of this any consciously worked-out theology of guilt must reflect either the one or the other basic decision (together with the process of consciously reflecting upon both attitudes as possible and as attempted). The classic theology of guilt, therefore, will presumably have to be viewed as a conscious reflection upon that hope of forgiveness in which guilt is in principle already overcome by God. For otherwise it would not be able to avoid the suspicion that it was representing guilt as innocuous. This of course is precisely not to say that it is possible for the Christian to develop a theology of guilt in which the factor of hope is eliminated. In theology too we remain those who have been redeemed by God's grace. For even the speculative reason has need of the compassion of God, and it is possible for it to have found this. Now on this showing we should so speak of guilt as the classic theology of guilt speaks of it, *so long as* in doing so we do nor forget the basis from which we speak, and we must make this standpoint from which we speak clear, seeing that freedom and its final and definitive character can be interpreted in a radical sense to the point of becoming a hypothetical atheism (in this way man can be free and this freedom of his can really create something final and definitive). But this radical interpretation may give rise to the impression that Christianity is representing human guilt as innocuous, at least in its consciously explicitated theology.

10

THEOLOGICAL OBSERVATIONS ON THE CONCEPT OF 'WITNESS'

I F we take the data of a Christian theology as a basis for an enquiry into the concept of 'witness', then presumably this approach should throw into relief certain special aspects and factors, even though precisely in *this* consideration what we have in mind is not an exegetical investigation but one which is based on dogmatics. Admittedly so far as the question of the nature of witness is concerned the data of a systematic Christian theology are (as will shortly appear) not so much the starting-point from which the enquiry will be conducted as the point to which it will lead up. Nevertheless this will not have any effect on the theological character of the considerations which follow.[1]

---

[1] The theological literature on the concept of 'witness' consists almost exclusively in exegesis and biblical theology (but cf. below K. Hemmerle). Alternatively it is concerned with the question of the difference and connection between the New Testament concept of witness and the idea found in early Christianity and in the Church of 'martyrdom'. Considerations of the concept of witness from the side of systematic theology, therefore, have to be sought in treatises on the theology of the word (on this cf. the author's remarks in the article 'Was ist ein Sakrament?', *Schriften zur Theologie* X (Einsiedeln, 1972), pp. 377–391 (to be translated in *Theological Investigations* XIV). While in Protestant theology an extensive literature is available on this, in Catholic theology there is no very wide coverage. Any attempt at supplying a full and precise list would exceed the limits of the present article. Only a few studies may be mentioned, which are directly concerned with the concept of 'witness' itself, and are either especially important, or have been published very recently. Earlier literature is to be found in N. Brox, *Zeuge und Märtyrer*. H. Strathmann, μάρτυς', *ThW* IV (Stuttgart, 1942), pp. 477–520; R. Koch, 'Witness', *Encyclopaedia of Biblical Theology* III (London, 1969), J. B. Bauer ed., pp. 976–985; E. Neuhäusler, 'Zeugnis in der Schrift', *LTK* X (Freiburg, 1965), cols. 1361 f.; N. Brox, 'Zeugnis', *HthG* II (Munich, 1963), pp. 903–911; G. Harbsmeier, *Ihr werdet meine Zeugen sein!*, Theol. Existenz Heute 8 (Munich, 1947); K. Rahner, *On the Theology of Death*, 2nd ed. (London, 1969); K. H. Rengstorff, *Die Auferstehung Jesu* (Witten, 4th ed., 1960) (Exkurs 3, Zum Begriff des Zeugen im Osterkerygma), pp. 136–145; N. Brox, *Zeuge und Märtyrer. Untersuchungen zur frühchristlichen Zeugnis-Terminologie*, Studien zum Alten und Neuen Testament V (Munich, 1961) (Bibliography, pp. 241–243). But the

It is true that 'witness' is a term which involves an intrinsic reference to someone else. Manifestly, however, it is also a term signifying not the imparting of some other *thing*, but rather that in which someone communicates himself, and, moreover, by the most intense use of his own freedom in so disposing of himself that thereby a corresponding decision is evoked in some other person too.[2] If 'witness' were concerned only with a *'something'*, then it would amount merely to a piece of information delivered by an expert on some specific topic, or an eye-witness's account of some occurrence which he had observed. In other words it would amount to evidence in a sense which is (ultimately) forensic. Now all this cannot be what is being referred to in any primary sense – at least not taken in isolation – when we speak of a bearing of witness in a religious sense. In this provisional description of witness we have not yet arrived at a stage at which it makes any notable difference whether or not we have already brought out with sufficient clarity that which constitutes the formal specification (the specific difference) of witness. Thus we are aware that our description might, in an extreme case, also be applied to functions of the human person which do not properly constitute witness, as, for instance, a totally committed love for another.

We are assuming straightway that the real factors included in this provisional description of witness do *de facto* exist: a man endowed with freedom and having power over his own self; the possibility of disposing

---

references contain some errors); U. Wilckens, *Die Missionsreden der ApG* (Neukirchen, 1961) (The 'Twelve' commissioned to act as witnesses, pp. 144–149); G. Stählin, 'Zum Gebrauch von Beteuerungsformeln im NT', *Novum Testamentum* 5 (1962), pp. 115–145 (The Synoptics and Paul); J. D. M. Derret, 'Law in the New Testament; The Story of the Woman Taken in Adultery', *NTS* 10 (1963), pp. 1–26 (on the juridical aspects of the concept of witness in the New Testament); R. Schnackenburg, *Die Johannesbriefe* (Freiburg, 2nd ed., 1963) (Exkurs 1: Sinn und Tragweite der 'Zeugen'-Aussagen von 1 Joh. 1:1 ff., pp. 52–58, and Exkurs 11: Das Gotteszeugnis und der Glaube, pp. 267–271); H. von Campenhausen, *Die Idee des Martyriums in der Alten Kirche* (Göttingen, 2nd ed., 1964); W. Bieder, *Segnen und Bekennen. Eine biblische und historische Studie* (Basle, 1965); N. Brox, *Der Glaube als Zeugnis* (Munich, 1966); K. Bornkamm, *Wunder und Zeugnis* (Tübingen, 1968); H. Fries, *Heraufgeforderte Glaube* (Munich, 1968); T. Lippert, *Leben als Zeugnis*, Stuttgarter biblische Monographien 4 (Stuttgart, 1969) (The Pastoral Epistles, 1 Peter); K. Hemmerle, 'Wahrheit und Zeugnis', *Theologie als Wissenschaft*, Quaest. Disp. 45 (Freiburg, 1970) (Systematic and Philosophical Aspects of 'Witness' in its Bearing on the Question of Truth).

[2] cf. the ideas of the Second Vatican Council on Revelation as self-communication on God's part in 'Dei Verbum', The Dogmatic Constitution on Divine Revelation No 2, and the ideas of witness, *ibid.*, No. 3.

of himself in an ultimate and 'absolute' sense so far as the concrete conditions of human life are concerned (or at least the power to attempt this
in the hope that at any rate within the course of a lifetime the man concerned will actually succeed in achieving it); the significance of an ultimate
understanding of himself in freedom for some other man as well; the
possibility of so using this power of self-determination as to achieve
contact with another, to make himself 'intelligible'; the character which
such communication has as a summons or appeal; the understanding of
such communication by the other leading to a state in which each party is
orientated towards the other, a state which must ultimately be called love.
Let us take all this as established for our present purposes, and leave any
further consideration to the philosophers to work out in an existential
ontology.

Our intention here is to throw light upon a few specifically theological
implications of the (provisional) description given above. For once these
have been explicitated, they can enable us to understand the specifically
theological sense of 'witness' which belongs to it absolutely and necessarily. Nor do we fear, in using this method of arriving at a specifically
theological concept, the reproach that philosophy is seeking to produce a
specifically theological concept on its own authority, and thereby doing
damage to itself and to theology. For by this approach it will also be
possible to make clear the point at which a certain reality of human life
begins; a reality, namely, in which, as a matter either of hypothesis or of
actual experience, an experience accessible at the level of philosophical
insight is elevated to a higher level on the basis of a transcendental experience. Now since this reality which we are pointing to is arrived at by a
process of transcending and radicalizing man's own experience of himself, it must not be excluded from a philosophical view merely on the
grounds that it belongs to theology – in other words that what it stands for
is precisely that which Christian faith expresses as a reality graciously
bestowed upon man by God, and understands to be supernatural revelation. Theology does not begin only at that point at which we begin to
study the scriptural sources of revelation (Scripture and Church tradition). On the contrary, it has already begun at that point at which, prior
to any such positive studies, man attains to such *de facto* realities in his
own reflections upon himself, realities which – whether reflected upon or
not, or reflected upon precisely *as such* or not – are already constituted,
amongst other things, by that which Christian theology calls grace. The
fact that there is a grace of this kind, which modifies the actual *awareness*
of man (and, moreover, as an abiding existential of human life) – this is a

point that a Molinist might possibly deny. A genuine Thomist cannot do so. On the contrary he must concede that theology (as the process of reflecting upon realities and experiences which are grace-given and inspired by the Spirit) is already present incipiently and in principle at the very heart of philosophy (considered as the process of reflecting upon man's own experience, which does not allow any external limits to be imposed upon it).

In witness man exercises his freedom at the most ultimate level of which he is capable of directing himself. In doing so it is of course conceivable that this process of directing himself in freedom may, in the individual case, be prior to the act by which it is communicated in the word of witness to another.[3] But if we assume (as we may assume here) that even the truest form of subjectivity as realized in freedom still always consists in an encounter with a being outside oneself (and, moreover, ultimately speaking not a thing outside but a person outside oneself) in which one receives that person and gives oneself to him, if subjectivity essentially consists in intercommunication, then in the last analysis witness is not a *subsequent* declaration of a basic decision which the subject has previously taken about himself, but rather is in itself the concrete form of this decision. In saying this there is a further question which can remain unresolved for our present purposes, the question namely of whether every decision which a human subject takes about himself, and in which he directs himself towards another, must be called witness, or whether such an act of decision in which he communicates himself should be called witness only provided certain further specific conditions are fulfilled, and the act concerned has certain specific properties. But regarded as a disposing of the subject's own self, and as such a process in which freedom acts upon itself, witness necessarily takes place as an act of self-transcendence in which the subject reaches up to the unsurpassable and sovereign Mystery

---

[3] Viewed from a purely tempora laspect, this can actually be accounted the normal state of affairs. But this does not alter the fact that witness is, after all, precisely not a mere subsequent announcement of a pre-existing reality which would still exist even without this announcement, and which has no intrinsic connection with it. The space of time during which an individual comes to his own fulness should not obscure the intrinsic unity of that through which the essence of this fulfilment is, in a real sense, constantly present in all sections of time in which it takes place. We encounter this phenomenon frequently in theology. Baptism is the sacrament of faith in which this faith is itself posited, and yet the baptized person normally comes to baptism with this faith already present in him. The sacrament of penance is the event of *metanoia* and conversion to God, and yet it presupposes that the *metanoia* which is made full and declared in the sacrament has already been present prior to it.

which we call God.[4] Transcendence as knowledge and freedom is always that openness, deriving from the Mystery itself (we distinguish it, therefore, from the idealism of an autonomous subject) to that Mystery beyond all comprehension which exceeds every experience of a conceivable 'subject', but constitutes the condition enabling knowledge to be achieved of 'classifiable' subjects. It is the openness to this Mystery as the basis of knowledge and reality both at the same time, this Mystery which we call God. Now given that this movement (initially, of course, not consciously reflected upon or explicitated, yet present in any and every act of cognition as that which makes it possible) towards the Mystery is sustained and empowered by that Mystery itself, it is necessarily open to the question of *how far* this Mystery allows itself to be attained to by the movement it initiates and sustains. Is it *merely* that which remains forever remote, forever forbidding, the asymptotic point towards which is orientated a movement which, while it does indeed proceed *outwards to* the infinite, nevertheless remains forever enclosed within the finite? Or does this movement contain the promise in which we hope that this Mystery bestows itself as itself (while remaining incomprehensible to us) to be, in a true sense, a *goal* which will be attained, and therefore even as itself sustains this movement from within itself? Christianity is a religion which acknowledges precisely *this* hope, regarded as an explicit theme, as the centre of its faith. It calls this goal, as we have understood it here, the *visio beatifica*, and that factor which sustains the movement from within and directs it towards *this particular* goal is called grace (*Pneuma*). Man can make this hope his own, and for this he finds within himself an inner power and (albeit never as something which he can fully reflect upon or realize) an enlightenment (called the grace of faith), and he seizes upon that in which this hope is actually fulfilled in exemplary form in the historical experience of Jesus of Nazareth. The experience of the Christ event in Jesus may or may not be achieved at a fully conscious level. But in any case it remains true that where the transcendental movement of the Spirit is unreservedly accepted it constitutes (according to the Christian interpretation of it) a movement sustained by God himself outwards towards the immediacy of

[4] This statement, and the considerations which follow, can of course be nothing more than brief indications within the present context. We say that the (human) spirit endowed with knowledge and freedom implies a limitless transcendentality, and that this transcendentality (as opened up from the basis of being regarded as mystery) implies an affirmation of the infinite Mystery which we call God. But this and much else besides can merely be asserted here without our being able to attempt any more precise explanation or justification. On this, however, cf., in the present volume, the observations on the subject of 'Thomas Aquinas on Truth'.

God, because it *de facto* and inescapably has as its intrinsic principle God himself. And this remains true even as we recognize that this state of being sustained, this openness of human transcendence to the immediacy of the absolute Mystery, is to be interpreted as (supernatural) 'grace' and as 'unmerited'. In those cases, therefore, in which 'witness' is achieved in the sense indicated in our provisional description (and so as an act of self-determination in which man positively and unconditionally accepts that which is within himself), there also takes place invariably and in all cases so far as Christianity is concerned the event of grace, the acceptance of this grace, the movement outwards towards the immediacy of God regardless of whether this is explicitly reflected upon or not. Witness is *de facto* a grace-given event, or it is not really witness at all. In this connection we are assuming that it can be present only in those cases in which man accepts himself in it unconditionally, and so bears witness to *himself* as he is. We are assuming, therefore, that the attempt, for instance, to attest the absolute absurdity of existence can be one of two things: first it can be regarded as no witness at all, seeing that man cannot introduce himself into his own witness in any way he likes, cannot interpret himself in any way he likes (is not the absolute creator of himself, but always proceeds from something previously offered him, always takes up his attitude *towards* something which he himself has not posited); or second, his false interpretation of himself is false only on the surface (which is perfectly possible), is merely the mistaken objectification of an original act of self-interpretation which, ultimately speaking and in its innermost depths, is, nevertheless, successful. In other words precisely *in it* there can be a witness for one who can distinguish between the witness itself and him who bears it. Witness, therefore, is, precisely inasmuch as it seeks to communicate the bearer of witness in his act of self-interpretation to his fellow, a bearing of witness of God himself as him who communicates himself in grace and offers himself as the subject of a direct relationship. Witness is an attestation of the grace of God whether this is consciously realized or not, whether it is objectified and expressed verbally or not. The imparting of oneself in witness to one's fellow constitutes, if it is really achieved (i.e. if it consists in an act of unreserved self-acceptance in the transcendence which is *de facto* elevated by grace to a higher plane), a witness of God himself. Any explicit statements about God (such as can of course arise in witness, though they do not necessarily have to) are merely the objectification in words of an ultimate depth which is always present in witness. The witness is always a theological one. What is different is simply the degree of conscious objectification of this theological character inherent in *every* witness, even though, as it has been presented in the provisional description with which we began, it appeared quite untheological and merely anthropological in character. This witness, therefore, can be Christian in an 'anonymous' sense. It can be an *'anony-mous'* fulfilment of human nature in which man reaches out to God,[5] and so (because sustained by God's self-bestowal = grace) salvific. But it is always (at least at the subconscious level) Christian. It would, of course, be advisable at this point to describe in greater detail the forms of witness of anonymous Christianity as they arise in concrete history, and also their specific content, if we were able to do so. For instance a commitment to sheer self-sacrifice for the sake of social justice; the unreserved champion-ing of truth and one's own genuine personal convictions. With regard to a witness of anonymous Christianity of this kind, we should guard against the criticism that any such Christian and theological interpretation of this kind of witness runs counter to the repeatedly declared intention and the (verbal) self-interpretation of him who bears the witness in this way. But all these are questions which cannot be entered into any further in the present context. Witness is directed towards *someone else*. The one bearing the witness seeks to communicate himself to *him*. Is this possible? What this question is concerned with is not the problems in the forefront, of how, and by what means, one person can communicate himself to another, or the question of how any such thing can be possible seeing that after all he who bears witness in this way can only impart, communicate, or bear witness in words *about* himself and, furthermore, ultimately speaking, can only communicate some objectified message, even if this message which is to be the medium of his self-giving consists in gestures and acts belonging to his own physical nature. Such questions as to the possibility of witness in the sense incipiently described above are certainly important too in enabling us to understand how such communication of self is possible. But we shall not concern ourselves with them here because they are questions concerning the process of imparting or communicating oneself, and not questions concerning witness in itself and the specific and ultimate possibility of this. Here we are assuming *the fact that* there can be such self-communication, which is realized in witness, or at least (to express it more cautiously) that it is possible to form the purpose, and make the claim of bringing such self-communication to reality. (In this connection, again, it makes no immediate difference *here* whether such self-imparting

---

[5] On this cf. 'Bemerkungen zum Problem des "anonymen Christen" ', *Schriften zur Theologie* X (Einsiedeln, 1972), pp. 531–546 (to be translated in *Theological Investigations* XIV).

is achieved precisely and exclusively in witness, or, for instance, whether it is achieved primarily in the love between two individuals, or whether there are very different kinds and modes of such self-communication. What we are presupposing for our present consideration is simply that such self-communication is achieved at least in witness too, and in this in a specific manner.) Now that we have demarcated the question in this way, it seems that we are justified in arriving at the following conclusion about it: If we are to say that there can in any sense be such self-communication on the part of a person endowed with freedom, unique in each individual case, a self-communication that is of its nature unrepeatable and incapable of being fully realized at the conscious level, then this can be only to the extent that both sides to this relationship have an ultimate bond of love with the one God, who, as the single and selfsame ground of these unique and, in themselves, incommensurable individualities, at once affirms them in their difference, unites them as providing their common basis, and sustains and guarantees the absolute character of their (mutual) self-communication. When an individual commits himself to his fellow absolutely, though in himself, in view of the finitude of his nature and the threats to which he is subject from forces within himself, he cannot guarantee the absolute character of this commitment, then, whether he recognizes it consciously or not, he is *ipso facto* appealing in hope to the one sustaining and reconciling basis of all free and unique acts. Witness, inasmuch as it is directed to another, and that too in an unconditional commitment[6] to this other, is, whether we realize it consciously or not, theological in character. It is sustained by that which, in Christian terms, is called 'grace', i.e. through the self-bestowal of the one God upon both of the two finite individuals who have achieved union with one another. And in this way the ultimate union between them, and at the same time the difference between them, are both assured, and God is made the interior

---

[6] It might be objected that so far as the witness of truth and his claims are concerned, it makes no difference, ultimately speaking, whether he is hearkened to or not. But it is precisely an intrinsic part of his 'martyrdom' to maintain his witness, despite contradiction, even to death. This is correct. But a witness which did not involve the hope, despite all disappointments, really to take effect and to be hearkened to, would be giving up its own nature in respect of its truth and its universal claims. The witness must necessarily hope that the contradiction which he encounters will be merely temporary. In him who bears witness, therefore, there is always a tendency, in the expression of the truth which he is bearing witness to in concrete human life, to reach out to a point at which that truth will be accepted by the hearer as well. The one bearing the witness, therefore, seeks himself to be assented to and accepted in the truth he proclaims.

principle of their mutual relationship. Of course we can conceive of a relationship between two individuals, and it can be such that it does not have God as its intrinsic constitutive principle. But to the extent that this relationship constantly tends to an absolute proximity and ultimate validity, and hopes to have attained to this at a radical level and as a real fact (precisely through God), God is (whether explicitly or implicitly) incidentally asserted as the intrinsic principle of this relationship. In this respect too witness has a theological character.

Of course witness always has also and necessarily a content 'classifiable in terms of this-worldly categories'.[7] In witness man can commit himself in his ultimate free decision to his fellow only in that he says a 'something'

---

[7] It is true that fairly explicit consideration has already been given to these points in the context of different key concepts in Christian theology (e.g. under the heading of 'Proofs of God's existence', in the light of the limitless transcendentality of man, or in the context of the idea of the radical unity between love of God and love of man). At the same time, however, it is probably true that hardly any explicit consideration has been given in Christian theology to the points which follow. Death in general and the death of Christ in particular have hardly been considered at all in the light of an existential ontology. Death in general is first and foremost a biological event, and the standard theology constructs a genuine interpretation of the death of Christ by regarding it from the outset as a moral act on Jesus' part, supposing that this could just as well have been achieved in a different way and still have had a salvific significance. Of course here we can provide no more than an indication of the intrinsic connection between a final and 'eschatological' revelation (and, together with this, its attestation) on the one hand, and the event of the death of him who was essentially the last of the prophets and the bringer of eschatological salvation on the other. When we speak of the 'blessed' death, we are referring to the death which, by the very fact of being undergone, leads to that which in Christian terms we call the 'resurrection'. By this term we are seeking to bring out as clearly as possible the intrinsic unity between death and resurrection, and, moreover, in such a way that death does not appear as a mere misfortune to be made good once more by 'resurrection'. When in what follows we interpret witness as the attestation of God's gracious imparting of himself, and for this purpose determine the content of this witness in terms of specific 'this-worldly' categories as a witness of death, then obviously we have still not arrived at any decision as to whether this bearing witness to death has to present its content explicitly and in so many words as death. The 'anonymous' forms of Christian witness already envisaged above do not, of course, need to bear witness in so explicit and conscious a sense to a blessed death as we would wish to work out in view of the full form of witness in the full realization of its own nature. The absolute and unconditional nature of the resolve, taken in hope, in virtue of which witness is borne even at the cost of endangering one's life can perfectly well take the form of an 'anonymous' (taking place in the hope of some other outcome) attestation to the blessedness of death, even when it has not yet been realized as a matter of conscious historical experience where this blessed death that is hoped for has occurred or will occur.

to that fellow. This gives rise to the question of what the nature of this particular and specific content of witness must be in order that it can constitute the content, classifiable in terms of specific categories, of a *self-commitment* to the other in which on the one hand the individual bearing witness commits *himself* in the totality of his free existence, while on the other, thereby and therein (whether consciously or unconsciously) he bears witness to the reality of the Mystery which commits itself to man, and which is called God. Manifestly this content, classifiable in terms of specific categories, cannot in any *primary* sense be an objectification in verbal form of the original transcendentality as opened up by God's grace to an immediate relationship with God, and accepted as such in freedom. Certainly something like this is possible, as, for instance *here*, in the present consideration, and as in every explicitly religious statement.[8] But this cannot be the first and primary content. For otherwise the only possible forms of witness would be statements which were explicitly and *ex professo* religious in subject-matter. Up to now we have consistently proceeded from the opposite assumption, because we have been seeking to discover the theological character of witness in a line of investigation which seems to be merely at the human level, and which we began by evaluating as a provisional description of witness. But how can the content of a witness of this kind be constituted, classifiable in terms of specific categories, and still not in any sense pertaining to a consciously religious statement? It must (without on this account *ipso facto* having to constitute a consciously religious statement at the secondary level) point on to that transcendentality which gives a statement the force of witness. If we look at the history of revelation in the Old and New Testaments we might very quickly come to the conclusion that the content of this as assignable to particular categories is related to the deeds of power wrought in history by God, who in them manifests himself as the bringer of salvation. This piece of information may be formally speaking correct, but it does nothing to solve the problem with which we are here confronted. For how is any historical event of this kind, expressible in terms of 'this-worldly' categories, to be recognized precisely *as* a deed of God? To this question we might seek to reply with the usual answer supplied by traditional theology, namely that it is in virtue of the fact that the salvific deed of power wrought by God in history is a *miracle*, or is accompanied by a miracle. But this would merely be to shift the question to a different level

---

[8] The necessity of an explicitly religious statement, and precisely the statement here being questioned, does not need to be treated of from different points of view, though of course we are in no sense either disputing it or trifling with it.

without solving it. Presumably too such a reply would constitute merely a piece of information applicable to the purely formal and abstract concept of revelation as such, but not capable of working out that which is specific to the New Testament revelation in Christ. A further point is that on these assumptions, and in the face of this reply, it might reasonably be asked whether on this showing there could be any basis at all for an *absolute* witness in the sense of a genuinely achieved absolute relationship between him who attests and him to whom his message is addressed (even if such a witness can in itself be assumed to have taken place without any such basis). The appeal to some kind of miracle is questionable in view of the difficulty of recognizing it as such (if it is to be regarded as some kind of occurrence assignable to a particular 'this worldly' category), and in view of its function as providing a basis for an *absolute*[9] witness. It could have significance only in connection with a *hope*, not yet established on any adequate basis, in a manifestation still to emerge in history, which subsequently enables us to apprehend the basis for an absolute witness of this kind in history as definable in terms of particular categories. The content of a witness classifiable in these terms, which attests the absolute immediacy of God as a grace that is posited in history, is thereby intended to enable man, by an exercise of his own freedom, radically to give himself to his fellow. Now this content of witness can only consist (in the 'order' in which this self-comminication on God's part is not of itself simply or absolutely manifest, so that it no longer needs any witness bearing to it) in a reference to an event of this kind, in which an individual, in all the reality of his effective human life (and not merely in some ideological 'interior' dimension and attitude) radically makes himself over to God, and in which this giving of himself is seen to be achieved by God's own acceptance of it. In other words the particular and 'this worldly' content of witness at this radical level can consist only in the proclamation of that death which, as it takes place, leads to the absolute life of God. Only a death of this kind, as 'accepted' by God, can be something more than an event of self-transcendence as sustained by God (though in fact we do intend to express this in witness). Also, and more than this, it consists in the fact that the actual achievement of such self-transcendence is

[9] As used in this context 'absolute' simply means: a witness for a final eschatologically victorious and unsurpassable self-communication on God's part as that which constitutes (albeit 'unmerited' and so grace-given) the radical fulfilment of that transcendentality which man represents, which he possesses, which as freely affirmed in the witness given to his fellow, is itself attested to. Cf. on the whole question the author's study in the present volume, 'Ideas for a Theology of Death'.

made apprehensible to us.[10] For all the 'this-worldly' positivity of a human event, it can indeed perfectly well (whether explicitated or not) be the process by which such self-transcendence is achieved (because in fact it takes place in the power of that God, that Mystery which human transcendence positively affirms in knowledge and freedom). But precisely because of this positivity and in it, such an event cannot enable it to be *made manifest* that the process is intended precisely *as* self-transcendence, and the transcendentality of this event constitutes something more than the enabling condition and the means by which such a process in its free intention seeks *merely* to achieve a reality definable in 'this-worldly' categories, and to achieve the immanent meaning of this. The acknowledgement of that death which has been blessed with happiness constitutes the content, assignable to a specific category, of a witness which, in respect of God and the individual personhood of him who bears the witness, is intended to be absolute. Of course this transcendental deduction of the content is not a deduction of the death of *Jesus* at this death which is sought as the source of blessedness. This belongs to the concrete event in which this content is realized, something, therefore, which remains at the historical level, and does not *have to be* so as a matter of transcendental necessity. Nor do we seek to maintain by this deductive argument that it would *de facto* take place without the historical encounter with the death of Jesus. But neither of these two factors in any sense changes the insight that a witness at the radical level can have its content as assignable to a specific category only in our acknowledgement of a death that brings us into the immediate presence of God, so long as such a witness needs to have any such content assigned to it at all.

We have said that witness is directed towards one's fellow. Now (in order to simplify the matter) let us make this more precise. Him to whom the witness is addressed is one's fellow not in his private individuality, but one's fellow to the extent that he exists in the life of society, to the extent that he is a 'political' being. Witness has a political character. It is public proclamation. If witness were directed to one's fellow as an individual person, and to the extent that he is, in any given case, that particular, unique,

---

[10] Of course in a fuller development of the idea the distinction, and at the same time the connection, would have to be described more precisely. The witness borne to the blessed death which is not itself a death of the one who bears the witness, and the witness of the assent of him who bears the witness to this death in a spirit of faith and hope. To the extent that the latter element too belongs to witness, even though *de facto* it may also be lacking in a process which claims to be witness, it can come to be present in the false forms of witness in the individual 'bearer of witness' which still await discussion.

and private individual, or to the extent that he does not represent the whole multitude of society at large, over and above any value we may attach to him as an individual, this self-communication would be that which we call love, or a pairing off at the purely biological level. Witness as such has a public and political character. This statement is initially simply a definition of terms. We call witness simply that which has a public character (and that which, to this extent, has a material affinity with witness in a strictly forensic sense). A transcendental necessity is to be ascribed to this statement (but then in a genuine sense) only to the extent that on the one hand man is in all cases a political and social being, and yet on the other precisely *as* such one which is no less invariably always unique and different from all the rest in his free individuality. Belonging to a society, and being unique and different from all others in free individuality are not two 'qualities' of man existing side by side with one another, but are present as mutually complementary, as (ontological) transcendentals in the scholastic sense. They are, in their relationship to one another, not one and the same, and yet at the same time they are inconceivable in isolation from one another. And to that extent the subject of the summons which we call witness and the one to whom it is addressed can express themselves and accept each other by listening to its message in a unique decision of freedom, and thereby act precisely *as* political beings. But then we have precisely that which we call witness, with all the qualities which we have hitherto claimed that witness has, whenever and wherever it really has realized its full nature. The public and social character of this witness is, by a special inter-involvement, that of the 'world' and that of the 'Church'. 'World', because, and to the extent that, this witness appears as a 'claimant', i.e. one who demands agreement and who essentially incurs the risk of remaining unheeded and being rejected. In other words it is addressed in public to another who can also be one who rejects this witness and is called the 'world' in the sense usually intended in Christian terminology in that here it is (rightly) assumed that in principle all men can and must be summoned by this witness, i.e. this witness cannot be regarded as having, in the fulness of its nature, a particular application, but constitutes, rather, a universal message. Wherever, by contrast, this witness is expressed and also hearkened to, something is constituted in him who bears the witness and him who hearkens to it (because both attitudes are public ones) which we here call (employing the same terminology) the 'Church'.

To the extent that the content of witness as classifiable in terms of 'this-worldly' categories is in its full nature the historical event of the

death of Jesus as blessed and as leading to God, it can, as a factor in concrete human life, only be realized aright when he who bears the witness
has in principle decided to accept his own death. The spirit of faith and
hope that one's own death will lead blessedly into the freedom and se-
curity of God's presence constitutes the mode in which alone witness is
possible. To that extent there is a real and effective connection between the
act of bearing witness to the truth and 'martyrdom'. For that which (in
terms of content) is attested in witness is (from a Christian point of view)
nothing else than the belief that this death has, in Jesus, achieved its goal
and the hope of the witness himself that in his own death he will be able to
follow after the dying Jesus. Now this necessarily involves the will to
incur the risk of this death, and, moreover, precisely as something occa-
sioned by the witness itself, to take upon oneself the act of 'martyrdom'.
The development which takes place, starting from the New Testament
idea of witness which does not yet (explicitly) contain the idea of a
'witness of the blood', leading to the concept of witness of the early
Church in which death (as freely accepted) is itself regarded as witness, is
therefore perfectly legitimate. For the truth which is attested to in the
verbal witness of Christianity is precisely the truth of death as constituting
salvation.

In Luke a witness is essentially a witness to the 'Resurrection', and,
moreover, an 'eye-witness' who as such has an 'official' position and a
special function. Now on this showing we must notice this point as something that follows directly from what has been said so far: every (Christian)
witness must bear witness not merely to the blessedness of death which we
await and hope for (and so the 'resurrection') in general, but must also
include in its concrete and specific content precisely the blessedness of the
death of Jesus. And to this extent such a witness, whenever it is borne, and
whatever authority and power is attached to it, is related to the 'eye-
witnesses' of the origins, without whom we could never assign to that
blessedness of death which we await and hope for the historical name of
Jesus. But in saying this we are not saying at the same time that this
witness handed down through history of the Resurrection of Jesus is
exclusively, or taken in isolation, the sustaining basis for the witness of
faith of subsequent generations and of Christian belief. For the credibility
of this historical witness ('the Lord is risen indeed') is itself sustained by
the transcendental expectation of resurrection which is inherent in man's
basic attitude. It is because (whether he explicitates it to himself or not) he
entertains a hope for himself, for his own final and definitive state – in
other words for the blessedness of his own death – that he has 'ears' to

hear this witness to an historical fact. A further factor is that this transcendental and inalienable hope (albeit either accepted or rejected in freedom) in the possibility of achieving blessedness in human death is always present. Moreover this hope recognizes that sooner or later in history it either has become, or will become, a real fact, and because of this and to this extent too, all such hope and the witness borne to it is 'Jesus-orientated'.

From what has been said it becomes clear what is involved (chiefly in the Johannine theology of the New Testament) in the witness borne from within oneself, and in its attestation by the Spirit. The very nature of the reality involved is such as not to admit of any justification or authentication of the witness from without. Witness involves a total human act (albeit one that is specified with reference to the world at large). And this can neither be authenticated by any factor outside itself, nor consist of a combination of individual acts or elements such that this combination could be justified by the individual elements making it up. For the first hypothesis is ruled out by the totality of the act involved inasmuch as it lays claim to the whole man and therefore does not admit of anything 'outside'. The second hypothesis is equally impossible, if only because freedom as the all-embracing self-comprehension of man, constitutes, despite all the plurality of the elements making it up, precisely the original unity and not the final result of the plurality which is in man. We are not maintaining, in what has been said, that this act constitutes sheer self-identity, or that it does not have within it any pluralism of constitutive elements which are irreducible one to another. Hence, of course, there is an *intrinsic* connection in that they have a common basis, and a mutual reference of the elements of such an act one to another. Hence, we may notice in passing, such a discipline as a fundamental theology is, if rightly understood, perfectly possible even if it does not construct the act of faith from without but makes its subject the intrinsic self-basis of this act in the mutual reference to one another of the elements constituting it. Witness is borne for the attester and the hearer themselves, and there are two reasons for this. First, it constitutes the movement of the spirit in knowledge and freedom in all its limitless, all-embracing, and radicalized breadth, comprising that which is at once self-evident and beyond our apprehension (incomprehensible), and it supplies its own authentication. Second, the content of this witness as assignable to 'this-worldly' categories contains nothing else than precisely the blessed acceptance of this limitless breadth as the salvation of man. The fact that this content is interpreted in Christian terms as Jesus of Nazareth and as his victorious death of course accounts for the factor of 'uncertainty' and of hazardousness which is inherent in every historical event where it is taken as the medium through which freedom reaches out to that which is transcendentally necessary. But on this point the Christian does not really need to say anything more than 'to whom else shall we go?'. And he can point to the fact that according to the witness of many consciences freedom's leap outwards towards the transcendental necessity is achieved in this name, and therefore this name in history can be appealed to in the witness. The breadth of human transcendentality, freed from all limits and radicalized (i.e. vivified by the hope of the immediacy of God), which carries its own authentication within itself because it is, and *ex definitione* can have no basis outside itself, is called, in Christian terminology, the state of being engraced and sustained by the Holy Spirit. In Christian terms, therefore, we can say that, as a witness affected by the Spirit, a witness is true and authenticated in itself. As such is also renders the specific and concrete content of this witness credible. God himself bears witness to himself in the witness. And only in this selfsame grace can it be hearkened to and accepted.

As a free and autonomous act of the individual bearing witness, the witness calls upon the freedom of the hearer. Because, and to the extent that, this witness has a specific content, classifiable in terms of 'this-worldly' categories, and thereby 'locates' the ultimate autonomous act of man in history, and since too it constitutes an appeal to the freedom of the other, it also brings to concrete and apprehensible form in history the ultimate decision of that other about himself. At the same time, however, it must be admitted that this objectification, as achieved in this sense in specific and historical terms, of a total free decision in accepting or rejecting the message attested to, contains an ultimate ambivalence or ambiguity within it. Thus for instance the concrete historical form in which rejection is manifested does not yield any absolute certainty of the fact that this rejection has also really been made at the heart and centre of the person endowed with freedom. And for this reason we cannot 'judge' him at this point. With this proviso, however, we can say that the effect of the witness is to lay bare the hostility with which the individual appealed to responds to God's self-communication to him, as made known to him in the witness. To that extent the witness has a revelatory character with regard to the 'sins of the world'.

There are two further points to be made about the witness: first that it constitutes the ('one') event of God's self-communication to man, and second that, as an event to which a concrete name can be assigned ('Jesus') it remains related to the historical series of those who bear witness to the

'Resurrection' of Jesus. And for both of these reasons this witness (precisely as it is presented in the Lucan theology) constitutes the bridge between the age of Jesus and his 'return', and at the same time is *ipso facto* truly eschatological in character. For the eschatological event of the self-communication of God is already present in faith and hope, and already apprehensible in the witness that has been uttered and hearkened to in history. Nevertheless the witness points us on to the future, to the unveiled immediacy of God, at the consummation of the world and of human freedom, which at present is still 'in course of development'.

What has been said about the unveiled form in which the witness is accepted also applies, of course, to the actual process of giving witness as apprehensible at the historical and social levels. Even while preaching to others, we can ourselves become castaways. Admittedly, in this case which Paul emphasizes, the witness too is not such as it is presented to be. For in fact in the very act of uttering the witness man should be surrendering himself to the Mystery of existence which we call God. This surrender can be lacking. The witness of the individual can be a lie to the extent that this making over of man to the God of grace as an act of concrete human living can *de facto* be wanting. But in that case this witness too is itself no true witness. The 'objective' validity which the Christian interpretation nevertheless ascribes to it, even when it fails to correspond to the interior attitude of the individual who proclaims it, is intelligible only if we recognize clearly that this witness takes place within a society precisely *as* a witness of this society which also as a whole effectively fulfils the witness which it bears. 'Holy Church' is, as Christians understand it, that which ensures that its witness (even when borne by an 'unworthy' individual) is a true witness, i.e. makes real that which it attests.

Of course, as in human discourse in general so too with witness, there are not only the full form and the radical realization of the very nature of witness, but also derived and deficient modes of witness. Religious or moral instruction, theological discourse, etc. are derived modes of witness, but still deficient ones, not even coming close to witness itself. This is all the more true since such religious discourses, which, for the most varied reasons, cannot be called witness in the true sense, nevertheless would be deprived of any meaning at all, or become statements belonging to the science of religion at the secular level without any concrete bearing on human life, if every element of witness were to be eliminated from them.

11

IDEAS FOR A THEOLOGY OF DEATH

IF the theologian is to follow the philosopher, the psychologist, and the physician in having something to say about death and dying, he will find himself in great difficulties,[1] and, moreover, for a whole variety of reasons. However normal and everyday an occurrence dying and death may seem to be, no one can have anything to say about them as a result of having actually undergone dying and death, as a matter of his own physical and spiritual experience. For even the experience of being in danger of death, whether from internal or external causes, does not provide any guarantee of the fact that this experience is substantially the same as that which is undergone by one in whom this state of mortal need really does lead to death itself. In this respect the theologian too is no more an expert so far as dying and death are concerned than the rest. A further difficulty, this time affecting the theologian precisely as such, is that what he has to say about death in particular, as distinct from the other specialists, is in any case more withdrawn from everyday experience than what the other experts have to report. For this reason his message is most of all liable to the suspicion of being mythology, a fantasy designed to provide false consolation, and mere empty talk. A further factor in the difficulties with which the theologian finds himself surrounded is the fact that the question of what he has to say about death as such, and the further question of 'survival after death', the 'immortality of the soul', 'eternal life' as attained to through the 'resurrection of the flesh' constitute two questions which in themselves are very different, but which cannot be treated of apart here because otherwise the impression might be given that the theologian is here speaking of death as such and taken in isolation, in

[1] The author has already published earlier studies under similar titles. Cf. *On the Theology of Death* (2nd ed., Eng. transl., 1969). In the foreword to this work some references will be found to important earlier studies on the question. Cf. also in this volume 'Theological Observations on the Concept of "Witness" '.

order to avoid the question of what, according to his convictions, will become of man 'after' and 'beyond' death.[2] But if he regards it as his task to discuss both questions at once, his subject-matter will become immeasurably obscure and ill-defined. One further and final point is that each of these two questions in its turn involves a whole series of further particular questions, questions of biblical theology, history of dogma, history of theology, philosophy, and existential ontology – questions, therefore, which are, again, totally incapable of being answered directly or unambiguously within the terms of any system of Christian theology or according to the particular interpretation of faith upheld by any Church. The result is that the individual theologian is forced to take personal responsibility for many statements which he makes on such particular questions, even though in himself he is not seeking in any way to go beyond a simple statement of the beliefs of Christianity and of the Church, and, indeed, of an immense tradition in human thinking which, for all the variations introduced by the use of conceptual models drawn from mythology, are ultimately all pointing to one and the same reality.

In this situation, then, beset as he is with difficulties, the theologian has no other course open to him than to seize upon certain aspects of the matter, chosen somewhat arbitrarily. Such a course may involve an intermingling of philosophical and theological propositions, principles which are, in a real sense, held in common by all the Churches as well as individual interpretations of such principles, and all this may take place without always being explicitly adverted to. But there is simply no way of avoiding this, a point which we must explicitly emphasize here right at the outset. And a further point, likewise following from the situation as it exists, is that the approach we are adopting cannot be one in which we explicitly quote passages from the writings of the Old and New Testaments, or refer to declarations of the Church's teaching authority. One final proviso: when the sceptic hears the message of faith and hope concerning a definitive finality of human existence which man will arrive at through death as the outcome of the history of his personal freedom, let him not be too hasty or too prejudiced from the outset in suspecting that the theologian is being moved by some personal egoism of his own, or is being excessively naïve and taking things too much for granted in setting such a value on 'eternal life'. One factor alone which might deter the theologian from doing this is what he finds in the earlier strata of the Old Testament itself. On the one hand it records how a living partnership,

[2] For a concise survey cf. the author's article, 'Death', *Sacramentum Mundi* II (New York and London, 1968), pp. 58–62.

finding expression in prayer and trust, was forged between the individual and the God of the covenant of his people. And on the other, despite this fact, any real prospect of a positive fulfilment of individual life after death is as good as totally ruled out for this same individual so far as these earlier stages of Old Testament history are concerned. It may be true that the individual stages in a history of revelation are not interchangeable with one another and, in the unilinear development of sacred history, no one of them ever recurs or is really the same as any other. At the same time, however, the theologian should take warning from the Old Testament not to be excessively triumphalist in his proclaiming of the principle, 'Non omnis moriar'.

With regard to the theology of death, many themes must be set aside from the outset, even though in the traditional and established theology of death they are explicitly treated of. Thus, for instance, we shall be omitting any discussion of the universality of death, even though a whole range of theological problems are implicitly contained even here, in what seems to be a self-evident truth. We shall be compelled to set aside the question of whether what the tradition of Christian faith has to say about death and the last things really applies to every being which we can account as human in a *biological* sense, and so, for instance, even to one who dies at the embryonic stage, or whether, on the other hand, all this applies only to those endowed with a genuine certainty of faith, who have really used their human freedom to achieve a personal history for which they themselves are responsible. Nor will we be able to enter into the doctrine of the relationship between sin and death, although in itself this is theologically speaking of radical importance.[3] In this connection we must confine ourselves in passing simply to the remark that for Christianity's understanding of existence a point that must in any case be taken into account is that specific interpretations of death are far from having that objectivity which merely confirms further views which they themselves feel that they possess. Rather such interpretations themselves in turn derive from that darkness of death, borne of human guilt, which pervades the whole of life, and so too this interpretation of self, even if the individual interpreter may be personally blameless and honest.

LINGUISTIC FORMS AND REALITY

It seems appropriate to me to exclude from the outset (i.e. before we enter

[3] On this cf. the studies of one of the author's pupils: L. Boros, 'Strukturen christlicher Vollendung', *Strukturen christlicher Existenz*, H. Schlier, E. von Severus,

directly into the question of the Christian understanding of death) to clear up certain misunderstandings, especially with regard to the question of the 'continuance of life after death', a question which, in fact, we shall not be attempting to separate from the question of death as such. First, in all Christian statements (as in all other human statements which are not mere signals of biological needs and requirements) a distinction has to be drawn between the form of language and that which is actually signified by it, a distinction such that the sense intended and the conceptual model used are neither identified nor yet fully distinguished from one another in the processes of conscious human thought, nor again can they be totally separated from one another. For there is no such thing as an idea without perception, a concept (as Thomas Aquinas already recognized) without a *conversio ad phantasma*.[4] And even the process of criticizing a perception at the conceptual level will always be undertaken by means of concepts which themselves in turn have to work with some other apprehension, even though they are not always simultaneously conscious that the perceptual and the conceptual elements in the concept are not identical. Given that human conceptuality and language have this special quality, which cannot be eliminated by any kind of meta-language, nor yet by computers or other technical attempts at a total rationalization of language, we have fully to take this quality into our calculations in the particular case we are considering here.

It may be true, therefore, that Christian statements about death and the 'continuance of life after death' make use of conceptual models of a mythological kind when they use conceptual systems which, in themselves and in their origins, are spatial or physico-temporal in character in their references to 'heaven', to 'the life beyond', to the 'after-' life, to the 'continuance' of existence after death, to the parting of the soul from the body, etc. But the use of such conceptual systems and forms of language does not in any sense invalidate the reality referred to by means of them, even though, by contrast with earlier ages of the human interpretation of existence, the elements of imagery or mythology and the inadequacies inherent in such systems and forms, have now come to be consciously recognized and felt to be such. Perhaps, indeed, those inadequacies are felt with such intensity that it is now totally impossible to use earlier systems and forms, at least if these are not to give rise to fatal misunder-

---

J. Sudbrack, A. Pereira edd. (Würzburg, 1968), pp. 251–262, and also the well-known study by L. Boros, '*Mysterium Mortis. Der Mensch in der letzten Entscheidung*' (Olten/Freiburg, 1962).

[4] On this cf. the author's article in this volume, 'Thomas Aquinas on Truth'.

standings in men of a certain level of education, with their knowledge of the natural sciences, their technical and historical equipment, and their new perspectives of thought. On this point it seems that, as a matter of ultimate principle, a difference of this kind, between the perceptual model and the reality to which it relates is present even in modern physics, and even in those conceptual models which, within their own dimension, are contrary to one another, as for instance particles and waves, which at once assert and, by the contradiction between them, at the same time obscure, the reality to which they refer. It is, therefore, perfectly conceivable that at some point in the future men will have learnt once more freely to use conceptual models and images which are now felt to be intolerably mythological and so rejected, because by means of these they perceive and express the reality referred to without incurring the danger of succumbing to the misunderstandings of earlier times thereby evoked. In all this the situation is, as we have said, not such that a reality referred to could be expressed in non-image form and without the aid of such conceptual models, the moment we consciously reflected upon the difference between that which is referred to and the form in which it is expressed in our previous statement of it. The new statement still contains this dualism also; only it is not reflected upon, or at least not so clearly, and it is not felt as so unsatisfactory. The dualism is still present even in a negative statement. It would be eliminated only if the question itself too which such a statement is designed to answer were eliminated, i.e. if it never arose at all. Someone who denies something must have understood that which he believes he has to deny. But even here it is only in a dualism of concept and image of this kind that he can make clear to himself in virtue of his denial precisely what this is that he is denying. And he must constantly ask himself whether what he is really denying is simply the image which he rightly finds to be inadequate or erroneous, or whether he is indeed denying the reality itself signified by this mental picture. The situation is in any case a difficult one, and particularly so in the case of a negative finding. But the only way in which the difficulties could be resolved by a sceptically negative reply would be if the situation itself and the question giving rise to it simply did not exist at all.

THE END OF THE TEMPORAL DIMENSION

On the basis of these assumptions we can now consider the misinterpretations which have to be eliminated from the outset in dealing with our present subject. On these misinterpretations the following must be said:

the 'continuance of life' after death is not to be thought of as the self-prolongation of time, or as a further extension in time of acts and experiences following one upon another in a series arising from some neutral substantial entity which impels itself forward through ever fresh epochs, and is forever engaging in some fresh activity within these constantly changing sections of time. On the contrary it is obvious that death is in *this* sense the absolute *end* of the temporal dimension of a being of the kind to which man belongs. What takes place after death is not something new in a temporal sense, or something that is constantly changing. Man does not wander through it in a dimension beyond death of a spatial or temporal kind such that between it and our former life a frontier in space and time would be constituted within what was ultimately one and the same dimension of spatiality and temporality. The opposite conception, originating from the traditional conceptual models, and giving rise again and again to the danger of radical misunderstanding and so too of radical rejection, is ruled out if only because otherwise we would have logically to accept something like a transmigration of souls or a radical change in the ultimate basic attitude of an individual in the so-called dimension beyond death, interpretations of existence which the Christian faith radically rejects because it takes seriously the fact that this life is one and single, and is brought to its fulness in a single and definitive historical development. Life 'after death', on the contrary, is something radically withdrawn from the former temporal dimension and the former spatially conceived time, and a state of final and definitive completion and immediacy to God which is absolutely disparate from space and time, and is the end-point of a life lived once and for all in freedom precisely *here*, the end-point of that personal history which is brought to its completion in itself. Now someone might say that a life after death would be totally inconceivable to him unless it involved other activities and interests, unless it 'went on' after a 'change of horses', as Feuerbach would put it, and, moreover, more joyfully than before. Again someone might object that it would, after all, be terrible if our former life, with all its banalities and questionable aspects were itself to be frozen in a final and definitive state. But to this we should have to answer that it is perfectly possible to conceive of 'eternal life' in some sense, even without having to imagine anything new over and above our former life by a process of mythological fantasizing, and further that the definitive state of our former life in its historical development is far from implying a petrification of its former banalities and questionable factors. For provided that this former life of ours was accepted in the freedom of love (at the moment we do not need to take into consideration the possibility of our culpably having allowed it to be lost) it included sufficient of the content of an eternal life and of infinite freedom for us to have some understanding of what these mean. For even in our present state the infinite Mystery which we call God is experienced in love and adoration; even in our present state we take absolute responsibility for our lives, experience that freedom, give and receive that love which, when they are exercised in that spirit of hope of which we shall have to speak further, are themselves experienced as having a radical validity and as final and definitive. We cannot withdraw ourselves from the absolute claim to validity which such freedom and such love have upon us by quietly, each in his own identity, vanishing into nothingness (whether in despair or in joy is ultimately speaking a matter of indifference here).[5] It must be said straight away here that this ultimately speaking entails no *objection* whatever to him who supposes that he is unable to believe in this 'eternal life' even as rightly understood. Rather it is only addressed *to* him so that despite the opposite interpretation of existence he may understand and savour the meaning of eternity in this sense as a matter of conscious reflection so long as in his freedom he takes the radical responsibility of loving. Eternal life is not the 'other side' so far as our personal history is concerned, but rather the radical interiority, now liberated and brought to full self-realization, of that personal history of freedom of ours which we are living through even now and which, once it has been fully brought to birth in death, can no longer be lost. The only further development which it can still achieve then is to lose itself in a loving immediacy to the ultimate Mystery of existence called God, and thereby discover its own fulness. We have mentioned above certain misinterpretations of the Christian faith with regard to 'eternal life'. Side by side with these, and subject to certain provisos consisting in more precise theological distinctions which it might perhaps be necessary to draw, we can now go on to make a further statement, even though it may entail a possible crude over-simplification of the theological propositions involved. It is this: statements about the 'continued existence of the soul after death', about its 'separation from the body', and about the 'resurrection of the body' must be accounted, so far as we are concerned, and at least for the purposes of *this* consideration, not as statements about different objective states of affairs, but as statements about one and the same state of affairs that is being pointed to by means of different conceptual models, statements, that is to say, about the final and

[5] On this cf. the author's article in this volume, 'Experience of Self and Experience of God'.

definitive state of the personal history of man as brought to its fulness in freedom. In view of this it is neither necessary nor helpful, at least for the range of problems with which we are concerned, to introduce a dichotomy between body and soul as a necessary assumption for the Christian conviction being referred to here. Nor are we absolutely forced to posit a temporal interval between the death of the individual and that which we really mean when we speak of the 'resurrection of the flesh'.

THE HOPE OF ETERNAL LIFE

Up to now we have been indicating how certain misinterpretations can be cleared away concerning the meaning of eternal life, which, precisely according to Christian theology, takes place at the moment of death. We can now apply ourselves to our real subject-matter, namely the hope of eternal life. Certainly so far as a Christian philosophy of belief is concerned, it is far from being so obvious as might perhaps appear at first sight that we can develop our Christian interpretation of death more or less directly from our idea of that eternal life which we hope to achieve through death. It would be just as legitimate a course to proceed in the opposite direction, attempting from a radical acceptance of death to achieve a genuine understanding of that which is meant by eternal life. But without in principle debarring ourselves from arguing in either of these two directions, let us attempt to achieve an understanding of the true nature of death on the basis of hope of eternal life.

The Christian has this hope of eternal life.[6] Such a statement is easy to make. Not only because it is far from being all that clear whether the individual Christian in concrete practice really does hope, really does hope for this eternal life, or merely uses this hope which we assert to exist as a façade and an analgesic so as to conceal an ultimate despair, this being the real truth of that Christian's existence. It is not only that to a man who is critical of himself and on his guard against his own deep-rooted egoism the word 'hope' all too easily comes to sound like some facile consolation, although in its true sense it implies the most radical exercise of the human spirit when subject to the bitterest pain, and even though hope is present only in him who first and foremost hopes on behalf of *others* – hopes in the responsibility he takes for them, hopes in that love for him whom we call God, and in the face of whom even authentic hope must in its turn forget its own nature. Over and above this, and on a theological

---

[6] On this cf. the author's article, 'On the Theology of Hope', *Theological Investigations* X (London and New York, 1973), pp. 242–259.

understanding, the word 'hope' in relation to eternal life involves a great gnoseological obscurity. Its significance is very far from having been reflected on in a really adequate sense in the traditional standard theology of the seminaries. Willy nilly the mental picture of hope which we entertain is such that that which is hoped for is something of which we already have a neutral knowledge even beforehand as in principle possible. From this the individual who entertains the hope then has to go on to a further stage because of specific difficulties in attaining the known object in the particular case envisaged, and actually *hope* for it. But in this view of hope we are *ipso facto* failing to realize its true nature in a radically theological sense. We are confusing that which is hoped for, that which is only present at all in hope, with that which is planned, that which is undertaken as the outcome of neutral speculation, that which, under certain predetermined conditions and according to certain specific methods, we have to bring to reality in the concrete. On this showing we are no longer in any real position to speak of the 'hope against all hope', of a hope such that it is only *within* it that that which is hoped for can be discerned at all, of a hope which constitutes the basic dimension of the Christian understanding of existence as such. Instead we have, right from the outset, missed the real theological nature of this hope, and degraded it to a more or less accurate calculation of chances which are entertained even by one who has no hope in the real sense in striving to achieve a still conceivable goal. Theological hope, on the other hand – to speak in wholly general terms – is the free and trustful commitment of love to the 'impossible', i.e. to that which can no longer be constructed from materials already present to the individual himself and at his disposal. It is called the expectation of that which is absolute gift, the giver of which withdraws himself into an unnameable incomprehensibility and can only be encountered in himself by actively engaging in such hope. This is called building on that which is without foundation, self-commitment to that which is beyond one's power to control. Christian hope never for one moment conceals or denies this character which it has. It freely exposes itself to the charge of being 'irrational'. It merely declares that it continuously discovers at the basis of existence that an offering is being made at this level of the power freely to commit oneself in such hope, even if it is possible to reject this offer or to suppose that one has rejected it. It says only, in an attitude that is 'inoffensive' and at the same time one of ultimate decision, that it cannot forbid itself to conceive of the inconceivable, because that inconceivable is precisely and inescapably present in existence and Christian hope cannot see why it should not also be spoken of, seeing that in fact it is spoken of by the very ones who condemn such statements or obstinately persist in holding that such statements cannot have any meaning because we cannot represent the reality concerned to ourselves or have any *comprehensive* knowledge of it.

Christian hope does indeed hold that, in the words of Anselm of Canterbury, it can '*rationabiliter irrationalia cogitare*', because the recognition of the inconceivable itself constitutes in its turn a prerogative and a function of reason, which must be unprejudiced in its encounter with reality as it is in itself. Nevertheless this hope also constitutes its own light. It carries its own authentication within itself, and is not the mere outcome of a rational insight which – itself not involving hope – would on this theory generate and release hope. On the contrary it is a primordial exercise of human freedom which commits itself to the unity of that which it cannot synthesize by its own power, the unity which it no longer comprehends, and yet recognizes as valid. It commits itself to the unification of that which has been divided, a unification which cannot be achieved by ourselves in some higher unity which we ourselves perceive and possess as something that we recognize within ourselves. Hope is itself a unique and underived mode of knowledge in which the creative element and the element which accepts from without in an ultimate passivity constitute a paradoxical unity, because that which is hoped for is present to us only within the hope itself, and is otherwise not even present as really conceivable. At the same time it is also that which constitutes pure gift, and which is received as such. We might go on to say much more about the nature of Christian hope in general. One point which should of course be emphasized is that the word 'Christian' as applied to it is not intended to have an exclusive sense such that it could only be engaged in by the kind of individual who considers himself a Christian in an explicit sense and as a matter of Christian and social indoctrination from without. We might go on to develop the gnoseological significance of hope in more precise terms, its place in the sphere of the practical reason which does not merely follow the speculative reason as its simple outcome and as something to be achieved of man's freedom. We might go on to enquire the extent to which it belongs to a subject endowed with intellect and freedom as a matter of transcendental necessity or, over and above this, how far it is sustained (albeit unconsciously) by that which we call Christian grace, in which the goal, namely God himself, sustains the movement even as it reaches out towards this selfsame goal. But these and many other matters cannot be treated of any further at the moment.

DYING AND DEATH

We shall shortly have to speak of death and the process of dying which actually leads to death.[7] We shall have to say that it constitutes the one situation for this hope, and that in which it is at its most radical, or, to put it better, that it can constitute this. But before going on to explain this we must first say something about death itself. It is precisely to the extent that in his death the Christian has to be he who hopes that it is both possible and necessary for him not to conceal from himself the comfortless absurdity of death. One day he will actually suffer it, and for this reason he should accord it its full significance in his theology of death too, as well as he can. Precisely from the point of view of a Christian theology it would be a failure to recognize the reality of death if we sought to approach it from an attitude of anthropological dichotomy by supposing that death affects only the so-called body of man, while the so-called soul, at least if it boldly resolves upon an attitude of Stoic transcendence, will be able to view the fate of its former partner called the body unaffected and undismayed as from above. Of course we do have to draw a distinction within the single individual between a number of different elements and dimensions. We must do this if we wish to avoid stupidly joining the *terribles simplificateurs* of anthropology. But however true this may be, still man is *one* in being and act, and death is something that affects the whole man.

At this point man in all that he is has arrived at a conclusion. It may be questioned whether this conclusion constitutes the consummation or the termination of him, but in any case in death he arrives at a radical conclusion, one which, on any showing, he cannot bring under his own power. Some may, in all calmness, describe this conclusion as absurd and an arch-contradiction. So it is, if only because we may in all calmness say that death is a contradiction to positive *and* to negative thinking. For the absolute conclusion as such provides neither thinking of a positive kind with any subject-matter, nor yet thinking of a negative kind, seeing that this latter is in all cases capable of operating only from the basis of a positive subject-matter, and its shift away from this is only partial. Even as the object of thought, death is, in relation to the individual existence of each person, as inconceivable as absolute nothingness in relationship to the sum total of reality. Death as a conclusion is the absolute powerlessness of man, in which we certainly also become too powerless to conceive of death or of God. But the dying man, who of his freedom possesses his

[7] E. Kübler-Ross, 'On Death and Dying', *Amer. Eccl. Rev.* 161 (1969), pp. 351 ff.

own life, nevertheless inescapably confronts death with a demand that it must constitute the sum total of his life as an act of freedom in which the whole of life is gathered up. For the very nature of freedom and its claim to the absolute dignity of responsibility and of love belonging to it cannot give its assent to a mere empty draining away of life. If there is anything that is of concern to man it is death. And it is precisely this that radically repels him. We can say in all calmness that to think about death is as impossible as the thought *of* death, because, in contrast to all other objects of thought, whether possible or actual, one's own death (incidentally just as God himself) is something that we cannot comprehend in our thoughts, bring under our power, and so manipulate, and hence one who, in his thinking, seeks always to bring that which he is thinking about under his control will be thwarted in the case of death.[8] It is, and remains, a fact that from all the points of view already mentioned and many more besides, death is the absurd arch-contradiction of existence. If it were not both possible and necessary for the Christian too to experience it as such, how could the Christian assert and recognize that death is the manifestation of sin, of that 'no' to the absolute truth and love which dwell in God, which is at once free and overthrows freedom?[9]

In this connection it must be said that we, presumably different in this from animals, cannot refrain from thinking about death, that we cannot 'pigeonhole' the fact of death. That the opinion of Epicurus to the effect that death does not concern us so long as we are alive, and, when we are dead, cannot be of concern to anyone, simply does not correspond to the reality of human existence, because in fact this advice in itself, and in the very act of consigning death to oblivion, gives it a place in life and so betrays the impossibility of putting the advice into practice. Death is not merely any kind of occurrence within our life, or coming at its conclusion. Rather, whether we suppress it or admit it, it is that in virtue of which we are continually discovering the nature of our own existence as finite and so mortal through that supreme apprehension in which we transcend everything assignable to categories within the space-time dimension. Among other factors, this one is of constant concern to us: the absurd arch-contradiction of our life. This is something more than a mere quality or attribute of death belonging to it to the extent that we seek to set our-

---

[8] Joh. Hofmeier, 'Vom gewussten zum gelebten Tod', *StdZ* 186 (1970), pp. 338–352 (a survey of the relevant literature).

[9] On the character of death as mystery cf. e.g. Y. Congar, J. Daniélou, H. M. Féret, *et. al.*, *Le mystère de la mort et sa célébration* (Paris, 1951), and also I. Lepp, *Death and its Mysteries* (New York, 1968).

selves apart from it as those who live. Rather it is something that we ourselves are.

THE EXERCISE OF FREEDOM IN DEATH

We shall now attempt to show that this situation of death constitutes
precisely the true and necessary situation of Christian hope. And the first
point to emphasize is that the state of hopelessness or (in order to avoid
unnecessary verbal conflicts) the radical inescapability of this situation of
death constitutes precisely the prior condition which makes hope in the
strictly theological sense possible. In other words it is something which
the Christian is least of all in a position to conceal from himself. Hope, in
contrast to foresight, with its function of planning and controlling, is
possible from the outset only in a situation in which we really are radically
at the end; where the possibility of acting for ourselves is really and
finally closed to us; where we can find absolutely no further resources
whatever within ourselves by which to achieve a higher synthesis between
a state of radical powerlessness and the supreme exercise of freedom in
death; where we become those who are utterly delivered up to forces from
without; where even the possibility of a heroic attitude of faith or a stoic
apatheia, or even a wild protest against the absurdity of existence, is withdrawn from us; where we are deprived of even the innermost and ultimate
subjectivity of our existence in its absolute depths. This is the situation of
Christian hope.

Of course it is open to us to object straightway at this point that if
death constitutes the ultimate state of absolute and dreary powerlessness,
while Christian hope must still be conceived of as an *activity* on man's
part, then there is no longer any place or any possibility of existence even
for Christian hope. Certainly as a matter of sober logic we must assign
Christian hope to a place during *life*, and, as far as it goes, in the process
of *dying*, and not assign it to that point of absolute void which we have to
understand death to be. But if we have to do with death even in life, the
question both can and must be posed of *what attitude* we are to take, can
take, or ought to take, towards this absolute null point. And it is precisely
here that the answer of Christianity comes: hope in eternal life – though
admittedly in that sense which we have previously sought to give to the
phrase eternal life in order to prevent misunderstandings of it. Of course
on a radical view of it this hope does view God and eternal life as one and
the same, and the exercise of this hope does not draw upon a reason un-
threatened by death or a knowledge of God already acquired from some

other source such that from it an innocuous reduplication of the real Christian hope could easily be constructed. Real Christian hope, faced with death, hopes in fact precisely while recognizing to the full the powerlessness of man either in thinking or willing when confronted with the absurd arch-contradiction of existence. And what it hopes for is a unity, a reconciliation of the contradictory elements, a meaning for existence, an eternal validity for love as freely entered into, an assent to absolute truth, so that all this that is hoped for is truly *hoped* for, i.e. is neither to be manipulated by one's own autonomous thinking, nor controlled by one's own autonomous power. All is hope, even the act of thinking in one who can still only think about the meaning of death, and is no longer in a position to think 'through' it comprehensively.

NOTHINGNESS AND FINALITY

To hope for this, however, since it is and remains hope which cannot be authenticated from any other source, but only in itself, could not be simply an exercise of sheer arbitrary choice, as if someone might hope here and now to become emperor of China tomorrow. This hope draws its life from that finality, as from an element inherent in itself, one of which we have already spoken briefly, that finality with which the individual freely decides for himself what is to constitute the good that he aims at, his personal love, his radical responsibility beyond any considerations of reward. The nature of this moral act is such that unless we are to deny the fact that it is demanded of us in an absolute sense, it cannot be regarded as radically transitory. It itself would surrender its absolute character if it were to recognize the death of itself as its appropriate end and as an element inherent in its own nature. In fact even one who feels death to be the radical and absurd arch-contradiction of existence does also concede this in principle. For what could prompt him to feel that death was so contradictory if in the act of dying *everything* were, of its very nature, to seek out the finality of finalities and to accept it as appropriate to itself. It might be said that in the very moment in which someone does what is proper to himself, the act of greatness, the total commitment, the act of love or duty in the most radical sense, he should of course not think of this as sheer finality, and should not thereby himself destroy himself in an attitude of ultimate cynicism, the only alternative being that he should, despite all, perform the supreme act open to man in an attitude of inconceivable, indeed absurd, heroism in response to this absurd finality. But if someone were to say this, then we should have to reply along these lines: in a moment of this kind of a free act of love, radical loyalty, etc. there is one reason why man cannot think of the nothingness, in a temporal sense, inherent in this act that is proper to his own nature, namely that it is *precisely* not subject to time. A further question might be what place there can still be for a protest against the absurdity of the nothingness of existence once we take up the following position: the moment we seek to be honest and truthful we have to accept this same nothingness as having a legitimate place in existence seeing that it is an intrinsic element in that which is proper to it. On this showing we ought to identify ourselves with Paul and ask why the maxim 'Let us eat and drink, for tomorrow we die' (1 Cor. 15:32) is in that case so meaningless or unworthy, if after all it can be claimed to have the value of sober truth. And if in reply someone made the further rejoinder that it is, after all, precisely the greatness and glory of human existence to maintain this protest against absurdity in the midst, and in view of, the absurdity inherent in human existence itself, and to practise love without recompense, loyalty etc., then such heroism under protest of its very nature excludes at least this finality which renders all meaningless. And then we should have to ask why at least this which is most deeply proper to oneself, namely our protest against the absurdity of being delivered over to death, cannot allow the truth to be borne in upon us as it really is. How too can it be that it is only the *appearance* of a definitive finality that we encounter, seeing that everything carries within itself from the outset the marks of that death which brings an end to all as the genuine truth?

All this should not be taken to mean that hope should be generated and built up through some factor which, in the last analysis, is exterior to itself. The very fact that this which is eternally valid is present in and with the absurdity of the experience of death is in itself enough to show that this is not what is meant. But hope is offered a choice. It *must* choose precisely because that which is valid in this sense on the one hand and death on the other cannot be reconciled on the basis of human nature itself. And hope opts for that which is offered to it as the eternally valid in the midst of an existence in process of dying. It chooses the eternally valid, rejects the death as the final and definitive factor, and gives the name of God to that power which is not its own, yet which removes, by reconciliation, the absurd arch-contradiction present in existence through death. This hope is exercised on behalf of all men, for all men are loved in it and it is not confined merely to the hoping subject himself. And hence the subject of this hope hopes too concerning his fellow men, who suppose that the only realistic interpretation they are able to come to about themselves is that they are the hopeless, that they too, beneath and beyond this supposed hopelessness, are the hope*ful*. How could hope think otherwise? In fact it experiences these fellow men as those who love and those who are radically loyal and selfless, and it refuses to interpret all this as a mere ideological façade in a world made up only of an egoistic and merciless struggle for existence, an existence which for all ends in the void of death. But if hope discovers itself afresh in the love and loyalty which it encounters in others – because in this hope is brought to its fulness in its protest against the absurdity of a life that is dedicated to death – then it will be giving no offence and doing no injustice to him who supposes that he has, in a spirit of defiant honesty, to interpret existence in a sense that is hopeless. For why should it not be the case that for some individuals their concrete situation is such that the only way in which it is possible for them to achieve a radical acceptance of death in which nothing is veiled (and this, after all, is the condition of true Christian hope) is for them to abandon themselves to the darkness of death even though it brings them despair? Why should it not be the case that many who die can only cry aloud with the dying Jesus: 'My God why hast thou forsaken me?', and in the midst of this abandonment that other word rises up silently in their innermost depths: 'Father, into thy hands I commend my spirit'? If even we Christians are in constant danger of using the words which, properly speaking, only Christian hope as such should pronounce, as a false consolation, which can never form any true basis for hope but represents an attempt to cover over the darkness and terror of death? Why should it not be possible even for such as these to entertain Christian hope unwittingly in the very depths of their souls. The borderline between real and final despair on the one hand, and illusion with regard to death on the other, is difficult to draw. We could here adapt a saying of Jesus so as to run like this: With men it is impossible, but in the power of God it is possible to draw this borderline, so that man finds his strength neither in despair nor in the illusion of self-sufficiency, but rather, believing and loving in hope, commits himself to the incomprehensible Mystery which comes to him and takes effect upon him in death.[10] We call this mystery the God of hope (Rom. 15:13).

FREEDOM AS THE EVENT OF DEFINITIVE FINALITY

Perhaps in conclusion we should return to a difficulty in the Christian

[10] For the foregoing ideas cf. for instance F. F. Wiplinger, *Der personal verstandener Tod* (Freiburg, 1970), and E. Jüngel, *Tod* (Stuttgart, 1971); but also 'Der

interpretation of death to provide a fuller explanation of it. It is one which in my opinion is more covered over than solved in the language of popular theology. In seeking to understand our own basic tenets we inevitably proceed from a basis of ideas drawn from the physical and temporal world. Right from the first we are conditioned by these ideas, and so we constantly think of all reality in terms of space and time extending in a linear prolongation in two opposite directions. We assign all reality to a place in the future as the past or the future as parts of a linear prolongation of time extending to infinitude between two poles. Unless we have learnt to subject this conceptual model to critical questioning (though obviously this does not mean simply to do away with it) the question arises of how on this showing something can continue forever into the future in this linear prolongation when manifestly it only began a short time ago in the past, and its existence does not extend backwards in this direction into infinity at all. It is not surprising that the idea has been seized upon of a transmigration of souls or a pre-earthly existence of 'souls' (an idea which appeared even within Christianity, for instance in Origen). These ideas have been developed in order to eliminate the apparent anomaly that a future extending into infinitude is ascribed to a being which has not had any past extending backwards into infinitude.[11] So long as we subject ourselves uncritically to this image of time, we will necessarily limit man in both directions as being radically subject to time. Obviously we have no intention here of contesting the fact that the physical man, compelled to seek his own identity from within space and time by relating himself to that which is alien and other to himself, is also a being subject to space and time. But it is not on this basis that we should think of his ultimate and free subjectivity if we are to avoid involving ourselves in this insoluble dilemma. At a level more ultimate than his state of belonging to space and time or time conceived of in spatial terms, he is a being endowed with a freedom which must achieve its own fulness. Now freedom precisely does not consist in a quest to achieve ever fresh changes at will. Rather it is of its very nature the event of a real and definitive finality which cannot be

Treffer aus dem Absoluten. Informationen zu einer Theologie des Todes', *Evang. Kommentare* 2 (1969), pp. 623–630.

[11] On the problems of time in connection with the question of death cf. also R. Ochs, *The Death in Every Now* (New York, 1969), and the reports or interpretations of experiences with drugs, N. W. Pahnke, 'The Psychedelic Mystical Experience in the Human Encounter with Death', *Harv. Theol. Rev.* 62 (1969), pp. 1–20, and the reply by a natural scientist published in the same number (H. K. Beecher, pp. 21–25), as well as a reply by a theologian (G. D. Kaufmann, pp. 26–32).

conceived of otherwise than something that is freely achieved once and for all. And to that extent man is the event of that state of definitive finality which we call eternity, and falsely, or by a misinterpretation, reduce in its turn to the dimension of linear time extending endlessly backwards and forwards. To the extent that this freedom is such that it must achieve its own fulness, it has laws of its own and conditioning factors of its own which are not at its disposal even when it is free precisely in the attitude it adopts towards these, and has in *this* sense a 'beginning'. This beginning, however, is as such not the mere occurrence of events and circumstances which precede freedom in time. Rather it signifies something which is ultimately and underivably new, and which, therefore, can be allotted to a specific point in the external linear development of time only in a secondary sense.

Now in order to picture to ourselves this modality of the event of freedom, namely the fact that it has a beginning and a definitive end, we have not at our command, of course, any such convenient conceptual scheme as is available to us through the experiences of spatial movement and the kind of time that is ultimately acceptable in this. The only way in which we can objectify in words this free occurrence which we ultimately experience and produce is for us to make use of the conceptual schemes which belong to external time. But even as we use these, and cannot avoid using them, we have also at the same time to adopt a critical attitude to them.

In fact we are gradually educated by the natural sciences rather than by any philosophical critique to realize how cautious we have to be in supposing that reality as it in fact exists can be apprehended by means of these popular conceptual models drawn from everyday life. If, therefore, again and again we feel ourselves oppressed by the real experience that we cannot see beyond death as the true end in a vision which could advance further within the same linear concept of time, then this still does not represent any argument against, or any condemnation of, the Christian hope of eternal life in the real meaning which this has. Where love and loyalty are truly exercised, and where the absolute truth which guides us is accepted, there *ipso facto* that definitive finality is achieved which we must seek not in some linear development of time after death, but in that state of definitive liberation which is achieved and brought to its fulness in death. This is the Christian hope, this alone, but this in a very true sense.[12]

[12] Two authors approach the question from the basis of the Bible, R. Pesch, 'Zur Theologie des Todes', *Bibel und Leben* 10 (1969), pp. 9–15, and M. Laconi, 'La morte nei vangeli', *Sac. Doc.* 13 (1968), pp. 395–426.

PART THREE

Christology

12

HUMAN ASPECTS OF THE BIRTH OF CHRIST

THE decisive factor in the mystery which we believe in and celebrate at Christmas is, of course, the advent of the eternal word of God as our Redemption in the flesh, and so as something which affects all Christians alike, and is in principle no different in its effect upon the Christian doctor than upon other Christians.[1] Of course Christian faith is also aware of the special factors in the conception and birth of Jesus (something which we shall have to treat of rather more fully at a later stage) precisely *from that* experience which the disciples *subsequently* had of Jesus in his acts, his words, his witness to himself, his death, and his Resurrection. This retrospective view, proceeding from Jesus hmiself to his origins, is legitimate. To the extent that he has proved himself in his life and Resurrection to be the absolute Word of divine grace, addressed to us through the deed of God wrought in him, Christian believers know that he was this Word of God in our flesh right from his origins, and did not merely become so gradually in the course of his life, though this is not to rule out a development of Jesus' human awareness at the level of conscious explicitation in terms of concepts and words, and thereby the character of Jesus' ultimate understanding of himself as mediated. Of course there are certain basic historical data with regard to Jesus' origins, some of which are obvious (e.g. Nazareth as his place of origin, the name of his mother, the existence of a group of relatives still known in the early Christian community etc.), and some of which can be deduced over and above that which we can accept as assured. But we are still forced to conclude that there are some factors acknowledged by believers as belonging to the origins of Jesus' life, which are not properly speaking handed down by historical tradition, factors which, while they are indeed rooted in the

[1] On this subject cf. the author's article, 'Virginitas in Partu', *Theological Investigations* IV (London and Baltimore, 1966), pp. 134–162, and also 'Dogmatische Bemerkungen zur Jungfrauengeburt', *Zum Thema Jungfrauengeburt*, Frank, Kilian, Knoch. Lattke, and Rahner edd. (Stuttgart, 1970), pp. 121–158.

actual event concerned, are theologically speaking known to us by a fully justified process of retrospection from what we know about the 'adult' Jesus himself. Thus from our knowledge of him at this stage we deduce what must have been the case 'at the beginning'. Now when retrospective theological deductions to the origins of Jesus are involved in certain of the statements which faith makes about those origins, then we can also go on to say that the content and the limits of such statements are determined by that which really follows compellingly from a retrospective process of this kind and what does not. This retrospective process may yield a legitimate stock of findings with a specific content. But it is possible that in the concrete, in dealing with an event thus arrived at by a process of retrospective deduction, we are unable to recognize where such distinctions should be drawn, even though we would be able to know them if it were a question of a historical datum following from the direct experience of the origin as a phenomenon in itself. What we mean in more precise detail by what has just been said, and why this abstract principle has a practical importance, will appear straightway the moment we apply this principle to the case with which we are concerned in the present study.

When the Christian doctor applies himself to the question of Jesus' birth, he will surely feel especially inclined to concern himself, over and above that which is of crucial importance in this Christmas mystery, with the biological aspects of this birth of the Lord. By this we do not mean the conception of Jesus by his mother without the intervention of a human father. This doctrine of Christian tradition raises too many questions for the theologian for it to be capable of being treated of here, within the space of so brief a consideration. What we are referring to here, rather, is the biological aspects of the actual process of the *birth* itself. At Christmas the Christian doctor may turn his mind to this biological side of Jesus' birth, and if he is theologically well instructed, then what will straightway strike him will be the traditional Christian doctrine of the 'virginity of the Blessed Virgin in the actual *moment* of the birth'. And so today the question arises for Christians in general, and for the Christian doctor in particular, of what really is meant by this 'virginitas *in* partu', in which the special factor in the birth of Jesus is represented as consisting in its physical aspect. For after all, once we abstract from this doctrine of 'virginitas in partu', it is obvious that since Jesus is truly man, his birth too is the same as that of all other men.

But how should the Christian and the Christian doctor conceive of what is meant by this 'virginitas in partu'? On the one hand he wants unreservedly to respect the traditional Christian doctrine, yet on the other he does not want to think of the *kind* of 'miracles' which strike him, conditioned as he is by modern outlooks and the modern environment, as too incredible, or which give him the impression of being too strongly mythological in character.

At this point we do not want to concern ourselves with the question of what theological qualification is to be ascribed to the doctrine of the 'virginitas in partu'. We will also pass over a question which might perhaps be of concern to the discerning biologist, namely whether the word 'virginity' as used in this phrase, 'virginitas in partu', is in its real meaning altogether suitable in its application here, or whether it would not be better to use some other term than 'virginity' to express what is meant, drawing our expressions from a clearer, more accurate, and more informed terminology. For our present purposes we are accepting the traditional understanding of the statement of the 'virginitas in partu'. Those who understand it in this sense explain it as follows: the process of birth takes place without any pain to the mother, and without the *hymen virginale* being destroyed by the passage of the child as it is born. The question is this: whether the concrete conception of the 'virginitas in partu' is simply identical with the doctrine of such a 'virginitas in partu', and therefore whether this particular conception remains binding so long as the doctrine itself is maintained, or whether *alternatively* we can maintain and formulate the real content of this doctrine without simply having to assent to this conception in its entirety, which traditional theology uses to explain that which is unique in the birth of Jesus. From the observation of various factors in the development of this doctrine's dogmatic history we can surely feel free to draw the conclusion that the 'virginitas in partu' has come down to us not as a record ultimately deriving from Mary herself and relating what she herself experienced in the birth of Jesus, but that on the contrary it involves a retrospective theological deduction as to how this birth must have taken place for theological reasons based on the unique character of the child himself. We cannot, within the present context, accord a separate presentation to each of these factors as observed, which belong to the category of the history of dogma. We must confine ourselves to pointing out that the New Testament itself contains no record of a 'virginitas in partu', and that it is only a very long time after the origins of belief in Christ that we encounter this doctrine for the first time in recognizable form, and, moreover, primarily in theological circles which are suspected of having been Docetist. But even if we assume that what we have in this doctrine of the 'virginitas in partu' is a retrospective theological deduction to a reality, and not a historical tradition of that reality, deriving from its initial occurrence in itself, this still does not mean that such a retrospective deduction is illegitimate. It is perfectly possible that the conclusion to which it leads constitutes an objective state of affairs. But the meaning and the limitations of what is thus concluded to needs to be tested and subjected to the question of what we can or cannot come to know by a retrospective deduction of this kind in view of its premises.

In any attempt we make to carry out a retrospective deduction of this kind our attempt will be accounted legitimate from a theological point of view provided it concludes to the substance of the traditional doctrine concerning the 'virginitas in partu'. And it will still be legitimate even though it does not in any sense justify us in concluding that this necessarily entails assenting to all the conceptions and mental images which have been employed in the attempt to provide vivid illustrations of what this 'virginitas in partu' signifies. It is true that what we are enquiring into is the human aspect of the birth of *Jesus* himself. Nevertheless, in accordance with the traditional view of the question we may concentrate more explicitly in our enquiry on the birth of Jesus precisely in its aspect as an event in the life of his mother Mary. For precisely this phrase 'virginitas in partu' is traditionally interpreted first and foremost as a statement about Mary herself. On the basis of dogmatic christology taken as a whole we must say first and foremost that when Mary gave birth to Jesus it was a genuinely human birth. Such a statement is to be understood not as a concession to those who shrink from the miraculous, or as a mere statement of human experience. Rather it is a genuine statement of faith, for the true, genuine, and full humanity of Jesus is a dogma of faith, so that without fear of contradiction we can modify the saying of the teacher of the early Church to the effect that our own birth would not be redeemed unless *it* had been 'accepted' too in the birth of Jesus. But in interpreting this statement we must invoke a no less obvious theological truth, namely that at the moment of the birth the mother and the child were human beings capable of suffering. And so at least initially we should presume that they were in fact subject to the pains of birth until the contrary is shown to have been the case. In this respect if there is something special, something in the nature of an exception to be asserted about this particular birth, then it must in a real sense be based on theological arguments, and should not *ipso facto* simply be assumed to be the case as the only fitting conclusion to be drawn in relation to such a birth as this. Jesus is truly man, and it is only as man that he was able to be our Redeemer. And for him and his mother pains are, in the fullest sense, 'fitting'. A doctor is least of all likely to see anything unfitting in the pains of birth. Nor can Gen. 3:16 be invoked as an argument against this, for the Redeemer, and so too his mother, precisely accept a position in which they are subject to the consequences of sin (Gal. 4:4; 2 Cor. 5:21). If, and to the extent that Gen. 3:16 is to be taken, therefore, in the sense that the pains of birth are an expression and a manifestation of the universal situation of sin in mankind, the birth of Jesus from Mary is not in itself such that it needs to be made an exception to this law. So far as the naturalness of Jesus' birth is concerned, it must be emphasized once more that it also includes the fact that Jesus came into the world through the natural processes of human birth. The traditional idea that Jesus came forth from the body of his mother in a manner similar to that in which he came forth from the closed tomb at the Resurrection must, therefore, be understood in the light of this, or else abandoned. Even Rathramnus, the 9th century Benedictine, took his stand against such Docetist or Manichee ideas, which all too easily come to enter into this question.

Now every doctor knows that the concrete processes of birth, in their effect upon mother and child, can vary very greatly from one individual to another despite their overall similarity. For all that the same physiological laws apply, the birth of a human being, at least as first and foremost an act on the mother's part, is an event affecting the *whole* of human nature, and hence, as it takes place in the concrete, depends to a large extent upon the particular disposition and attitude of the individual mother concerned. Taken even in a purely general sense, pain (regarded as a physiological occurrence) can be experienced in very different ways, according to whether the individual subject is in a position positively to integrate this 'pain' into the totality of his active living or not. Pain as lived through is itself from the outset pain that is interpreted by the free and intelligent subject, and so true is this that under certain circumstances one and the same physiological process, taken subjectively and as affecting the whole of the individual concerned, constitutes a pain (in the popular sense of the term) for one individual and not for another. On this basis when we say that as a matter of general principle Jesus and Mary were liable to pain, and when we presume in principle that in the case of Jesus' birth they were subject to the ordinary birth pangs, these statements must, once more, be subject to a certain crucial proviso. If we are thinking of the sinlessness of the Blessed Virgin, her integrity (i.e. her freedom from concupiscence,[2] taking this to mean a state in which it is impossible fully

[2] cf. the author's 'The Theological Concept of Concupiscentia', *Theological Investigations* I (London, 1961), pp. 347–382.

to integrate the impulses of the physical side of our natures and those deriving from the environment about us within our personal decisions as subjects), then it is clear that that which, in physiological terms, we would call 'pain' would be, and actually was, in her case experienced quite differently than with us. With us this occurrence is experienced as pain. Whether or not we still wish to call it by this name as experienced by Mary is perhaps ultimately speaking a mere question of terminology. For in any case the believing Christian can say this: the birth which took place here was, after all, different from birth as we know it, because she who gave birth and he who was born were different from ourselves in virtue of their sinlessness and their integrity (though this should not be conceived of in a 'paradisal' sense), for all that they made themselves one with us. Now once we recognize this as a starting-point for a true interpretation of the phrase 'virginitas in partu', albeit one that is not decked out in mythological hues, we can surely go on to regard the conception of the *hymen virginale* being unbroken as one of which we have no historical knowledge at all. Moreover even without this we can continue to maintain a positive meaning for the phrase 'virginitas in partu'. This conception, then, even considered as a theological conclusion, can be shown not to have any compelling force, and therefore is not binding as a matter of faith, the more so since in this respect the theological tradition is not so univocal as is sometimes supposed.

13

THE QUEST FOR APPROACHES
LEADING TO AN UNDERSTANDING OF
THE MYSTERY OF THE GOD-MAN JESUS

T HE situation may possibly be otherwise than I suppose. But I
believe that there are three possible approaches to that mysterious
relationship with Jesus through which, in the very act of living
itself, that is achieved and really comes to be understood ('realized')
which the Church's faith recognizes about Jesus. Approaches to a mysterious relationship, I say. What we have to recognize here is both the
distinction and the connection between the approach as such and the
reference of our whole personal existence to Jesus.

These three approaches are constituted by the following factors: one's
fellow man (one's neighbour), death, and the future. They are closely
interconnected. But we have to have taken these factors of our neighbour,
death (to the extent that we can do this as a matter of 'living' experience)
and hope in the future in full and radical seriousness in order that they
may point us on to that relationship with Jesus which alone constitutes
the basis for an explicit and genuine Christianity.[1]

Before we go any further, before we proceed to speak of each of these
three approaches in turn, one point of concern which we encounter particularly often nowadays requires an answer: we do not really know (at
least at the level of conscious reflection) what is properly speaking meant
by this Christian relationship with Jesus, and why such a thing constitutes something more than a mere 'ideology' which we 'conjure up' for
ourselves in order to escape from the harsh realities of the real world.

[1] The considerations here presented are intended as preliminaries leading both to
the development of a personal attitude towards Jesus as a matter of one's own faith,
and also to a consciously worked out christological process of reflection within
theology. But since such approaches actually belong, so far as we are concerned, to
the 'reality of Jesus' (in order so to express it) they also have their place – once we
have explicitly thought them out – in christology.

What has to be said on this point? First and foremost: Can we really love Jesus? Whatever his fate may have been 'after' death, has he not been withdrawn from us and from any possible relationship of love with us by this death? When the question is put in these terms, then we are really referring to that person who once lived, him himself in his earthly lot, rather than as an ideal to which we have assigned an historical name more or less adventitiously and of our own volition. It is the historical Jesus – not an ideal or an ideology – whom we are referring to when we ask whether we can 'still' love Jesus. In rejoinder it might be asked: Can we love anyone whom we have loved in life and who has died? Must we not go on loving him if our love for him during his life was such that it embraced the individual who was loved unreservedly? Have we not pre-cisely a responsibility for the dead – in other words a radical connection with them? Can we, or should we, simply turn away from them with a shrug of the shoulders, on the grounds that they are precisely no more, or at least that they have been withdrawn by death from any conceivable sphere of life available to us? No! Love and responsibility cannot detach themselves from the beloved once they are dead. They still have a claim upon us. We may, perhaps, forget them, because we do not really know what we can 'do' for them, because, precisely, we are unable really to pre-serve and integrate our own life in its various sections, from which they cannot be blotted out within the flux of time. But what we cannot say is this: the dead are in principle of no further concern to us. Their abiding claim upon us is such that they are not transformed into an ideal ideo-logical demand upon us which has to be respected for the future (our attitude to those fallen in war or murdered at Auschwitz etc. is often misinterpreted somewhat in this sense, as though a state of affairs belong-ing to the past remained in force throughout a quite different future to which these dead do not belong). Rather their life, as still laying a con-stant demand upon us *is* forever both for them and for us. They do not prolong their existence in a different life, one with which, admittedly, on this hypothesis we could not really have any genuine relationship. They remain as real factors forever, with this life of theirs which we ourselves have experienced. This is why they both can be, and are, loved. The concrete manner in which they enjoyed a real relationship with us during their lives may vary very greatly. But in the last analysis this is not of fundamental importance for our relationship to one who, though he has 'died', is still living. A child too can love his mother and accept that her life still in a real sense continues as a force that lays demands upon him even when this same mother died in giving birth. Nor do any of these genuine possibilities of an abiding relationship of love with those who, though they have died are still living, gainsay the fact that the majority of men have only very rudimentary experiences of this relationship, indeed may perhaps go so far as explicitly to deny it when they are explicitly brought face to face with it. We men are, in fact, beings who realize their ultimate potentialities only gradually and in fragmentary form, and not all epochs necessarily offer equally favourable situations for the realization of such potentialities.[2]

From all this it follows that we can love Jesus too, accept as of radical significance the demands which his life lays upon us, and in accepting these demands affirm this life as an abiding and continuing force, as 'existing'. We have not yet reached a stage at which we can straightway proceed to raise the question of what approach we should adopt so that this love can include precisely those special qualities (in its actual nature and in what we can recognize about it) which belong precisely to it, as distinct from the love we bear to other men. All that we are attempting to establish at this point is that he who regards Jesus and his life as entailing a final and definite demand upon him personally, is in effect affirming that he is living, and has been delivered from death. On any other showing he would not be assenting to Jesus himself in his claims upon us, but assenting to him only as an abstract ideal, an 'idea' which we have conjured up for ourselves at most in connection with the past life of Jesus, but which ultimately speaking would be independent of him.

Now that we have drawn attention to this point we can go on to enquire into the three approaches already mentioned, enabling us to understand what the Christian faith acknowledges about Jesus.

The first approach consists in *love of neighbour*.[3] Jesus himself shows us what this means in Mt. 25, where he asserts an identity between himself and our neighbour. Every love for one's fellow man has, at least in its nature, the character of an absolute commitment of one's personal existence to that fellow man. Hence where there is real love, it is achieved whether consciously or unconsciously, in the hope that, despite all the questionableness and fragility by reason of which that fellow man cannot in any sense supply a complete justification of the absolute character of

[2] On this line of argument cf. the author's ideas as presented in the article immediately following the present one and entitled 'Remarks on the Importance of the History of Jesus for Catholic Dogmatics'.

[3] On this see also the author's article 'Reflections on the Unity Between the Love of Neighbour and the Love of God' in *Theological Investigations* IV (London and Baltimore, 1969), pp. 231–249.

the love that is borne to him, such a commitment is reasonable, and need not necessarily meet with ultimate disappointment. Now in Jesus and through him this hope has been confirmed. In his person a man appears in palpable and historical guise for whom and in whom it is manifest (to those who believe) that that love in which man lovingly commits himself to him can, in its absolute character, no longer meet with disappointment. This man, therefore, can enable us to commit ourselves in love to our fellow man too, justifying us in this and enabling us to hope in the total and unreserved character of this commitment. But let us imagine a man who, in virtue of his very existence, his human lot, and the final and definitive outcome of this, provides an absolute justification for a total and unreserved love for himself and his brethren, and overcomes all ultimate reserves on the part of himself as the subject of this love with regard to the ultimate questionability of the beloved. Such a man as this is (though this is a point which we cannot develop further here) precisely he whom the Christian faith in its traditional formulation acknowledges as the God-man, as that man who is one with God to such an extent that if we commit ourselves to him unconditionally in the sureness of faith and hope, then the goal of this love of ours, which embraces both the beloved and ourselves, becomes God himself, and no longer solely an individual man in all his radical questionability. But for the same reason the converse is also true: he who loves Jesus as one who lives, with a love that is justified and sure of itself, and in an attitude of absolute trust that recognizes its absolute basis in Jesus himself, such a one has already accepted Jesus as him whom the Christian faith proclaims, whether he does or does not understand the classic and abidingly valid formulae of christology.

A second approach, leading to an understanding of what Jesus is and is for us, can be discovered in the *experience of death*.[4] This approach is primarily connected with that which has been said with regard to love of neighbour as leading to an understanding of Jesus. The absolute character of such love seems in fact to be threatened in the most radical sense by the very fact of experiencing the death of the beloved. And even if we say that such love is asserting that the beloved survives as a final and definitive force, still this would in its turn lead to the further question of what grounds there can be for so boldly hoping that the beloved does remain as a final and definitive force in this sense, and where *that* man is whose fate, regarded as brought about by God, enables the victory which such a

---

[4] On this cf. also the author's ideas as presented in this volume in 'Ideas for a Theology of Death', and also in *On the Theology of Death* (2nd ed., Eng. transl. 1969).

final and definitive state represents to be manifested to our eyes in historical terms. But even apart from this, the experience of death constitutes an approach enabling us to understand the reality of Jesus and his significance for us. However much each individual may die his own death, it still remains true in the deepest sense that death is the common fate of all men, and that in it they are united among themselves by having to endure that which is most extreme and most ultimate. And no one is justified in adopting an attitude of indifference to his fellow. But at what point in our personal history do we achieve the concrete hope that this that is most ultimate and extreme in our existence, in which we are absolutely torn apart from ourselves, is not the victory of the sheer empty nothingness of man, but in the contrary opens onto the absolute blessedness of the love of God and his eternity? In the end it is only in a man whose 'resurrection' is experienced in faith and hope as the crown and fulfilment of our common death. But if in such a resurrection the final and definitive assent of God to us is recognized as the true reality of the death of Jesus and of our own death, then the risen Lord is believed in as the unsurpassable word of salvation uttered by God to us, and as the bringer of eschatological salvation. And again we can assert this: he who is thus believed in in the power of a hope that overcomes death and as the basis of this hope, is precisely he who is acknowledged in the Christian faith as the incarnate Word in whom God has definitively and victoriously uttered himself to man.

On this basis it becomes, properly speaking, *ipso facto* intelligible why and how we can designate the factor of *hope in the absolute future*[5] as an approach enabling us to understand what Jesus is and what he means for us. We are speaking of a hope which hopes on behalf of all, and, moreover, hopes for a final and definitive victory as the outcome of the history of mankind, even though it cannot point to any definable goal already filled out with a content which we can recognize (for to do this would be to turn from the inconceivable and mysterious God of the future to make an idol of the future itself fashioned by our own hands). Such a hope as this must necessarily search history to discover how far it has already advanced in its course towards the future. This is not in order to anticipate the absolute future by already formulating it in ideological terms, or in order falsely to transform it into a goal to be constituted as such by man himself.

[5] On this see also the author's article, 'On the Theology of Hope', *Theological Investigations* V (London and New York, 1973), pp. 242–259, and the various studies in which the future is treated of from one point of view or another as an active factor.

Rather it is because this hope must render an account of itself in the concrete. It should not be prohibited from enquiring into the 'signs of the times', seeing that it is genuinely hoping for its own fulfilment, and that this, after all, is destined to be achieved in and through history. Nor should it restrain itself, from motives of false diffidence, from itself noticing in history that history itself has already entered upon a phase in which the possibility of an ultimate collapse of history into the void of God as its absolute future is already past. Once we have, in a spirit of faith, seized upon the 'Resurrection' of Jesus, then we have grasped the fact that the one and single history of the world as a whole can no longer fail, even though the question of how the personal history of the individual will turn out remains open, and belongs to the absolute future of God which brings blessing indeed, but still at the same time remains at the level of inconceivable and indefinable mystery. But once the word of God's self utterance, in the case of a concrete individual in history, is present never again to be withdrawn, and accepted in faith as the absolute future of history, then that unity between God and man is present and believed in too which Christian faith acknowledges in the 'hypostatic union'.

The question must be asked how we can love our neighbour unreservedly, committing our own lives in a radical sense on his behalf, how such a love is not rendered invalid even by death, and whether we can hope in death to discover not the end but the consummation in that absolute future which is called God. And anyone who does ask these questions is seeking thereby, whether he recognizes it or not, for Jesus. He who really keeps alive this threefold question and does not suppress it will not find it in itself so difficult to discover the answer to these questions in history in the person of Jesus, provided Jesus is preached to him aright. And provided he opens himself to the answer to this threefold question, constituted by Jesus and his life in death and Resurrection, then he gains too an approach which will enable him to understand the traditional christology, which at first sight seems so difficult to understand, but ultimately speaking conveys no other message than that in Jesus God has uttered himself to man victoriously and unsurpassably as the blessed response to that threefold question which is not merely something which man may possibly raise within himself, but rather which, at basis, he himself is.

14

REMARKS ON THE IMPORTANCE OF THE HISTORY OF JESUS FOR CATHOLIC DOGMATICS

B Y way of introduction to my short essay I may be permitted to re-
call a brief episode, though in itself it is of no great importance. A
few years ago, on a visit to the U.S.A., I met a Catholic professor of
dogmatics from Europe. In the course of a theological discussion he ex-
plained to me that though of course he did not doubt the existence of
Jesus of Nazareth, still he felt that even if this were not a historical fact it
would make no difference to Christianity as he understood it. However
unimportant this little story may be in itself – the more so since this position was put forward with a gentle undertone of doubt and self-criticism
– it is, nevertheless, not altogether without significance as a symptom of
what is taking place in Catholic theology today. I say Catholic theology
because it is well known that in Protestant theology the tendency radically to emancipate the beliefs of Christianity and its 'dogmatics' (to the
extent that any such discipline still survives) from history is of far longer
standing.[1]

The *first* thesis which I would put forward here on the complex problems pointed to by this anecdote runs as follows: Catholic faith and its
dogmatics as they have been understood up to now, and also as they will
have to be understood in the future, remain indissolubly bound up not
only with the historical existence of Jesus of Nazareth, but also with the
historical events of a specific kind which took place during his life. This
thesis, precisely in its universality, has of course become a sheer obvious
truism from the earliest times of Christianity onwards (in the struggle
against gnostic tendencies which are already discernible in the New
Testament itself) right down to the struggle of the Catholic Church

[1] A survey of the treatment of the question and the importance accorded to it in
the Protestant sphere is provided by H. Zahrnt, *Es begann mis Jesus von Nazareth*
(Gütersloh, 2nd ed., 1968).

against Modernism at the beginning of the twentieth century. But abstracting from the difficulties which this thesis has to face, and to which we shall be returning in our second thesis, it turns out after all, on a more careful and precise presentation, to be less self-evident to our understanding of the Catholic faith and Catholic theology's understanding of its own nature than appears at first sight. For the thesis does in fact become more difficult and more obscure the moment we ask the following question: Is it intended as a *dogmatic* statement of faith or as a thesis of fundamental theology which (on a right understanding) has the function of *supplying a basis for* our faith? In putting forward this question we are, of course, not from the outset insinuating that the question as presented in this twofold form has to be answered in precisely the same sense or with the same *range* in view of the historical events of the life of Jesus that are pointed to. But even if we do not make this insinuation, the question as presented in these two alternative forms remains difficult for us of today. I believe that we have to presume that today not a few Catholic dogmatic theologians and exegetes would answer the question in the affirmative in its *dogmatic* sense, but in the negative if it is taken as pertaining to fundamental theology.

If we deny from the outset that there is any kind of difference between dogmatics and fundamental theology, or at most are prepared to conceive of a fundamental theology which from the outset has nothing to do with the facts of history, precisely, for instance, the history of Jesus' life, then of course, while it is still open to us on the most favourable view to regard the first theis as intended in a dogmatic sense, it can no longer possibly be intended from the point of view of fundamental theology. But there are many who, even though they would not defend any such radical elimination of fundamental theology in general, or have never entered into a question of this kind very profoundly (for in fact even in theology there are a few strange 'obsessional specialists'), nevertheless in the concrete they will deny the first thesis when taken in a fundamental theological sense, even while they accept it when taken in a dogmatic sense. For instance nowadays even respectable theologians should be subjected to the question: Do you believe *that* Jesus is risen from the dead, or do you believe also *because* he has risen from the dead (as, despite Bultmann, Paul was allowed to believe)? And to this not a few among even the Catholic theologians of today will be found to reply: Obviously I believe only *that* he has risen from the dead. Such theologians, therefore, reject, at least with regard to the Resurrection, an interpretation of the first thesis in a sense pertaining to fundamental theology. It should be noticed that here we are still abstracting from the more general question of *which* realities and events in the life of Jesus the interpretation of the first thesis in the sense of fundamental theology necessarily has to concern itself with. But allowing for this, the first point to be made is that it seems to me that any absolute denial of the first thesis is thoroughly false and heretical. The proof of this assertion from Scripture, tradition, and declarations of the Church's teaching office, can of course not be adduced *here*. It is true that in the course of the struggle against Modernism at the beginning of the present century many regrettable wrong judgements were made at the individual level by the official institutions of the Church's teaching authority. Nevertheless, on this crucial point that which it was sought to hold firm to and to defend in this struggle was right, was Catholic, and must endure. (In this connection it is a secondary question what degree of success was achieved in arriving at a correct understanding of Modernism itself considered as an historical entity and in a way that did positive justice to its basic concerns.)[2]

Now that we have established the fundamental theological meaning of our first thesis, which still remains in force even today, we can go on to the more precise question of exactly what the real interrelationship is between dogmatic theology and fundamental theology, faith and the historical experience on which faith is based. This is a question which still remains completely open. Certainly since the apologetics of the 19th century right down to the first few decades of the 20th century an extrinsicist approach has been pursued in fundamental theology which has made itself felt even in many of the individual declarations of the Church's teaching authority against Modernism. This extrinsicism, however, fails to do justice to the realities, or to express aright the true relationship between faith and that which provides the basis for faith.[3] There has been a widespread failure (as, for instance, the charge of heresy made against Rousselot has shown) to recognize how faith and the historical findings of fundamental theology mutually condition one another, and are immanently present within one another, even though they are not to be identified, and to perceive the relationship between the light of faith and the basis for faith as capable of being reflected upon by human reason. In a fundamental theological demonstration of Christian revelation of the kind we

---

[2] On this cf. e.g. K. Rahner and J. Ratzinger, *Offenbarung und Überlieferung* (Freiburg, 1965), pp. 11 ff.

[3] Among many other studies which should be cited on this question, cf. G. Muschalek, *Glaubensgewissheit in Freiheit* (Freiburg, 1968); E. Kunz, *Glaube – Gnade – Geschichte. Die Glaubenstheologie des Pierre Rousselot* (Frankfurt, 1970).

are thinking of it was fondly imagined that properly speaking we could only be surprised at how, in that case, men who could not be presumed to be stupid or ill-willed did not embrace Christianity in its Catholic form as soon as they had heard only a little of this fundamental theology. But even if today we no longer accept the idea which has held sway for at least a hundred years of how, in more precise terms, dogmatic theology and fundamental theology are related one to the other (not even if today, once more, a somewhat similar version is seeking to assert itself in a certain current of Protestant theology), then this is still, despite all, far from meaning that the Catholic dogmatic theologian, or even the Catholic exegete, should seek to get rid of his difficulties by saying that he rejects the fundamental theological significance of the first thesis totally and from the outset. Even when we have defined this thesis in such precise terms, we are still far from having arrived at any decision as to the full scope of what the Catholic theologian is to regard as indispensable in the life of Jesus as being relevant to fundamental theology. Even when we have interpreted the thesis in this sense, we have still not decided anything on the point of whether the historical findings in fundamental theology of such real events in the life of Jesus are or are not in *all* cases *univocally* the same.[4]

This brings us to a *second* thesis. It runs as follows: Catholic fundamental theology, and also present-day dogmatics (each in its own way) must nowadays take quite new factors into account, affecting points of individual detail. These consist in the findings and problems of present-day exegesis with regard to the historicity, whether asserted or assumed, of the events of the life of Jesus. Fundamental and dogmatic theologians must reckon with the fact that the degree of historicity to be ascribed to these may vary very greatly and in very vital respects. Their approach, therefore, must be quite different from that which it has formerly been. I am aware that so far as the majority of modern Catholic *exegetes* is concerned, in presenting such a thesis we are merely beating an open door. But I believe that unfortunately even today this thesis is still far from being regarded as established so far as the dogmatic theologians are concerned, and above all in the teaching of dogmatic theology in the seminaries. One point of detail, in itself insignificant, may serve to indicate this.

---

[4] This is certainly not the case, and these distinctions should be worked out in any fundamental theology. In doing this we should not act as though, for instance, our knowledge that the Eucharist was instituted by the pre-Easter Jesus is arrived at by a process of speculation univocally the same as the experience of his Resurrection and of the reception of this experience on our part.

It is intended not as a hostile criticism of the Second Vatican Council, but as a simple statement of fact. Let us take as our example what it means to read the third chapter of 'Lumen Gentium', concerning the hierarchical constitution of the Church, or other passages concerning the priesthood in the Church, through the eyes of a modern exegete, and in the light of the New Trstament passages there adduced. Unless we choose to regard these passages as mere pious biblical embellishment of statements of doctrine which could equally well have been expressed without these New Testament quotations, we must come to the following conclusion: a modern exegete would not have had the audacity to produce such naïvely asserted *dicta probantia* from the New Testament, and, moreover, would have maintained this attitude even if, with his colleagues from the department of dogmatic theology, he were to hold that such passages should obviously be included in documents of the Church's official teaching and in a context which intrinsically belongs to the modern awareness of faith and tradition. But it must be conceded that nowadays they should not be included in such documents in a way that reduces them to the status of mere pious embellishments devised by those who rejoice in biblical jargon. What we have said here does not, of course, apply to all such Scriptural quotations, but conversely, not all the quotations concerned can be allowed to escape this criticism.

The modern dogmatic theologian needs to adduce arguments from Scripture and to present them seriously as such, instead of merely repeating the Church's doctrines in biblical formulations. And if he is to do this he must take serious and exact cognizance of the findings, and also the problems, of modern exegesis. Nowadays he can precisely not simply present every saying placed upon the lips of Jesus by the evangelists as his *ipsissima verba*.[5] *He*, the dogmatic theologian, must also allow for the possibility of very early theological developments within the primitive Christian community, dating even from before the earliest writings of the New Testament. Again in drawing theological quotations from the Apostolic writings, he should not simply treat them as though the individual sentence cannot and should not be submitted to further enquiry against the background of the whole of Christian revelation and of its

[5] Although this still is a widespread practice in the current textbooks of dogmatic theology. We cannot justify these methods simply by saying that the inspiration and inerrancy of Scripture is presupposed from fundamental theology. For the pupil will rightly recognize who is the immediate author of the statement which is adduced, and, moreover, it is of the utmost importance for the meaning and the theological significance of such a quotation to recognize this.

real origins[6] (in accordance with the *analogia fidei* and the ultimate unity
of the New Testament, which, however, is not always immediately
apparent, and which the dogmatic theologian must always in principle
uphold). The doctrine of a canon within the canon is, in its real content,
a sound and ancient principle of hermeneutics for Catholic dogmatics.
But we should not conclude from it that we have the right to set aside
certain writings of the New Testament or even individual sentences
(though admittedly these have to be interpreted aright) as not being in any
sense binding upon us. The Catholic theologian must achieve a genuine
understanding of the fact that even in the New Testament itself there are
different levels and certain theological developments of the most varied
kind, and which are far from admitting any direct or easy harmony between their various parts. Once he has grasped this fact, he has no reason
whatever to despair of an argument from Scripture on a right understanding of it, provided he takes with all due seriousness modern exegesis
and the refinements of biblical theology. The only prior condition is that
he must have sufficient confidence in himself thoroughly to think out and
bring to maturity in the context of the Church what he has already in
principle observed in the New Testament, namely a living theological
development which proceeds from the original experience of revelation,
produces further theological developments, and even at the end of the
New Testament, despite the division between the New Testament itself
and the theological developments which follow (a division which itself
has theological relevance) does not cease to advance to further ideas,
taking the New Testament as its standard. A further prior condition is,
admittedly, that the dogmatic theologian, in his use of arguments from
biblical theology, must make clear the true nature of his approach through
biblical arguments to his pupils. He must try to avoid giving the impression that all that is needed is to cite some passages from Scripture, perhaps
to add a verbal paraphrase, and one has *ipso facto* proved what a Council
has taught on the subject a thousand years later. Of course we can say that
the statements just referred to constitute the outward presentation of
something which a serious dogmatic theologian has actually achieved at
an earlier stage, but when we view the average approach in dogmatic
studies from *this* aspect (not from any other) right down to the present,
we see that in fact it has not been such as has been described above, even
though much in this approach can be excused on grounds of sheer lack of
time. For a seminary teacher in dogmatics too inevitably suffers from this.

[6] cf. K. Rahner, 'Theology in the New Testament', *Theological Investigations*
V (London and Baltimore, 1966), pp. 23–41.

With regard to former interpretations of the second thesis, we are, once more, still stuck fast at a very general level, so that what has been said up to now must still seem to be nothing very exciting. The situation completely changes once a more precise question is posed. It is a question for the theologian who is not an exegete. What, in more precise terms, is he to hold firm to as historical in the life of Jesus, and as indispensable for him from the point of view of fundamental theology? This means too what he can and must expect from the exegete working in the field of fundamental theology. For whether the exegete notices it or not, he too, whether in a positive or a negative sense, is constantly working in this field. To mention just a few examples chosen at random, and purely for the sake of illustrating what is meant: must such a theologian expect the exegete to present the command to baptize in Mt. 28 as the *ipsissimum verbum* of Jesus? Must the exegete hand over to him the institution of the Eucharist, with at least a few words of interpretation and historical reconstruction? Innumerable questions of this and similar kinds are manifestly raised between exegetes and dogmatic theologians, and however true it may be that the dogmatic theologian should not prejudice the methods intrinsic to exegesis and biblical theology as historical disciplines, it is no less true that the dogmatic theologian cannot dispense the exegete from the duty of finding the answer to these questions which he puts to him, provided this exegete himself intends to be a Catholic theologian in the true sense, and not merely a historian of religion who by chance is concerned with the writings which are called the New Testament as mere texts of the history of religion.

I believe that the problem as here presented in more precise terms sharpens into a twofold question for the Catholic dogmatic theologian, with his special interest in the history of Jesus:

(a) According to the findings of historical research, did Jesus, prior to his death, say anything expressive of a messianic awareness in some way that is *apprehensible* to us, or *alternatively* are the indications of this such that historical research can be in a position positively and actually to *contest* them?

(b) Did Jesus rise from the dead in a way that does not simply reduce this event to a mere figure, and to something belonging only to the realm of the disciples' conscious faith? Or alternatively is this conscious faith of theirs based rather upon the Resurrection (however this may be interpreted in more precise terms) as something which is prior to the faith itself, albeit only apprehensible *in* that faith?

In connection with these two questions we must add a few further observations before going on to our third thesis, so as to understand what the two questions mean. So far as the 'messianic' consciousness of Jesus is concerned a question *of this kind* is ultimately speaking independent of the question of whether Jesus really claimed for himself the title of Messiah in his own words. The same applies to the other titles of dignity ascribed to him. The one point of concern for our present question is whether prior to his death he in some sense understood himself to have a significance of such a kind that he required other men to enter into a state of unity with him (a state to which the name faith, or any other name, may be given) of such a kind that the believer recognizes salvation as objectively and indissolubly bound up with him. If we can say this, then, I believe, we can trace the development of all that the subsequent strata in the New Testament present us with in the way of interpretations of Jesus, and which are found later still in the Church's teaching concerning divine Sonship at the metaphysical level (together with the doctrine of the pre-existence of the Logos as rightly interpreted) from Jesus' own understanding of himself as here described. In this connection it still makes no difference whether a particular exegete formulates the point of departure in New Testament and ecclesiastical christology referred to above as historical or merely as being more or less *of such a kind* as we have just indicated. He may formulate it quite differently. What is essential is that this point of departure, so long as the individual wants to remain a Catholic exegete, is adequate so far as he himself is concerned, and so far as the Church's own conscious faith is concerned, as such a point of departure.

The second observation is this: so far as the question formulated under (b) is concerned, the Catholic dogmatic theologian (and the exegete, who in fact should never cease to be a dogmatic theologian as well) has not only the right but the duty too (generally much neglected) clearly to work out the uniqueness, deriving from the reality itself, of the knowledge of the Resurrection of Jesus achieved in fundamental theology as distinct from all other historical knowledge. This is a point which cannot be developed or rendered more comprehensible any further here, yet it is of crucial importance for a right understanding of the question formulated under (b).

Only at this stage can we proceed to formulate the *third* thesis, and it is only by so formulating it that we can show how the problems we have developed up to this point come to their full sharpness. The thesis runs as follows: there is one question which Catholic dogmatic theologies have not yet thought out in any explicit sense at all, and so which has not been answered even at the implicit level by them in any clear sense. The question is whether the dogmatic theologian can be satisfied *solely* with a positive answer from the exegete to the *second* question (that concerning the Resurrection of Jesus), and whether he can develop the statements of christology concerning Jesus himself solely from faith in the Resurrection as based on the findings of fundamental theology, even when he dispenses with the historical witness which the exegete provides to a 'messianic' awareness of the pre-Easter Jesus as a positive assertion.

The thesis we have stated lays down that there is a question here concerning which the dogmatic theologian still has to make his own position clear. Is it for him still an open question, or *alternatively* is it one which has already been decided in the affirmative on dogmatic grounds (obviously in collaboration with the exegete)? Obviously no such question is being presented as open so far as Jesus' own messianic awareness is concerned 'in itself', nor even with regard to any *dogmatic* statement about it. It is a question only of the knowledge of this messianic consciousness as a matter of *fundamental theological* enquiry into the history of Jesus, and *quoad nos*. Alternatively, and in more precise terms, it is a question of whether the dogmatic theologian's knowledge of this awareness as derived from fundamental theology constitutes an absolutely indispensable prior condition so far as he is concerned for his dogmatic statements about Jesus. In my opinion it has been sufficiently demonstrated elsewhere[7] that we can so think of the messianic awareness of Jesus, or Jesus' human awareness of his 'metaphysical' divine sonship in the sense of the theological orthodoxy of the Council of Chalcedon, that the exegete will not feel compelled to raise any objection on the basis of his data.

We are asserting, then, that there is here a question which, so far as the specialist in dogmatics or fundamental theology is concerned, is still an open one. It is the question of what demands such a theologian must make upon the exegete from the standpoint of his dogmatic theology with regard to the possibility of knowing about the messianic consciousness of the pre-Easter Jesus (this question is, of course, still independent of the further question of what the exegete's reply will be to this question and this demand from the side of fundamental and dogmatic theology). Again in asserting that the question is open, we are not of course in any

---

[7] cf. K. Rahner, 'Dogmatic Reflections on the Knowledge and Selfconsciousness of Christ', *Theological Investigations* V (London and Baltimore, 1966), pp. 193–215; A. Vögtle, 'Exegetische Erwägungen über das Wissen und Selbstbewusstsein Jesu', *Gott in Welt. Festgabe Rahner* I (Freiburg, 1964), pp. 608–667; H. Riedlinger, *Geschichtlichkeit und Vollendung des Wissens Christi* (Freiburg, 1966).

sense biased against the fact that this question which is put to the exegete must inevitably, or at least with the utmost historical probability, meet with a negative answer from his side. Nor do we intend in any sense to insinuate by this third thesis that it is exegetically speaking certain, or at least extremely probable, that there was never any point in time in the 'development' of the pre-Easter Jesus (though from the point of view of dogmatics it is perfectly conceivable) in which he claimed for himself certain titles of dignity (it makes no difference which), which of their very nature contained that which we are nowadays able to call a messianic awareness, the awareness of being the eschatological bringer of salvation, the Son of God etc. Again in these questions, which are certainly exegetically speaking difficult, we should not proceed from the tacit assumption that the most sceptical and minimalizing interpretation has the greatest chance of arriving at the truth.

The situation nowadays, however, in exegesis is such not only on the Protestant but on the Catholic side too, that with regard to the pre-Easter Jesus' understanding of himself in so far as this is still historically attainable to us, very difficult and disputed problems arise, and hence the Catholic dogmatist and fundamental theologian must ask himself what he should or should not demand of the exegete from his own standpoint as in this respect unconditionally established. And with regard to this question our third thesis now purports to say that provisionally (at least until the whole problem has been thought out more precisely) it is not impossible from the outset to take the experience of faith of the Resurrection of Jesus as our sole basis, and so to achieve those theological conclusions which are already expressed in the New Testament itself, and then in the later credal pronouncements of the Church in her christology. Admittedly the Resurrection must be understood not as any kind of coming to life of a man, or even as the return of a man to the plane of temporal and biological existence, but rather as a unique event, though one that still takes place within the unfolding of our time, as the seal of God upon the 'reality of Jesus' (if we may avail ourselves of this somewhat obscure phrase) etc. To state the matter in other terms: it is perhaps conceivable (from the aspect of fundamental theology) that the risen Lord (who, of course had a religious mission with regard to the radical closeness of the kingdom of God, which claims our absolute obedience) can, solely on the basis of the Resurrection, be recognized with sufficient sureness as *that which* the statements of Christianity in its orthodox christology acknowledge him to be. It is true that we cannot at this point adduce the true arguments on which this thesis is based. This would go far beyond the scope of so brief an essay as this. The third thesis is, in fact, ultimately speaking intended merely as a question to be put to the fundamental theologian and the dogmatist as to whether they might possibly come to terms with a thesis of this kind, and thereby could give the Catholic exegete wider scope and greater freedom in his historical researches concerning the pre-Easter Jesus' understanding of himself than they have accorded to that exegete hitherto.

Of course an objection which might be advanced against this hypothetical third thesis might be that whatever reply might be made to it it would be of no real importance for the simple reason that the enquiry into the Resurrection of Jesus from the point of view of fundamental theology is no easier to answer than the question, likewise from the point of view of fundamental theology (not from that of dogmatics!) of the pre-Easter Jesus' understanding of himself. But for reasons which I cannot set forth here, this objection does not seem to me to be really justified. Provided our thought is not conditioned by the Platonist assumption that man is divided into body and soul, each 'part' having its own absolutely disparate destiny, provided we do not think of our Resurrection and Jesus' in the sense of a return to a biological mode of existence such as we experience in the present, or in some similar sense which is in reality mythological, provided we understand, on the basis of both these conditions, that the definitive mode of existence for a being of our kind endowed with freedom, when this definitive state is taken as the object of our hope, implies what we know as 'resurrection', then we are in a position to understand how there can be a 'transcendental' justification for a hope of resurrection (even though in history as it *de facto* exists this hope is always connected with the 'experience' of the Resurrection of Jesus in a *mutually* conditioning relationship). And so in the light of this the assured faith of the disciples comes to seem as though they had believed in a strange miracle which no-one nowadays can reproduce. But as we have said it is no part of our task here to provide a justification in terms of fundamental theology for the conviction that Jesus did indeed rise from the dead (regarding this as an element in faith in his Resurrection which comes into force only within this faith, but still as such can also be, in a genuine sense, the basis for this faith).

Even if this third thesis were to be taken as an enquiry into what it means to say that the Resurrection is an adequate point of departure in fundamental theology for christology, it would still always have a certain importance for the question of Jesus' own understanding of himself, something which is a matter for historical research. For the exegete who in his own faith reproduces the Easter faith of the disciples (without interpreting it away) must, in his realistic researches into the historical facts, precisely pose the question of how in all seriousness the first disciples could have arrived at their Easter faith if they had known nothing beforehand about Jesus from his own understanding of himself, except that he was a wandering religious preacher preaching a message which was totally independent of his person and his own faith.

It would be a satisfaction to me if this first sketch for a strategic approach to liberate the modern Catholic exegete were to be welcomed by the exegete himself and greeted by the specialists in dogmatic and fundamental theology at least with a certain good will and without immediate protest. Admittedly for this I am assuming that in both camps there is some understanding of such problems. For today it is the fashion to be fideist so far as the Christian faith is concerned and more or less schizophrenic so far as the relationship between faith and reason (taken in a philosophical and historical sense) is concerned. But this state of affairs need not necessarily always remain the same.

15

THE TWO BASIC TYPES OF CHRISTOLOGY

W E shall here be attempting to work out two basic types of christology, and so of christological statements which are put forward with the claim that they are *the* basic forms – in other words that in principle and taken together, they embrace the entire field of possible christological statements. Before attempting to give an outline of these two types, I shall have to make certain preliminary observations. The two types envisaged are, so far as I know, nowhere explicitly or precisely reflected upon as such, i.e. as distinct from one another. This means that I must take full responsibility for what I shall have to say about them, the special qualities which I shall be ascribing to each type exclusively, and the lines of demarcation by which they will be distinguished from one another. Both of these basic types (and of course from time to time various exceptional forms and hybrids appear), can be expressed in either an orthodox or a heterodox way, so that in the history of dogma as it actually exists both types figure repeatedly and in very many ways. In the christologies which have *de facto* been developed these basic types figure for the most part in mixed form, so that it is extremely difficult to draw a clear and explicit distinction between the two. I believe that these two forms are already present in the christologies of the New Testament, even if there too they have not been consciously adverted to as clearly distinguishable from one another. It is virtually impossible within the limits we have set ourselves to provide proofs from biblical theology and the history of dogma in support of our proposition. We must confine ourselves to delineating the two basic types envisaged in very abstract terms and without the safeguard of established historical facts. It is extremely difficult even to find names for the types referred to capable of designating them clearly and unmistakably. In fact any concise designation of them inevitably entails the danger of misunderstandings. With this very important proviso, I would like to call the first type the *'saving history'* type, a christology viewed from below, and the second

213

type the *metaphysical* type, a christology developing downwards from above. In saying this it must admittedly be recognized that the concepts of a rising and descending christology do not really cover what is here being pointed to in an unmistakable manner. For a 'saving history' christology, leading upwards from below, can as such obviously be re-expressed in the alternative christology proceeding downwards from above. For it understands, and must understand, this process of 'rising up' as an act proper to God himself. This does not of itself mean, however, that the 'movement downwards from above' here would lead to the same conclusions in terms of content as the 'downwards movement' in a meta-physical or 'descending' type of christology. In distinguishing these two types we are leaving the question open as to whether the second type is not in some sense logically contained in the first all along, and whether it cannot be explicitated from this under certain metaphysical and theo-logical conditions, especially those bearing upon the unity between the history of the natural world and the history of human thought. There is a further question which cannot be treated of here, namely to which of the two types here envisaged the classic christology of Chalcedon properly belongs. Despite the fact that at first sight this christology, which is strongly metaphysical in character, seems to correspond to a descending christology, it appears on closer examination that what we have in this classic christology is rather a mixed type, especially seeing that in it the development of ideas is markedly in terms of particular categories, and it is not the cosmological christology proper that determines the approach. Rather this is at most something that can be derived from it as a conclu-sion, especially since in a Western Trinitarian doctrine the cosmological function of the Logos (who becomes man) has ceased to be regarded as a special property of the Logos as distinct from the Father and the Holy Spirit.[1]

---

[1] The author has repeatedly made known his views on questions of christology. Cf., for instance: 'Current Problems in Christology', *Theological Investigations* I (London, 1961), pp. 149–200; 'The Eternal Significance of the Humanity of Jesus for Our Relationship with God', *Theological Investigations* III (London and Balti-more, 1967), pp. 35–46; 'On the Theology of the Incarnation', *Theological Investi-gations* IV (London and Baltimore, 1966), pp. 105–120; 'Christology within an Evolutionary View of the World', *Theological Investigations* V (London and Baltimore, 1966), pp. 157–192; 'One Mediator and the Many Mediations', *Theological Investiga-tions* IX (London and New York, 1972), pp. 169–184; 'The Position of Christology in the Church Between Exegesis and Dogmatics', *Theological Investigations* XI (London and New York, 1974), pp. 185–214. Also in the present volume, 'Remarks on the Importance of the History of Jesus for Catholic Dogmatics'.

THE CHRISTOLOGY OF SAVING HISTORY

We must now proceed to delineate the first type, the 'saving history' christology. In it the eye of the believer in his experience of saving history alights first on the man Jesus of Nazareth, and on him in his fully human reality, in his death, in the absolute powerless and in the abidingly definitive state which his reality and his fate have been brought to by God, something which we call his Resurrection, his glorification, his sitting at the right hand of the Father. The eye of faith rests upon this man Jesus. He is, in the concrete sense described, the content of the specifically Christian experience, and the experience of saving history. Through him, as faith sees it, God's ultimate and irrevocable utterance of salvation to man is made. The fact that God is gracious to man despite his attitude of culpable protest, and the fact that this grace imposes itself victoriously – this is something which becomes definitively and unsurpassably clear to the experience of faith in this man Jesus. Jesus of Nazareth is not merely *an* utterance of God to man which, viewed in the light of the development of the history of salvation and revelation always remains at the level of the provisional and conditional turning of God to man, but rather the definitive, unsurpassable, and victorious – in other words eschatological – utterance of God to man. And because of this, and to the extent that it is true, Jesus cannot be subsumed into the category of prophet and religious reformer.[2] On the contrary, it could be demonstrated, even if we must forego this here for want of time, that from this starting-point of christology which we have just defined, the classic statements of the Chalcedonian christology can be arrived at provided that we interpret these in themselves aright. And for this precisely the starting-point mentioned above has, conversely, an indispensable and crucial importance. The point of departure for this christology, therefore, is the simple experience of the man Jesus, and of the Resurrection in which his fate was brought to its conclusion. It is he whom man encounters in his existential need, in his quest for salvation. And in Jesus he experiences the fact that the mystery of man, which it is not for man himself to control, and which is bound up with the absurdity of guilt and death, is, nevertheless, hidden in the love

[2] Materially speaking, the subject here being treated of is the same as that which the author has sought to throw light upon in the articles entitled 'Mitte des Glaubens', *Hilfe zum Glauben*, Theol. Meditationen 27, A. Exeler, J. B. Metz, K. Rahner edd. (Einsiedeln, 1971), pp. 39–56. But cf. also in the same series, *Ich glaube an Jesus Christus*, Theol. Meditationen 21 (Einsiedeln, 1968) with references and bibliography.

of God. Where Jesus is present in this sense there is *ipso facto* present too an orthodox – a Chalcedonian, if we like to express it so – christology, even if, through our own limitations, or because of the liability to misunderstanding inherent in the Chalcedonian formula, the explicitation in terms of faith of this basic experience of Jesus and in Jesus in faith is *de facto* not attained to. We have already said that a basic experience of this kind of the fate of Jesus can be described as the deed of God wrought upon him and upon us, and so too the Chalcedonian interpretation of that fate can be expressed as a descending christology, though this does not mean that this *precise* descending christology, in contrast to the second basic type of christology, need necessarily be saying more than what was already clearly present at the starting-point: Jesus in his human lot is *the* (not *a*!) address of God to man, and as such eschatologically unsurpassable. In this basic type of christology, in which Jesus is from the outset seen within the context of the individual man's quest for salvation in the concrete human conditions of his life, the cosmos as such does not enter into the question.[3] As the creation of God and as the world which is in a fallen state, this is simply there beforehand as the stage on which the event of Jesus in saving history takes place. And properly speaking it makes no difference to this to say that this world has, in the providence of God, been conceived of all along in such a way that its true function is to be the stage for this saving event. This appears above all from the fact that the possibility and actuality of sin, to which this saving event represents the answer, does not itself in turn appear as conditioned, permitted, and mediated by this saving event. Any transition of this christology into the second basic type could at most be arrived at on the basis of the conviction that the promise of the Spirit given through Jesus signifies not merely the salvation of man, which is measured by his own personal need, but rather the self-communication of the absolute God as he is in himself to man.[4] For our present purposes we shall not attempt to show how the various exceptional varieties of this basic type, whether orthodox or heterodox in character, can be derived from it, and also how they make their appearance in history. And a further task which must likewise be foregone is that of devoting a fuller consideration to the question of what

---

[3] The consideration of these basic forms, and, arising from this, the working out of a programme for the presentation of christology was brought to fruition in the course of a study which the author undertook with his colleague, W. T. Thüsing in the Winter semester of 1970–71 at the University of Munster, Westphalia.

[4] On this cf. the pronouncements of the Second Vatican Council on Revelation in 'Dei Verbum', *The Decree on Revelation* Nos 2 and 6.

may be concluded from this basic starting-point of christology with reference to an orthodox, sober, and prudent theology of the Trinity, and also with regard to the question of the pre-existence of the divine Logos.

METAPHYSICAL CHRISTOLOGY

The second basic type of christology has, with all the necessary provisos, been called the metaphysical type, a descending christology. In this formulation the term 'metaphysical' is taken in its broadest sense – in other words not merely as having that meaning which is familiar to us from the classic Western philosophy of being. If, and to the extent that, a christology clearly goes beyond the original experience of Jesus by the believer (whether justifiably or unjustifiably, this is not the question for the present), then it is metaphysical. This also applies, for instance to a christology which originally, and not merely in a derived sense, speaks of a communication of idiomata from the *kenosis* and the death of God, and intends such paradoxical statements in their full seriousness. It would in fact be possible to speak in these terms in a derived sense of the conclusions following from the first basic type of christology. In any case the metaphysical christology as intended here clearly finds its point of departure and the possibility of verifying it in the first basic type of christology. But this does not alter the fact that what we are dealing with here is a basic type which is different in its entire conception. It can, of course, be present in various ways more intensively and more clearly. If we want to designate it in its fully characteristic form we can surely isolate two special characteristics in it. First the approach here consists in a markedly 'descending' christology, which, at least formally speaking constitutes something more than a mere inversion of the ascending christology found in the first basic type. The pre-existence of the Logos, his divinity, his distinction from the Father, the predicate 'Son of God' ascribed to the divine Logos as him who pre-exists in this christology, are regarded as manifestly belonging to him from the first, and assumed more or less to be statements based upon the verbal assertions and convictions of Jesus himself. This pre-existent Logos who is the Son of God descends from heaven, becomes man, i.e. assumes a human reality as his own, in such a way that this pre-existent Logos also achieves a visibly historical dimension and appears in the very history which as pre-existent he has already shaped and moulded.[1] In this statement of a 'descending' christology we

[5] At the New Testament level these basic forms seem particularly clear in passages of the christological hymns in the Pauline Captivity Epistles and in the Prologue to the Johannine gospel.

are not at present concerned with the question of whether and how it is covered as implicitly included also in the ascending christology of the first basic type. If we have rightly understood it, this is certainly the case. But the decisive factor in this descending christology is, after all, precisely that it proceeds, as something that is self-evident and does not need any further recourse to the experience of Jesus in saving history, from a doctrine of the Trinity, the Logos, and a pre-existing Son of God. And these assumptions are properly speaking based not upon the experience in saving history of the crucified and risen Jesus, but are made known through verbal teaching by this same Jesus, a teaching which is placed upon his lips and regarded as his *ipsissima verba*. And in this approach we are abstracting from the question of whether this is historically speaking justified or not. God has become man. For this second type of christology this is, from the point of view of religion and theology, not a justifiable interpretation of a more original experience of saving history, but the supreme and primary axiom of this christology, though of course we are also aware that there is a history behind the revelation of this axiom itself. Hence it comes that the statement of faith that Jesus Christ is God does not need any further explanation so far as this line of thought is concerned, whereas in the first basic type of christology the same statement has an interpretative force – though of course a justified one – and comes as the conclusion of an elaborate argument, since our critical understanding of it has to be acquired from the more original experience of saving history. Secondly this descending christology, as found in the second basic type, implies a doctrine concerning the cosmic and, if the term may be permitted, transcendental significance of the Incarnation. It is the Logos that created the world that becomes man. But from this there follows the further implication that this process of becoming man constitutes something more than a mere isolated event marking a particular point in space and time, and belonging to a particular category, in a world which for the rest is comprehensible even on other grounds, but is rather the supreme point in the relationship of the divine Logos to his world in general. Creation is then regarded as the enabling condition for an element in the self-emptying, self-uttering, and self-communicating of God. Because, and to the extent that, God will not empty himself and bestow himself in an act of love into a void of nothingness, the world becomes that which opens itself to receive its own glory, which is sufficient for it. Man, on this basic conception, is not that which is 'self-evident' in itself, or the empty question waiting to be answered by God, but precisely that which comes to be if, and to the extent that, God himself utters himself; that which is precisely contained within a question, and also an answer of God in which God himself expresses himself. World is not simply accepted as that which is already given, but comes to be in that God himself utters himself, and in this self-utterance of his in the Word become flesh, imposes the finality and unsurpassability of this self-utterance. The Incarnation is not so much an event in space and time, simply requiring to be accepted in its factualness, but is rather the historical supreme point of a transcendental, albeit free, relationship of God to that which is not divine, in which God, himself positing this non-divine, enters into it in order himself to have his own personal history of love within it. Saving history, as the history of the forgiveness and reconciliation of man in his guilt, is embraced and integrated within a relationship of God to the world which is established prior to guilt with a view to the history of God's own Incarnation within his world, and admits of the presence of guilt in the world only as a possibility of radicalizing this relationship of God to the world, sustaining it always and throughout from the first, the relationship of love in which God lavishes himself upon the world. For this basic type it is ultimately speaking not a decisive factor whether it is developed more in terms of existential ontology or of cosmology – whether, in other words, man is conceived of as belonging to a world or whether the world, together with man, is conceived of as God's self-utterance – provided only that this self-utterance of God is thought of as achieving its point of eschatological irreversibility in Jesus.

ON THE RELATIONSHIP BETWEEN THE TWO BASIC TYPES

The fact that these two types are not merely basic types but *the two* basic types of christology should surely be conceded. If we take sufficiently into account the formal character of the characterization of these two basic types, the two types concerned could, of course, materially speaking, be made to undergo extraordinary variations. And hence the impression may emerge that there are very many other types of christology which can likewise be claimed to be basic types. But if we take the transcendentality and the historicity of man as constituting the two poles of our basic understanding of humanity, then, for our understanding of what is meant by Jesus Christ, there can be only one conception, in which man remains freely within his history, from which in fact he can never be separated so as to achieve a state of total transcendentality, and in which he finds his salvation, and one conception according to which man radically brings to bear his metaphysical powers in order to proceed from the question of what he is as subject and what the whole of reality is in one, and attempts once more to understand what he has initially freely experienced in history as his salvation.

This in itself already provides a starting-point for a more precise definition of the relationship which the two basic types bear to one another. It is clear that the second basic type constantly presupposes that experience of sacred history which is experienced in the first basic type, as its abiding basis and as the necessary criterion for rightly understanding the assertions it contains. Precisely today it is necessary, for an understanding of faith which is appropriate to the modern situation, to make clear whence this second basic type derives. This is not to maintain, even implicitly, that the second basic type is really superfluous, and, especially today, simply makes it more difficult to believe in Jesus as the eschatological bringer of salvation. Even in the New Testament as a whole the frontiers are, after all, crossed, from a statement belonging to the sphere of the first basic type to statements belonging to the second. And in principle this procedure is justifiable even if the titles of dignity attributed to Jesus in the New Testament point to him as man in his function as bringer of salvation without directly or *ipso facto* consciously reflecting upon his pre-existence as a God who is on the one hand 'in himself' the inconceivable origin, and on the other he who can utter himself in historical terms and so justifies what is really meant in statements about the Trinity.[6] Man as a whole, and in the spiritual development of humanity as such, is always too he who asks questions at a metaphysical and transcendental level. He is always he who cannot have any eschatological hope as a man of this earth unless he affirms that a continuity exists through all the discontinuity between the history of the natural order and the history of the human spirit. Jesus constitutes the eschatological response of God primarily not in words but in the deliverance of concrete reality. And precisely if this is true, then this response of God is *ipso facto* an event of this material world, albeit one which brings about eschatological transformations in it. If we conceive of the deed of God as one, for all the freedom in virtue of which the individual realities and events of the world are both connected with one another and distinct from one another, then we should enquire into the intrinsic unity which exists between the creation of the world and that unique event within this world which we recognize in faith in Jesus of Nazareth. All descending christology of the second basic type may have a secondary and interpretative

[6] On this cf. the author's remarks in the article, 'Theos in the New Testament', *Theological Investigations* I (London, 1961), pp. 79–148.

character. It may again and again, in order to achieve intelligibility and to justify its own propositions, be forced to return to the quite simple experience of Jesus of Nazareth. Nevertheless it is legitimate, inevitable, and sanctioned by the fact that the Church, right from the earliest times down to the present day, has discovered Jesus of Nazareth precisely in these statements of a Chalcedonian christology which seem so abstractly metaphysical, almost irreligious, and strangely inquisitive in character. It has discovered him there afresh again and again.

ON THE SIGNIFICANCE AND CREDIBILITY OF THE TWO BASIC TYPES

Surely it is unnecessary to give any prolonged explanation of the fact that in modern times, and on the most different grounds, whether from missionary considerations or considerations of religious pedagogy (or however we like to put it), the first basic type of christology can more easily be understood in its credibility and significance for the concrete conditions of human living than the second, which, if, as is usual, it is presented in isolation and without connection with the first, all too easily gives the impression of mythology, and seems to run counter both to historical experience and to any genuine idea of God. If from considerations of missionary needs and religious pedagogy we set the first basic type in the foreground as our point of departure for christology in general, then a clearer distinction must be drawn between the two basic types than is normally the case in the preaching of the Church. For it is usual for this to present the saving history and soteriological significance of Jesus for us merely as the conclusion of arguments primarily put forward in a descending christology, and not as the point of departure, as an experiance of saving history, which we make first and foremost in the true man, Jesus. It is possible of course to take the statement 'The Word was made flesh' in the sense of the metaphysical and descending christology of Chalcedon. (This without prejudice to the question of how the statement was intended in its explicit sense in John.) But as understood in this sense it cannot nowadays constitute the point of departure for a preaching of christology which can only find any basis in fundamental theology by invoking the established authority of those who put forward such a statement.

With regard to the relationship which the two basic types bear one to another, a point which should be examined more precisely than has been the case hitherto or is possible here is whether we cannot discern an

exaggerated argument in the second or metaphysical basic type of christology, in that it goes beyond anything which can be regarded as an
implication or a clear and unambiguous consequence deduced from the
first basic type, and capable of being justified on these grounds. It could
in fact be the case that an exaggeration of this kind, even when it is
assumed to be binding in faith, is nevertheless incapable of being deduced
by formal logic from the propositions of the first basic type, but needs
other supplementary principles, so that it is only when these are brought
together with the propositions of the first basic type that the statement of
the second basic type can be arrived at. It might be the case that statements which sound to our Western ears, educated as they are by Chalcedon, as statements of this second or metaphysical basic type, and so
contain a supplementary element of this kind, are actually (and above
all in their place in Scripture), intended merely as emphatic statements
in the sense of the first basic type.

These two basic types and their mutual interrelationship surely enable
us to understand that in present-day Christian theology too there is room
for a pluralism of christologies. If these christologies respect the Church's
credal formulae concerning Christ where these are definitive, and constantly submit afresh to critical reappraisal by standards outside themselves, and provided that at the same time they include, and accord all due
respect to, the essential reference to Jesus as the bringer of eschatological
salvation, the different christologies can continue to be different, and still
be orthodox. Even the approach by way of fundamental theology to the
understanding of a certain essential point can assume very different
shapes. The point we refer to is that man, whether consciously or not,
seeks for a bringer of salvation in the absolute of this kind. Again very
different answers can presumably be given to the question of how far we
can advance into the second basic type of christology, if we start from the
first. For surely very different opinions can be held with regard to the
existence, content, and binding force (from the point of view of faith)
of the previously mentioned element of exaggeration in the second basic
type as compared with the first, and such differences of opinion cannot
straightway be eliminated by appealing to the decisions of the Church's
teaching authority, or by a discussion merely at the theological level. The
point of departure for a decision of faith in concrete human life varies
from one individual to another, and from one epoch to another. In practice it invariably and inevitably includes elements which are not the outcome of conscious reflection, and are incapable of being so. Now these
different points of departure for a decision of faith for Christ – something

which invariably plays its part in determining the christology of a man or a theologian – are quite incapable of being united, in any effective sense, within a higher synthesis. Certainly one can strive to achieve some such thing. It may well be legitimate to tackle such a task ever afresh. But whatever gains may be achieved by christologies of this kind, which reduce a pluralism as far as possible to a synthesis, they are achieved only at the cost of becoming more remote from one particular, but in the concrete conditions of human life essential, point of departure in human understanding, and the only one from which christology can be pursued. Even the two basic types of christology, and their mutual interrelationship, render such a pluralism of christologies both inevitable and legitimate.

LIST OF SOURCES

ON RECOGNIZING THE IMPORTANCE OF THOMAS AQUINAS
A lecture included in a special series broadcast on the Bavarian radio on
29 December 1970; unpublished hitherto.

THOMAS AQUINAS ON TRUTH
A slightly revised version of a lecture given on 26 January 1938 to the
Philosophical Society at Neukirch. It is here published for the first time
in German. A translation has already been published in *Rev. Portuguesa
de Philos.* 7 (1951), pp. 353–370.

POSSIBLE COURSES FOR THE THEOLOGY OF THE FUTURE
First published in *Bilanz der Theologie im 20. Jahrhundert* III, H.
Vorgrimler and R. van der Gucht edd. (Freiburg, 1970), pp. 530551. A
French translation in *Bilan de la théologie de XXe siècle* II (Tournai –
Paris, 1971), pp. 911–952. Published again in French in *Nouvelle Revue
Théologique* 93 (1971), pp. 3–27, and in Spanish in *Arbor* 75 (1970), No.
291, pp. 6–29.

ON THE CURRENT RELATIONSHIP BETWEEN PHILOSOPHY AND
THEOLOGY
A lecture delivered on 13 November 1971 at the formal opening of
the 'Hochschule für Philosophie/München' (The Jesuit Faculty of
Philosophy), and published in *Theologie und Philosophie* 47 (1972), pp.
1–15.

THEOLOGY AS ENGAGED IN AN INTERDISCIPLINARY DIALOGUE
WITH THE SCIENCES
Lecture delivered at a conference of the Centre for Interdisciplinary Research at the University of Bielefeld on 28 September 1970; published in *Die Theologie in der interdisizplinären Forschung*, J. B. Metz and Tr. Rendtorff edd. (Düsseldorf, 1971), pp. 27–34.

ON THE RELATIONSHIP BETWEEN THEOLOGY AND THE CONTEM-
PORARY SCIENCES
A lecture delivered at a conference of the 'Secrétariat International des Questions Scientifiques' of the *Pax Romana* at Rome on 20 March 1971.

INSTITUTION AND FREEDOM
A lecture first delivered on 5 November 1971 in the Institute of Education of the BASF/Mannheim. Published in *Die BASF* 20 (1970), E1 – E8; also published in *Internationale Dialogzeitschrift* 4 (1971), No. 1, pp. 39–49. A Portuguese translation has appeared in *Broteria* 93 (Lissabon, 1971), Nos 8–9, pp. 147–161.

EXPERIENCE OF SELF AND EXPERIENCE OF GOD
First published in J. Tenzler (ed.), *Urbild und Abglanz. Festschrift für Prof. H. Doms* (Regensburg, 1971), pp. 201–208.

DOES TRADITIONAL THEOLOGY REPRESENT GUILT AS INNOCUOUS
AS A FACTOR IN HUMAN LIFE?
Hitherto unpublished.

THEOLOGICAL OBSERVATIONS ON THE CONCEPT OF 'WITNESS'
Prepared for a symposium at Rome in January 1972. Unpublished in German.

IDEAS FOR A THEOLOGY OF DEATH

A Lecture delivered at a conference of the *Katholische Akademie in Bayern* on 15 November 1970 at Regensburg. Hitherto unpublished.

HUMAN ASPECTS OF THE BIRTH OF CHRIST

First published in *Tribuna Medica* 7 (Madrid, 1970), No. 368, pp. 14–15. Here published for the first time in German.

THE QUEST FOR APPROACHES LEADING TO AN UNDERSTANDING OF THE MYSTERY OF THE GOD-MAN JESUS

Published in *Geist und Leben* 44 (1971), pp. 404–408.

REMARKS ON THE IMPORTANCE OF THE HISTORY OF JESUS FOR CATHOLIC DOGMATICS

First published in *Die Zeit Jesu. Festschrift für H. Schlier*, G. Bornkamm and K. Rahner edd. (Freiburg, 1970), pp. 273–283.

THE TWO BASIC TYPES OF CHRISTOLOGY

A lecture given at the *Katholische Akademie in Bayern* on 16 December 1971 at Munich. Hitherto unpublished.

INDEX OF PERSONS

INDEX OF SUBJECTS